WEATHER SHAMANISM

"Nan Moss and David Corbin have written a wonderful and inspiring guide to living spiritually with weather. I greatly value their insights, as shamanic practitioners, into how we can be conscious and respectful partners with the great spiritual forces that pass across the sky, the land, and the seasons. A book for everyone who hopes to live more consciously with the natural elements."

TOM COWAN, AUTHOR OF *FIRE IN THE HEAD: SHAMANISM AND THE CELTIC SPIRIT, SHAMANISM AS A SPIRITUAL PRACTICE FOR EVERYDAY LIFE*, AND *YEARNING FOR THE WIND*

"Weather Shamanism *is quite simply a wonderful, profound, power-filled book, alive with sacred stories and loaded with cross-cultural indigenous wisdom. Nan Moss and David Corbin are master shamanic teachers who reveal what becomes possible when we intentionally align ourselves with the ancient forces of nature to alleviate suffering and help restore order when chaos moves in. This book contains very good medicine!"*

HANK WESSELMAN, PH.D., AUTHOR OF *THE SPIRITWALKER TRILOGY, THE JOURNEY TO THE SACRED GARDEN*, AND COAUTHOR OF *SPIRIT MEDICINE*

"With global climate change barreling down on us, the techniques of weather shamanism are essential to our collective survival. Nan Moss and David Corbin share their courageous exploration of these ancient spiritual ways of living with and learning from weather. They have brought timeless wisdom and wit into working with clouds, water, wind, and the ethics of believing humans are in control. This book matters—it has guided me through Hurricane Katrina; serious floods; ice storms; long, hotter and hotter summers; and an unpredicted winter tornado that hit my house in the middle of the night. Our ancestors practiced these ancient arts for countless millennia, and now they are even more relevant to the new world of weather we are experiencing. I say thank you to Nan and David and to this book."

MARTHA WARD, RESEARCH PROFESSOR OF ANTHROPOLOGY,
UNIVERSITY OF NEW ORLEANS, AND AUTHOR OF
VOODOO QUEEN: THE SPIRITED LIVES OF MARIE LAVEAU

WEATHER
SHAMANISM

HARMONIZING OUR CONNECTION
WITH THE ELEMENTS

NAN MOSS with DAVID CORBIN

Bear & Company
Rochester, Vermont

Bear & Company
One Park Street
Rochester, Vermont 05767
www.BearandCompanyBooks.com

Bear & Company is a division of Inner Traditions International

Library of Congress Cataloging-in-Publication Data
Moss, Nan, 1950–
  Weather shamanism : harmonizing our connection with the elements / Nan Moss with David Corbin.
    p. cm.
  Includes bibliographical references and index.
  ISBN-13: 978-1-59143-074-2 (pbk.)
  ISBN-10: 1-59143-074-7 (pbk.)
  1. Nature—Religious aspects. 2. Nature—Effect of human beings on. 3. Weather. 4. Shamanism. I. Corbin, David. II. Title.

  BL65.N35M68 2008
  202'.12—dc22
                                                                    2007042674

Printed and bound in Canada by Transcontinental Printing

10 9 8 7 6 5 4 3 2 1

Text design and layout by Priscilla Baker and Virginia Scott Bowman
This book was typeset in Garamond, with Trajan and Agenda used as display typefaces

To send correspondence to the authors of this book, mail a first-class letter to the authors c/o Inner Traditions • Bear & Company, One Park Street, Rochester, VT 05767, and we will forward the communication.

To the ancestors, who knew what was real.
To those with whom we have circled and will circle,
who have the heart for this work.
To Merlin and all of our descendants, may they
inherit an alive, beautiful, and vital Earth.

CONTENTS

PART THREE

WEATHER SHAMANISM

PART FOUR

THE PRACTICE OF
WEATHER DANCING

ACKNOWLEDGMENTS

There is a profound yearning in our culture for the experience of community and collaboration. As far as we know, shamanism has always been about partnering with helping spirits. The manifestation of this book is just that. As we each stumbled upon our invitation to the spiritual path of weather shamanism, it seemingly began with the "me"—the individual's response to a call to cross a spiritual threshold—to show up. It did not take us long to discover that we were on to something much greater than what our own particular lenses of perception could provide. To be truly accessible, and useful, to our modern world we needed to pull together the teachings of many—from the greater community of the ancestors and from those alive today. And so we extend our gratitude and appreciation to all the compassionate beings, of all the worlds, who are part of this work. It is because of and through you that we may find the truth, the beauty in it for ourselves.

The spirits of weather, and the compassionate helping spirits, were of course the most important influence behind this work. May we live up to their teachings.

Of Michael Harner, without whom most books on shamanism would not have been written, enough cannot be said. His vision and courage have helped bring shamanism back as a major force for healing in our world.

We also give our love and appreciation to Sandra Ingerman for her groundbreaking work, brilliant teachings, unfailing encouragement, and support. We also want to thank Tom Cowan for showing us the poetry of life, Bill Brunton for urging us forward and publishing our articles in *Shamanism,* Hank Wesselman and Jill Kuykendall for their integrity and inspired works in the world (and with much gratitude to Hank for his generous gift of "Lono the Rainmaker"), and to all of our ordinary reality teachers, who of course were anything but ordinary.

Of the people who supported and encouraged us through the years there are more than can be counted. Special thanks to the Port Clyde Drumming Circle (Bente Kjos, Carolyn Horn, Eric Anderson, Georgene Arbour, Glenn and Laurie Fenlason, and Meg Barclay) for providing a loving spiritual community, for keeping the hearth fires glowing while we are away, and for letting us experiment on them. Thanks also to Danny B. (the "heart and soul of Esalen"), Cynthia Johnson-Bianchetta, and Kashi for lighting up our lives; esteemed colleague Elaine Egidio and Larry Lima for helping us to be the best teachers we can be; Mara Bishop, Mia Bosna, Zoe Calder, Stephanie Campbell, Cynthia Crisp, Katharine Flebotte, Ailo Gaup, Peggy Goodale, Carol Irons, Sue Jamieson, Larry Kessler, Susan and Chris Marshall, Sharon Massoth, Victoria Post, and Eugenia Woods for sharing your insights; and to all the others—you know who you are.

Of those who helped craft this book's development, we want to thank Jenny Dowling for her creative expertise and her patience in teaching us how to write, Kathy Westra for her pathfinding in the publishing world and unrelenting attention to detail, and Carol Glegg for her "eyes" and enthusiasm. Many thanks also to Steve White, Renata Butera, and Kevin Quirk for helping us get started. And to Kate Gale, teacher, poet, and editor of Red Hen Press, we owe our gratitude for her savvy and confidence in the worthiness of our manuscript, giving us the boost we needed to send it out there.

To all of our contributors, whether or not your offerings appear in *Weather Shamanism,* each and every one of you are a part of this effort and we appreciate you all. Every time you asked how the work was coming along, or reminded us that you were eagerly waiting for the book, we felt sustained—and sometimes spurred on! Unless you are already mentioned, we wish to express our sincere gratitude to: Edda Arndal, Diana Atkins, Paul Beaulieu, Marguerite Cassin, Dory Cote, Tom Crockett, Heather Cumming, Connie Eiland, Myron Eshowsky, Joe Godwin, Dave Hanson, Linda Ierardi, Ramona Lapidas, John Lawrence, Michele Lessirard, Robert Levy, Wendyne Limber, Paul Lipton, Greg Murray, Joan Northrup, Priscilla Palmer, Sheila Porter, Linda Roe, Katie Rose-Walker, Kim Rothman, Jeanne-Rachel Salomon, Steve Snair, Carol Tietjan, Martha Ward, Sinead Wilder, Tom Winegarten, and Petra Wolf. Mary from Texas, you brought more to this work than you will ever know.

We wish to thank all of our workshop sponsors—we know how hard you worked, and may we meet again. We also wish to offer our gratitude to the staff, community, and spirits of Esalen Institute for your generous hospitality and willingness to host us year after year. Likewise we honor and thank the beings of our home realm in Maine for all their vital support and inspiration.

To those we know and all the rest at Inner Traditions • Bear & Company, we extend huge thanks and best wishes for your continued service to our society. Though it may sound self-serving, we applaud what you do and long may you prosper. You were always our first choice as a publisher, and Simon Buxton's praise was absolutely justified. Thank you, Jon Graham, for seeing the potential in *Weather Shamanism,* and many thanks to managing editor Jeanie Levitan, art director Peri Champine for the compelling cover design, and to our project editor, Laura Schlivek—we are so happy that you asked for this book!

Finally, we wish to mention our love and gratitude in memory of our good friend Linda Crane, who was part of our circles from the very beginning, who taught many of us about how to live a creative and inspired life, to have courage, and to take joy in all of Nature and her weathers.

INTRODUCTION

If I were to write a book about the weather, what
would it say?
It would need to talk about the beauty of weather.
About the miraculous and divine in the process
that sends swirls of moisture and air and heat and cold
around our planet,
providing life-giving nourishment where it is needed,
cleansing and renewing, destroying and rebuilding.
It would need to speak of the power and elegance
of this all-pervasive being that alters the shape
of the land,
even as it nourishes a single flower.
It would need to show how we are weather and
weather is us.

D. C.

Weather Shamanism is an invitation, a call to any who are curious, who care about where our world may be heading, and who sincerely wish to safeguard the viability of our planet. This book is for those who love beauty, who welcome wonderment, and

1

who are willing to dance with mystery. It is a calling to enter into the enlivened worldview of our ancestral shamans to learn that we are not alone, and that whether we realize it or not, we are in relationship with the elements of Nature—and weather is Nature. *Weather Shamanism* shows a way to begin walking a path of spiritual relationship with the seen and unseen, with the creative forces and spirits of weather.

This book taps in to the legacy of ancestral knowledge and more. Most importantly, it will introduce you to *weather dancing,* the heart of weather shamanism and its "miracles" of weather working. The practice of weather dancing will lead you toward a spiritual relationship with some of our planet's most fundamental elements and forces of creation—those of weather. The path of weather dancing is necessarily about your unfolding relationship with your self and your soul, in partnership with compassionate helping spirits. As such it is capable of inspiring profound change. This happens through your enhanced appreciation of the gift of life in this middle world, Earth; in the way you look at and understand the nature of reality; and in your ability to recognize yourself as an essential and vital cocreator of our world. Through your spiritual growth and empowerment as a weather dancer, you will be able to offer deep healing for our troubled ecosystems and human communities.

The primary aim of this work is to encourage you to perceive and relate to the elements of weather as live beings who are worthy of our attention and respect and, if you are willing, to inspire your own journey into weather shamanism. For those who wish to embark wholeheartedly upon this path, be forewarned that it is not enough to simply gain a lot of information. You must actively practice, finding ways to bring these teachings into your daily life. This is a process, and, as with relating to Nature overall, it is ultimately a personal one.

What this book is not, and can never be, is a "cookbook." Rather, it is the telling of a journey, David's and mine. So it is not possible to give you an exact recipe, and the path we ask you to follow is necessarily circuitous. What we can do is show you how it happened for us and share what we learned. We offer our own process to you with the intention of demonstrating that it is not that hard, that it's not a rare and highly unlikely thing to reach out to the weather spirits and learn to relate to them. What we do not wish to offer you is a work of unbelievable stories and events that serve only to create feelings of distance and futility. By walking with us in our journey, you will be able to see how available this path can be.

As David and I say in our workshops, our job is to teach you what teaches us—to help you see that there just might be something real and worthwhile going on in the shamanic world and that it's possible to find it for yourself. At the least, we hope to tweak your curiosity so that you will give more attention to the world outdoors and its weathers, and thus to the urgings of your soul. Every offering of the gift of your attention generates healing for the terrible dysfunctions we suffer when we are disconnected unduly from Nature.

For the "just curious" reader who wants to learn something new and is willing to try out a different perspective, *Weather Shamanism* offers much in the way of literary and anthropological research, including anecdotes and personal accounts from us and other contributors collected over a decade. These stories were not chosen solely for entertainment value (although this was certainly one of the characteristics we looked for). Most of them also contain embedded teachings, an ancient means of transmitting information that is still the way that the teachings come to many of us today. Some of the contributions also provide an intimate look at the shamanic journey itself, a chance to vicariously follow along and receive teachings about the spiritual nature of weather. For the experienced shamanic practitioner there is "buried treasure," and you know how to look for it. May this work enhance and support you in your spiritual practice.

As shamanic practitioners, we have opportunities to communicate directly with our helping spirits. This is how I received my calling to this path. I did not consciously ask for it; I knew nothing about weather shamanism. Yet when the call came, I was rash enough to make a promise that has resulted in this book. On the other hand, wisdom and guidance from the helping spirits can be very subtle—so much so that we are aware of the beginning stages of a process or transformation only from the perspective of hindsight.

For example, a few days ago David received, "out of the blue," via the U.S. Postal Service, a DVD of an outdoor concert from years ago in which he had played bass guitar in a jazz band. No letter or note came with the package. And when he reviewed it, David witnessed something he had forgotten: His band had opened with a long, somewhat hypnotic "droning" number, and just as it ended, a brief thundershower erupted. The band leader joked to the audience that this was the band's rain dance! It was 1984, and David was only months away from his formal introduction to shamanism. The process that would eventually result in the direction of his work today had already begun.

At present many fear that we are in a time of aberrant and worsening weather conditions such as megastorms, killer heat waves, El Niño– and La Niña–generated floods and droughts—the specter of global warming. Though we can see that the consequences of full-blown global warming can and will threaten the stability of our societies, we are only beginning to grapple with the reality that our extreme dependency upon fossil fuels exacerbates the problem.

Among the more obvious signs of a hotter world are increasing numbers of significant storms, for example, those of the infamous hurricane seasons of 2004 and 2005. We continue to receive data from around the planet confirming the surprisingly rapid and seemingly inexorable melting of the world's glaciers and polar ice caps. Concurrently, sea levels are rising, rendering coastal communities (New Orleans, for one) vulnerable to tragedy and necessitating a major reevaluation of our coastal living patterns. Predictions range from more droughts to more storms to more floods, or all of the above, and with increasing severity. Yet some areas will prosper with these changes, while other regions and their native flora and fauna will suffer.

Today we are undergoing an alarming trend of plant and animal extinctions, with many species teetering on the brink. If the earth and atmosphere continue to warm, we'll see more animal and plant losses. In the Arctic the diminishing ice cover and shortening length of the cold season are already significant stressors for resident polar bear populations as well as the Inuit peoples, who must face the likelihood of unwelcome changes in their traditional life patterns as their home realm undergoes the challenge of global warming. Few can escape a profound sense of loss as we contemplate a world without the features and beings we have always known in our lifetimes, from the continental shorelines to the magnificent glaciers to the great polar bears.

From another perspective, consider how today's and tomorrow's weather events are influenced by a worldview that provides little room for the personification of natural forces, much less an acceptance of the reality of spirits. David and I believe that to recognize the existence of spirits of weather is an essential step that is not yet beyond our ken and reach. We still have the ability, and hopefully the time, to reestablish aware and active relationships with these spirits, as well as all the other spirits with whom we share our world.

This book is not about how to control the weather; it is about changing ourselves. It is about raising our consciousness to a level that allows us to act as if we understand that all things are connected. What is barely known and remembered today is that as individuals and communities, we can and do collectively exert a real effect upon the weather *by our psyches and emotions and by our sense of connectedness or disconnectedness from the natural world*. The greatest and most important change we can make is to begin to accept a broader worldview: one that is supportive of an intentional relationship with Nature, a partnership that fosters the reality of an alive and vital Earth.

When we can look at a tree and say, "There is life," and when we can look at a rock or a cloud and say, "There is life," then we can look within ourselves and find respect for all life. Then we can see the true nature of our relationship with the world and better comprehend the need to exist in harmony with the earth. Then rain will fall where it is needed, and sun will shine on a beautiful and viable world.

The spirits of weather want us to work with them. They want us to take an active and conscious role in the healthy functioning of our planet. If these spirits see that we are interested in learning from them, that we are dedicated to working for the good of all, then they might take notice and gently teach us ways in which we can live in harmony with each other and with all of Nature. From this comes true healing, for ourselves and for all ecosystems on the planet.

Shamanic practitioners can take great heart from the alive and continually evolving ways of shamanism to bring forth the wisdom and relief of undue suffering that our world needs now. Through the practice of weather shamanism we can tap in to the incredible potential that awaits us all for creating and restoring balance and well-being to our lives and world. As weather shamans we can harmonize our connections with the elements, bridging earth and sky for love of the world.

Do David and I find this path challenging? You bet.

Wondrous? Infinitely.

And if you have the heart for it, it can be yours, too.

PART ONE

THE CALL

1

THE DOOR BLOWS OPEN

The great sea has set me in motion
Set me adrift,
Moving me as the weed moves in a river.
The arch of the sky and mightiness of storms
Have moved the spirit within me,
Till I am carried away
Trembling with joy.

SONG OF UVAVNUK,
AN INUIT WOMAN SHAMAN,
FROM *ACROSS ARCTIC AMERICA*
BY KNUD RASMUSSEN

It is Saturday afternoon at the Pathwork Center, deep in the heart of the Catskill Mountains of New York. Twenty-three people lie quietly on the floor with bandannas over their eyes. The resonance of drums fills the room with harmonious and compelling vibrations. I am drumming with my partner, David, in the center of the room by a simple altar cloth and lighted candle. We are drumming for people who vary in their ability and level of experience, but all have done this before. It is the celebrated shamanic journey to the nonordinary realms; worlds of compassion, wisdom, and grace. Today they attempt something new: the search for a spirit of weather. And if they find such a spirit, they each have a question to ask on behalf of our circle. The excitement is palpable.

The drumming continues, and I am somewhat surprised to feel the familiar desire to journey also, even as I drum. I gaze around the room and everything seems peaceful. I look at David, his eyes wide open and watchful. I indicate that I wish to journey and then close my eyes as I drum and drum and drum . . .

⌗

I fly to the upper world in the company of power animals, asking to meet a spirit of weather. I don't know why, but I feel ecstatic. We fly through a layer of storm clouds—up and up—searching until we finally are face to face with a cloud being. He is imposingly large, with lightning shimmering in his eyes, and when he speaks, snowballs tumble from his mouth. I feel glad to have my helping spirits nearby. I introduce myself and respectfully ask the cloud being for a teaching for our community. I am genuinely surprised and dismayed by his teaching. He is unmistakably annoyed! He tells me that, essentially, our culture has forgotten him, that in times past people all over the world spoke to him, prayed to him, and worked with him. Now he is ignored. Now our science and "knowledge" attempt to de-personalize, de-spirit him. So he creates aberrant, rough weather that we will notice, puzzle over, and know that we don't know. As I feel this spirit's mood, I am speechless. I offer a thank-you for his teaching and my promise to share this with the circle and community.[1]

⌗

I've held a passion for weather all my life, and as a practitioner of core shamanism for many years, I thought I recognized the spirit in all things. But from this journey I saw that I still carried our culture's concept of weather as chaotic interactions of purely physical forces. Meteorologists describe and attempt to predict general and specific outcomes from the interactions of such forces, while the rest of us, as the general public, alternately praise and ridicule—or curse—both those meteorologists and the weather. Though we lend our own names to hurricanes and enliven our language with a variety of weather-related expressions, most of us rarely venture further in our general understanding of weather beyond its physical nature. Without realizing it, I was participating in a collective cultural arrogance that leaves little room to see, hear, or feel the spiritual reality of weather. Furthermore, I saw the notion of weather working, such as rainmaking, as an elusive and extravagant concept, lodged somewhere between myth and that which is too complicated and dangerous.

Weather is, and probably always has been, prayed to, blamed, talked about, studied, and misunderstood, but never ignored. Weather happens all over the planet. Many of our most memorable experiences with the natural world are related to the forces of weather. No matter whether you were born and raised in a rural, suburban, or urban environment, you experienced weather and its power to shape you into who you are now. When outdoors, we are surrounded by it. Weather plays its part in determining the quality of our year, our work, and our play. It is what strangers talk about to one another. A weather event has the capacity to draw us out of the relative isolation of our daily routines. It brings us together; we all share the experience.

Weather changes us. As it shifts and transforms itself, it likewise alters us. Yet we remain only minimally aware of the unique and personal effects of weather's workings. We may notice how our mood and behavior respond to the weather, yet weather's capacity to affect our overall physiology is little understood and not well known in our general culture.

Biometeorology is the study of how the atmosphere and its weather conditions affect us in terms of our health. For example, the passage of cold and warm fronts can alter our blood pressure and acid/alkaline levels, affecting our tissues' ability to hold water and thus influencing our body weight as well as the well-known conditions of aching joints, bunions, and headaches. Even our white blood cells (leukocytes) are affected; their numbers tend to rise with the onset of cold polar fronts and fall with the passage of tropical fronts. And every summer we hear of deaths attributed to heat waves, especially among the very young and the elderly. In Germany the science of biometeorology is taken more seriously than in North America, so much so that it can influence the scheduling of certain medical procedures such as surgeries.[2]

Weather is a primary force of creation and is responsible for shaping the earth and all life as we know it. We know from geological records that in times gone by, the mass extinctions (estimated at nearly 90 percent during the Permian Age) that have periodically befallen countless animal and plant species may have been directly or indirectly caused by dramatic changes in climate. This is how we mammals got our start—we could flourish once the great dinosaurs left the earth.

For eons plants and animals, including humans, have adapted their physiology in order to thrive in a variety of climates. This coevolution continues to this day. As we grow familiar with the rhythms of our local climate, we learn what to expect from year to year and season to season and plan our lives accordingly—more or less. Yet climate change is inevitable, and to continue to live for generations in a place requires a willingness on the part of any community to adapt to weather's expressions, from the seasonal and daily variations to both the predictable and the unpredictable cycles of rain and drought, heat and cold, calm and storm. This has always been so.

Though we could not live without it, we often think of weather's immense influence in terms of loss of life and hardship, translated into billions of dollars spent each year due to the destruction of property and crop failures from weather-related disasters. The largest supercomputers in the world are hard at work modeling the complexity of weather patterns in order to understand the workings of our atmosphere so that we can predict and prepare for what is coming. Even as we seek a more comprehensive knowledge of weather and its effects on our lives, the by-products of our lifestyle are inflicting great damage to the environment—damage that is changing the climate and weather patterns all over the earth. For example, recent studies show that a new kind of smog in our skies, especially above and downwind of urban areas, contains particulates so small that they actually make it more difficult for rain or snowflakes to coalesce in the clouds, thus further troubling those regions already prone to drought. To bring it closer to home, today's extra-small particulates of pollution are also increasingly hazardous for our own respiratory and cardiovascular health.

Most disturbing and potentially devastating is the predicament of global warming, the effects of which have already wreaked havoc with what we have come to think of as "normal" in our climate. For years we have debated whether global warming is simply one of Earth's natural cycles or whether humans cause it. Today there is general agreement that it is likely both, and it is undeniable that the vast amounts of pollution and resource depletion fueled by the demands of our huge population directly impact the ongoing course of global warming.

Weather and its events make history, as in notable storms or droughts (consider, for example, biblical floods), and has played its definitive part in the successes and failures of human endeavors throughout our existence. Historical chronicles show us how the weather changes our plans or squashes our ambitions. In August of 1588, for example, in a conflict between Britain and Spain, the invading Spanish Armada, consisting of a formidable array of great warships, was decimated by an unusual month of severe storms off the coast of Scotland. Though the odds had originally been heavily in Spain's favor, from the surviving captains' logs we know that even as the remnants of the Armada retreated, the fleet was hammered by yet another storm off the coast of Ireland. It is said that the Armada lost more ships to the weather than to actual battles with the British.[3]

The weather also had an unusual influence on the earliest attempts by the British to settle in the New World. From 1587 to 1588 the first English colony in the United States was founded in North Carolina on Roanoke Island. Today this colony is called the "Lost Colony," as it disappeared without a trace; by the time it was revisited by another ship from England, in 1589, none of the four hundred colonists (among them Virginia Dare, the first recorded English birth in the New World) could be found. To this day no conclusions have been made as to their fate. We can speculate that the local native people either took them in or killed them (apparently this colony was involved in the murder of a chief), but there is also another piece of the puzzle, one that shows up during the second attempt at colonization by the English at the settlement founded at Jamestown, Virginia, in 1607.

According to the records, few of the Jamestown colonists survived the first year (38 out of 104), and 4,800 of the newcomers were challenged by famine and disease over the next seven years, from 1607 to 1614. Hardship in colonizing a new realm is not unexpected; however, as a result of the work of Matthew Therrell, we know something curious about the weather's contribution. According to Therrell, a University of Arkansas tree-ring specialist who examined the trunks of recently logged bald cypress trees dating from the years 1000 to 1997, in the very region that the Roanoke and Jamestown colonies shared, there were exactly two severe droughts, and both occurred during the founding years of the two colonies, 1587 to 1588 and 1607 to 1614.[4]

Could the timing of these droughts have been a case of weather working, of humans deliberately influencing the weather to discourage colonization? The English colonists were not moving in on empty lands. Many peoples had been living there for thousands of years. In fact, there were millions of people on this continent at the time of historical contact with Europeans. We'll never know for sure, but we can wonder.

Our earliest memories of weather events hold valuable keys to our understanding of how we respond to the world and life today. By cloud gazing or witnessing awesome displays of lightning or wind in our childhood, we learned to appreciate and even be thrilled by the beauty of the natural world. For a great many of us, early experiences of Nature nurtured our willingness, and need, to turn to the natural world for a communion, to receive a primal sustenance at the emotional, physical, and spiritual levels of our being.

I, for example, feel a surge of excitement and eager anticipation when a hurricane approaches—even as I worry about possible injury to those I love. And if the storm bypasses us, I feel let down, cheated of a rare encounter. But out of respect for the feelings of others, I have learned to keep quiet at these times.

Hurricane Hazel's "visit" to Virginia's Tidewater peninsula in 1954 was the earliest, most memorable weather event of my preschool years. Hazel instilled within my psyche an everlasting sense of awe and admiration for the power of Nature. During that afternoon I watched pine trees whip back and forth so wildly that some snapped in two, while many others lost branches to the hurricane-force winds. I saw the frothing waves of our normally placid tidal creek rise up and wash over the boundaries of its clay banks in an assault on the pine wood at the edge of my aunt's yard. I remember relishing the change in routine—no compulsory afternoon nap, no captive hours in nursery school. Most of all I can still feel the intense sense of adventure that night after Hazel had finished her blow, when my grandfather drove our family inland from the coast to check on relatives living on a farm, with whom we had lost telephone contact.

As we left I saw that there were no lights in town, and the night was as dark as night should be. My grandfather drove slowly, dodging branches and large puddles on the narrow and hilly back roads, yet we all felt his sense of urgency as we made our way deeper into the country. I knew my grandfather as a patient and playful man, always ready to indulge my cousins and me with a story or treat. This night he was different. His words were sparse and his tone terse as we drove through the storm-struck countryside.

Suddenly Grandaddy braked hard just as we came around a curve and there, illuminated through the headlights and light rain, lay an enormous and ancient oak tree, felled by the storm. Its massive form sprawled across the road. Peering ahead from the backseat, I could see its great limbs reaching out toward us, curled and broken. Startled to see such an enormous being lying so wretchedly, I remember suddenly feeling fear for the first time during that entire experience. I thought of my own oak tree at home and the dangling rope swing I spent so much time on, whirling and gazing up at its generous spread of branches. My grandfather got out of the car, leaving the rest of us inside, and again I felt a twinge of fear when I watched him walk over to the tree, as if he had to get a closer look to believe it himself.

We had to backtrack, and many turns and other roads later, we finally made it to the farm. The old farmhouse was battered but essentially in good shape, save for a few lost storm shutters. We cousins banded together much as the adults did, sharing our stories and eating good things, but unlike other times, we were soft spoken and content to gather for the rest of the evening in one room, where in moments of silence we could hear the rain sounding on the rusty tin roof. I eventually fell asleep, comfortably bedded on the floor, by the flickering glow of candlelight.

Some of us will remember weather phenomena as intensely frightening, crackling with a mysterious, wild power that, when unleashed, is capable of immense destruction. Perhaps we felt small, unprotected, and extremely vulnerable in the face of this aspect of Nature. Others may remember a time of great joy when a snowstorm gifted us with a world of sparkling beauty and delight—and an unscheduled day off from school! We may, as adults, find ourselves still anticipating snowstorms, despite the inconveniences and difficulties.

Now consider how we, in turn, influence the weather. The high levels of environmental pollution and resource depletion that go hand in hand with our current lifestyles demonstrably affect our weather patterns. Nearly every schoolchild has heard something of our well-founded fears of irreparable loss of rain forests and related issues of air and water pollution. Studies show, too, that we are not that far off in our complaints that the weather is more often rainy on weekends when we want to recreate outdoors. Indeed, in some metropolitan areas, such as the Northeast corridors, weekday patterns of commuting back and forth to work add increased numbers of particulates to the atmosphere, which does, in fact, enhance the chances of rain by the weekend. There are also studies under way to assess the atmospheric effects of high-altitude contrails from the thousands of jets flying around our planet every day and night.

In the "ordinary" sense, weather phenomena are neither designed nor created by human hands. We do not sculpt the clouds, hurl bolts of lightning, switch on the wind, adjust the thermostat for a heat wave or cold front, or dial up a sunny day. Yet this is not to say that we don't affect the weather. Both by our lifestyles and by our state of being, we can and do affect the weather. We respond to the weather, and weather, in turn, responds to us.

Though the concept is little understood or accepted by our prevailing worldview, we humans affect the weather by our psyches and emotions—and through our very sense of relatedness to the natural world. We often speak of emotion and weather in ways that relate the two, such as "raging storms" or "thundering anger," using images of one to describe the other. Are these just useful metaphors for one another, or do they reflect a deeper relationship?

In one of his old journals David found this entry:

Awakened at 5 a.m., aroused by a sudden wind pelting the house with projectile leaves and branches. In the distance the sound of cracking limbs and falling trees. As the wind howls, a fear arises in the gut—the suddenly violent weather evoking an eruption of adrenaline-filled emotion.

This is an example of frightening weather sparking a strong emotional response, but there are also stories in which strong emotions have provoked a particular weather phenomenon. In Greek mythology the god Zeus, when angered, was capable of hurling thunderbolts to Earth. And Norse mythology honors Odin, the deity whose hammer evokes lightning and thunder. Tom, a former Marine captain, has this story to share:

Several officers and I came over to help Dr. R. build a fence around his backyard. The ground was hard (Texas caliche), and in some areas we could dig no further than 4 or 5 inches. Rusty had us put the fence up anyway, with insufficient anchoring of the posts. We were inside because it had started raining when we noticed the fence was leaning from the wind. Five officers in their underwear were outside putting up braces and support. By now there was 2 inches of water on the ground. In a "beer-powered" exhibition of joy, I raised my hammer over my head and yelled, *"Odin!"* A lightning bolt struck the telephone pole 20 feet from me, sending sparks 200 feet down the power lines. After everybody had calmed down I heard someone ask, "Where's Tom?" They came over to where I was, and I was lying on my back in the mud and the water, staring up into the rain. I recall the exact moment I saw the bolt hit the pole: tongues of fire traveled down the wires, reflected by the water on the ground. I was surrounded by light brighter than the sun. I was relieved to find that I was still alive. I got up and we went inside and drank more beer. I have not mentioned any god's name around inclement weather since.

If the weather does respond to us, then we can ask, "What does weather react to, and how?" Remembering that our feelings, thoughts, and acts of living are all connected to the web of life, it is worthwhile to look at whatever is going on within us, in our everyday lives, and in the world at large.

In 1999 we received a letter from Mary, a seventy-seven-year-old woman from Texas, who responded to our article "Shamanism and the Spirits of Weather," published in the journal *Shamanism*.

I have known God all my life and Jesus has been a personal reality to me as long as I can remember, but having been raised in the orthodox understanding I was not told of the spirit in all things. . . . I met a shaman, who became my mentor. One evening we were in the park where we studied, prayed, and meditated together, and in meditation, which I am not always good at, I went into the clouds and communed with the spirits of the clouds, and they told me that the Creator had created them to give rain where it was needed and withhold it when it was not needed, but due to the erratic mental and emotional energy that man sends out they are no longer able to serve man as they were created to. It grieves them deeply.

Mary's experience suggests that we are indeed part of it all, as the ancestral teachings describe, and as such it may well be that our feelings, thoughts, and acts of living do exert an effect on those around us, including the weather. To be sure, we are not the whole show. On a grand scale the spirits and forces of weather must interact with all in our world, yet the reality is that we, as one of the more dominant and aggressive species on this planet, with our unmistakable "footprints," are in a significant and dynamic relationship with the weather. This relationship is built upon both physical and emotional dimensions, heavily influenced by our perceptions and experiences of the world. From the common perspective of our culture, it is harder to grasp the nonphysical aspect of our relationship with weather than the physical. Nevertheless, our emotional, mental, and psychic bond is real, as people like Mary are discovering through their journeys and meditations.

There are still viable cultures around the world that carry on in the knowledge that everything embodies *spirit,* a normally unseen life force and sentience that inhabits rocks, animals, plants, trees, places, rivers, storms, mountains, oceans—indeed, everything. Many of these cultures recognize and work with spirits of weather. The spiritual elders, wise men and women of widely separated peoples, understand the need for humans to honor and relate to the spirit world for the overall maintenance of harmony and balance and for the good of their people, including the good of the individual. They see this intentional relationship with the world of the spirits as a special duty for humans, and they attend to this responsibility through the enactment of community rituals, such as the Iroquois Midwinter Ceremony (a world renewal rite), the Lenape Big House Ceremony, and the Sun Dance of the Plains peoples. They consider individual relationships with the spirits as equally important, including expressions and acts of honoring and gratitude for our lives and for all our relations—seen and unseen—who share life with us on this beautiful planet.

For David and myself, that initial journey to the irate weather spirit was seminal, opening a path that we had not consciously dreamed. It marked the beginning of a new and powerful direction to our spiritual practice. We were about to discover that to embark upon a path of conscious relationship with the spirits of weather is to walk a path that helps us realize our connection with all of Nature. In so doing, we can reclaim the potential that is our birthright: to become fully *human* in our lifetime in the highest sense of the word, as conscious beings who appreciate the chance to live on this earth and who understand that we are all related. Along this path we may encounter opportunities to experience and foster harmony in ourselves and, hence, in the world. Following the lead of the spirits, we can heal the wounds of disconnection from Nature that most of us suffer from, thus enhancing our own well-being and that of Mother Earth.

The Salish of the Pacific Northwest have a word, *skalalitude,* that describes what life is like when true kinship with Nature exists: "When people and Nature are in perfect harmony, then magic and beauty are everywhere."[5]

2

A DIFFERENT VIEW—
A NEW STORY

The question is not what you look at, but what you see.

THOREAU

*In the darkness of our restricted modern lives, we need
new visions that can open up our hearts and give us a
hopeful metaphor by which to live. . . .*

*We turn to the shamans, the mystics, and the
visionaries who seek unity and harmony with all creation.*

*In our age of crisis, turning to the inner wisdom of the seer
may be the most practical, down-to-earth thing we can do.*

*Seeing the earth as one dwelling place for all living
beings and caring for that common ground is a necessity
if we are to survive.*

LINDA SCHIERSE LEONARD,
CREATION'S HEARTBEAT

What is the nature of weather beyond our physical description? Does weather possess an innate spiritual essence, one that we can intentionally relate to and interact with? To truly understand the weather means looking beyond physical explanations. Sometimes there are no obvious interpretations, and in these cases science tries hard to find one. The assumption in our modern worldview is that a purely physical cause is there, waiting for technology to reveal it. Though there may be a rational, physical explanation for a particular phenomenon, to the shaman this is only part of the story—the "ordinary reality" version. To grasp the concept of weather shamanism and the path of aliveness and harmony it holds for us, we need to look at the origins and scope of our own learned perspective of the world—our *worldview*.

Our worldview consists of all the ideas, ideals, definitions, descriptions, and rules of what reality is all about and how to properly live our lives that we have been taught since birth; likely we began to learn this worldview even while gestating in our mother's womb. Our worldview infiltrates everything. It is our inherited, culturally transmitted story, one that fashions for each of us the lens of perception through which we "see" and interpret our worldly experiences.

From the Talmud we have the adage, "We do not see things as they are. We see them as we are." Lacking this awareness, we can easily fall into the deception of regarding any particular worldview as the correct version of reality and defend it—sometimes with great hostility—by dismissing or denouncing the perspective of others. History is replete with examples of wars and other tragic tales caused by the collision of worldviews.

Everyone is supported by his or her own worldview, and everyone is in bondage to it. On the one hand this perceptual filter makes it possible for us to live and behave in a more or less coherent, consensual way with the other human inhabitants of our local environs. Within its parameters, we can live together in general agreement as to the nature of reality. However, the price we pay for this general agreement is that we forget that our worldview, though capable of penetrating the deepest recesses of our consciousness, is neither the only truth nor the entire truth of reality.

As children growing up in the modern world, we learn through our schooling and experiences of socialization to value concrete techniques of gathering and processing information. We are taught to analyze, classify, and deduce rather than intuit. We are urged to accept the overall, consensual agreement about the nature of reality as something akin to "what you see is what you get": that the world is a tangible realm, most usefully described and understood in terms of dichotomy—something is either this or that, and rarely both at the same time.

In Western culture we tend to discount and disavow that which is ambiguous or paradoxical. It is the artists, poets, theologians, and philosophers among us who are most readily sanctioned by society to convey their sense of the world in other than rational, mechanical terms.

When confronted with something that perplexes or confounds us, we tend to attribute our lack of understanding to not having enough facts or evidence, or we relegate it to the scrap heap of the supernatural. These are the modes of explanation available to us within the container of our standard worldview. What we consider supernatural is that which escapes the boundaries of our worldview, that which leaps beyond the contours of our maps of the *real* world. These maps show no place for an unknown entity. It is as if we live on a map of a flat world, and if we go too far, we'll fall off the edge into uncharted and dangerous waters.

To expand our worldview, we can take that flat, two-dimensional map and round it out into a sphere, like the shape of the earth, the sun and the moon, and the wheel of the seasons. We can include the mysterious and not have it banished to the netherworlds. There is no abyss to become hopelessly lost in; there is only the whole, where all things hold center place and what goes around comes back around, again and again. This shift in perspective can transform the supernatural into something multidimensional, where the mystery becomes approachable, but not at the cost of awe and wonder.

One evening over dinner in a restaurant, we enjoyed an animated conversation with friends as we described some of our research and explorations about the weather. When the waitress stopped by to refill our wineglasses, our friend Steve genially asked her if she had any interest in the weather—and if she had ever tried to influence the weather. She paused and then answered, "Maybe." Shortly after returning with our meals she waved her arm expansively toward the large window and said, "Let there be rain!" We chuckled and went on to eat our dinner.

Ten minutes later we looked out the window and saw rain falling! Immediately we beckoned to our waitress, who seemed just as surprised. The rain shower was gentle and ended by the time we emerged from the restaurant.

What happened here? Even as we asked this question, we realized there could be no absolute answer, that mystery would prevail. The incident carried a spaciousness of ambiguity that could accommodate more than our normal worldview. We could look at this as an interesting coincidence, or we could view this moment from another perspective, another paradigm of reality, and find the possibility of a teaching from the spirits of weather: that weather hears and responds to us, and that weather is alive and in communication with us, though we may or may not intend it so.

We affect the entire world, including the weather, by our relationship to it in countless ways, likely as much by what we do as by what we do not do. When we rigidly hold to a given worldview, when we are unwilling or unable to shift our perspective, we can exert an untoward effect on the outer world beyond our individual intentions, be they well meaning or otherwise.

What if we looked at the elements of weather with a worldview that told us we are related? The Yamana people of the Amazon region take notice of the particular weather that accompanies the birth of a child. In their worldview, an individual birthed during "good" weather may have a special connection to that kind of weather—an extra dose of relatedness—and will, at times, be asked to appeal to the "good weather spirits" on behalf of the community. Those born under "bad" weather conditions are carefully watched for episodes of unruly behavior, as such behavior may actually call in "bad" weather conditions.[1]

How would it feel to hear about what the weather was like on the day of our birth? Would we be able to find a greater sense of relatedness with the natural world, with our own natures—even our destiny? It is said that Samuel Clemens (Mark Twain) remarked that because his birth coincided with the appearance of Halley's Comet, his death would coincide with its return—and that prediction proved true. I once met a man of Caribbean Taino heritage who proudly shared that he was born during a hurricane and that another one "visited" on the day of his wedding. His people, as well as the Maya, honored a great creator-storm deity, Hurakan, whose name is the origin of our present-day word *hurricane*.

We live by our stories, including those experiences and memories from our childhood when we heard stories, from fairy tales and biblical accounts to family anecdotes, all of which compose the tales of ourselves—our personal history—and reveal our interpretation of reality. These stories are our dreams of ourselves and our surroundings and as such carry great power, as they continually shape us and our manifestations in the world.

If we can cultivate an awareness of our own personal stories as well as the stories we hold as a culture, we can then see how they describe our understanding of reality and of how we live today. Furthermore, they will point to where we are headed. The clarity that this awareness brings can motivate us to initiate the changes we need to create if we are to safeguard the vitality of our world. These changes can be made far more easily and effectively when we know how to reframe our worldview. Shamans speak of this as learning to dream a new dream of the world—and of ourselves in the world. This is the first and most important step in any creative act of manifestation.

Through our current worldview we have torn ourselves away from the natural world in our attempts to encapsulate, regulate, and dominate it. We have run away from home and have forgotten the way back. Our relentless acts of consumerism are rapidly eating away at our dwelling place, to the point where we may soon find ourselves in the predicament of no longer having a life-sustaining home to which we can finally return.

We are fast running into trouble. We face sobering issues of fossil fuel depletion, wars over resources and nuclear proliferation, and environmental degradation, some of it irreversible. These are but a few of the challenging problems we and our descendants must meet. But what if we could learn from the legacy of our ancestors? What if we could infuse our prevailing worldview with a spiritually oriented perspective founded upon respect and a sense of reverence for this world and its inhabitants, including ourselves? If we could marry such a worldview with our technological abilities, then we would have a far greater chance of solving the life-threatening problems of today.

Tamra Andrews writes in *Legends of the Earth, Sea, and Sky:*

We take nature's power for granted. We see the sunrise and call it science; the ancients witnessed the same sunrise and called it a miracle. We have long lost touch with miracles. We no longer recognize the sacred. The ancients had an intimate relationship with the sky. They lived close to the land and they respected it, because they learned that given proper respect, the earth fulfilled their needs.[2]

We can look, once again, to our hunter-gatherer ancestors and to those indigenous peoples alive and well today, with their vast experience and considerable achievements of successful living in the natural world. We look to their legacy for wisdom and guidance, for the help we need today to survive and thrive in good relationship with all, and not at the expense of all. We can study the literature, the ancient mythologies, and anthropological and historical accounts, which contain practical knowledge for living on the earth as well as spiritual and religious teachings.

To this day many people of Iceland recognize the reality of a spiritual side of Nature and the need to live in good relationship with those spirit beings who coinhabit their world. The ancient knowledge of the "Hidden Ones" is remembered by many. In fact, Iceland's government allows for official recognition of these nature spirits, and their sacred places are often protected. For example, the construction route of a new road once had to be changed when it threatened a large boulder said to be important to the Hidden Ones; obstacles such as machine breakdowns, injuries, and the like had beset the project until the path was altered so that the sacred space was out of harm's way. As Edda, a native of Iceland, once related to us, humans frequently cross paths with the Hidden Ones, but these are often respectful encounters and do not always involve a conflict of desires.

Our ancestral worldview is not lost. It can surface in a longing for more personal experiences of the sacred. Perhaps we once heard a song in the wind and are listening for another. The power of a snowstorm to quiet a city's doings or the overriding intensity of lightning and thunder may speak to places in our souls where we are longing for a fresh breath of chaos, and where the wildness of Nature enlivens our hearts. City parks can be our favorite places to visit, where we find animals to observe and trees to walk by or sit under. At a period in David's life when he was a resident of New York City, he would time his walk to the office to place himself at the precise spot and moment when a sunbeam could touch him directly, and not as a reflection from the window of a building. This became a "highlight" of his day.

We still have doorways left to us to recover our heritage of ancestral wisdom. Underlying the cosmologies and worldviews of indigenous peoples around the world is the tradition of shamanism. Largely eradi-

cated by oppressive political systems and religious fundamentalism, shamanism is reawakening. Today we are witnessing and benefiting from a
growing population of initiated shamanic practitioners. This spontaneous revival of the oldest form of spirituality known to humankind has
been fostered over the past few decades by those called to its promise
of healing, empowerment, knowledge, and gifts of well-being for our
world.

The tradition of shamanism embodies one of humankind's oldest
worldviews. There is clear evidence that humans on every continent
knew the methods and knowledge of what we now call "shamanism"
for at least tens of thousands of years. Despite the grievous loss of many
of the world's indigenous cultures and their shamanic knowledge, we
still have access to our original spiritual roots. This is possible because,
at its heart, shamanism embodies a unifying worldview, one that by
virtue of its inclusive nature is shared by peoples of vastly different cultures and times.

Michael Harner, founder of the Foundation for Shamanic Studies
and recognized by many as a shaman, has brought forth the working
concept of *core shamanism,* meaning the basic "bones" or skeleton of
this venerable tradition. Core shamanism embraces that which is held
in common—the underlying precepts, practices, and cosmology—no
matter where in the world we find practicing shamans. The existence
of this core in itself is akin to a miracle in that peoples everywhere,
regardless of their different bioregions and enormous possibilities for
cultural variations in speech, dress, art, lifeways, and so on, ended up
with a working spiritual technology that is so similar at its essence.

It is significant for us to reflect upon the fact that no matter who
we are or where we live, thanks to the nearly ageless presence of shamanism in the world we each have ancestral ties to one or more of the
world's shamanic traditions. Although its roots are archaic, by virtue
of its inherent aliveness and ability to evolve in technique and perspective according to the needs and ways of the times, shamanism cannot
become obsolete.

Dr. Harner has this to say regarding the resurgence of shamanism in our modern world:

> Another important reason that shamanism has wide appeal today is that it is spiritual ecology. In this time of worldwide environmental crisis, shamanism provides something largely lacking in the anthropocentric "great" religions: reverence for, and spiritual communication with, the other beings of the Earth and with the Planet itself. In shamanism, this is not simple Nature worship, but a two-way spiritual communication that resurrects the lost connections our human ancestors had with the awesome spiritual power and beauty of our garden Earth.[3]

In the shamanic worldview, all that exists is alive, and everything and everyone is interrelated with everything else. We are related not just to each other as families and humans but also to the beings and elements of Nature—to the trees, rocks, animals, clouds, wind—and we are privileged to live upon our relative, the earth. From this basic premise, we can say that the tradition and practice of shamanism works to promote personal and planetary health, empowerment, relatedness, and spiritual growth. Shamanism recognizes that we live in a universe of both *ordinary reality,* this physical world of space and time, and *nonordinary reality,* the usually hidden spirit world. Knowledge of both these worlds is vitally connected to the well-being of all.

In every sort of cultural background, our traditions originated from those in which we recognized and honored our kinship with the beings of all the domains of the earth, of the weather, of Creation. We did not see ourselves as apart from the body of our environs, for we knew that we belonged to the whole. We could be alone but not separate, yet to survive and thrive, we valued community and depended upon its life-enhancing interrelationships. From the perspective of this worldview, we were able to enjoy and benefit from our sense of real kinship with the outer world as well as with the unseen spirit realm. And as with many, if not most, ordinary-reality families, some spirit kin we could relate to in an easier, more congenial fashion than others. Above all, we understood that every one of our acts, and even our thoughts, had some kind of effect in the world.

Within the worldview of shamanism, with its techniques of communication and union with that which is alive in all things, we find the tools to learn directly from Nature. The shaman is one who learns more from her or his own experience than from the teachings of others. By accessing the wisdom that is inherent in our surroundings, we, too, can learn what is behind appearances. We can ask Nature herself, "What is it we need to know at this time, and what is required of us to maintain balance in the world?" In this way we can begin to forge our own personal relationship with all of Nature and with the spirits of weather. The shaman who practices in the interests of maintaining good relationships among the human community and the plant, animal, and spirit communities of the local environs is no stranger to the spirits and forces of weather. She or he works to cultivate friendly relationships with these beings and may be gifted with a greater ability to predict the weather, and to sometimes influence the course of storms.

It is the journey, or "flight of the soul," that distinguishes a shaman from other healers or mystics. Once in this altered state of consciousness, it is possible to travel into nonordinary reality to explore the otherworldly landscapes of the upper and lower worlds, as well as the nonordinary aspect of our home, the middle world, to seek those helping spirits who can provide the needed healing and wisdom. The shamanic journey experience is also a way to learn through direct revelation about the nature of reality and the oneness and sacredness of the cosmos. It is a state of ecstasy in which we remember that everything is connected.

Effort on behalf of another is at the heart of shamanism, and many of our contemporary spiritual and healing practices evolved directly from this most ancient calling. When asked to do so, a shaman will often journey to the nonordinary realms of compassionate spirits to obtain healing assistance and information for practical use in our ordinary world and reality. Sometimes, through their collaboration with the helping spirits, shamans can work a miracle on behalf of an individual or a community.

The highest calling of the shaman is to help maintain and restore balance and harmony and thus relieve pain and suffering in the world. Shamanic weather working, or the attempt to change the weather in a particular place, is ultimately healing work. As with all shamanic healing, it is not only about "curing" a symptom, be it a headache or a drought; rather, it is aimed at bringing the whole system back into balance, to "heal" the earth, so that each part can function harmoniously on its own and in relation to all other parts. To try to change only one thing, to make it rain here or shine there, will ultimately damage the whole, like trying to heal a disease by treating only one symptom.

There is another side to this effort as well. As important as the lessons of the past are, what we also need, perhaps even more so, are the teachings that can come to us today that are appropriate for our world in all of its present complexity. The teachings of the compassionate spirits of the worlds of nonordinary reality, and especially the helping spirits of this middle world, are what we must have now.

Barring catastrophe, we can't bring the world back to a preindustrial or preagricultural age, nor would we want to. Our population is far too great and our environment drastically different from that of earlier days in terms of plant and animal communities, habitats, air and water quality, and so forth. To survive as a species we must alter our course. To do this we need to find that which inspires a change of heart and to seek the counsel of those who can show us a better way. To change our hearts we have only to reach out to the natural world that is still available to us. We can start right where we are with an open heart and a desire for relatedness. To offer something in return, we begin simply with our presence, our willingness to show up. In this way we'll tend those wild seeds of our internal garden.

Through the practices of shamanism and the shifting of our worldview, David and I felt we could face the modern challenges of life and manage to be of some use in the world. Our experience has been that it takes time and sustained intentionality to successfully adopt and become one with a new paradigm of reality. It's like learning another language. We are taught the rudiments of vocabulary and grammar and then maybe become adept at pronunciation. Yet we still have to live the language—think in it, dream in it—before we can be truly fluent.

We are so engulfed by the worldview of our birth that as modern-day shamanic practitioners we have to struggle to wholeheartedly trust the reality of the numinous spiritual world our ancestors knew and related to so well. It is unlikely that the shamans from indigenous cultures were as perplexed or suffered in this way. Nonetheless, we can all set out to learn how to live in good relationship with our world, in our present evolution of self and times. We need to know how to restore balance where it is so sadly lost. To bring to light what the compassionate spirits can teach us about how to conduct our lives in sustainable and harmonious ways, we begin by expanding and transforming our worldview into a more inclusive paradigm. It is an enormous challenge, and the stakes couldn't be higher.

The weather is an ever-present portal to this end. Extreme weather events have an unerring way of shaking down the walls of our worldview and hence our perceived security. They fill us with awe—the kind of fear-inspired awe that can hurl us out of our comfort zone, away from the confines of our familiar preoccupations. In these moments we are capable of losing our preconceptions of the nature of things, and the opportunity awaits to enter into a spaciousness of being that is not normally available to us, if we manage to steer around fears of personal survival or loss of property. Our appetite for life is whetted, our sense of appreciation soars as we look at the world, each other, and ourselves with new eyes. It is notable that in the aftermath of a calamitous storm so many people readily move into a place of compassion for one another, whether in villages or big cities. Thrust out of our normal realms of relating to the world, we enter into an expanded openness of the heart.

Consider the story of John Newton, captain of his own schooner and a slave trader. He and his ship's crew, along with their cargo of suffering Africans, encountered a storm on the high seas, a storm so fierce and frightening that Newton gave up hope and communicated to his crew that they were all in the hands of the Almighty. But they survived that storm, and something drastically changed for John Newton. You might say his worldview shifted, because he renounced slavery altogether, became a Protestant minister, and gifted the world with the well-loved song *Amazing Grace*.

For thousands of years the shaman has deliberately set about to suspend, at will, the confines of ordinary worldview and, through experiencing that ecstatic state of oneness, has been able to bring back one more piece of the puzzle of the true nature of our cosmos. Each time any of us is able to experience this sense of unity, we touch upon a state of harmony and are changed. The shaman well knows that any change or shift in our awareness affects the world around us, sometimes subtly and sometimes dramatically. Again and again, the shaman seeks experiences to bring on that fire of illumination, of brilliant awareness. For all of us, life itself in this middle world offers countless initiations and moments of ecstatic insight and feeling—if we can manage to relax our hold on our operative worldview.

We are trained to see only one worldview. Some cultures are trained to see only the other. It is our challenge and responsibility to learn that there is more than one worldview, to see beyond our socialization to what is really there. This truly is the expression of oneness that can help us to establish a working, sustainable relationship with life, with Nature, and with weather. In a world that is struggling to survive our abuses and excesses, we need now more than ever to have people willing and able to heal the rift between Nature and ourselves. The worldview of shamanism provides us with an effective and profound way to reconnect with Nature and with the power and wisdom found in the spiritual world and to learn to live in harmony with all things and all beings on the planet.

3

CHANGING THE WEATHER

IS IT REAL?

And Jesus arose and rebuked the wind and said to the sea: Peace, be still. And the wind ceased and there was a great calm.

MARK 4:39

Everybody talks about the weather, but nobody does anything about it.

EDITORIAL IN THE HARTFORD COURANT, 1897

The summer had been unusually dry, even for the arid region around Santa Fe, New Mexico. A prolonged drought of several years was unabated, and the daytime temperatures were consistently running to 90 degrees or more, which was high for that altitude of 7,000 feet above sea level. The fire danger rating was posted as "extreme," recreational road closures were in effect, and there were restrictions on the use of city water. It was July, and Sandra Ingerman was leading a five-day "Medicine for the Earth" gathering just outside of town. By midweek Sandra had reached the point where she normally held a powerfully healing fire ceremony. But because of the drought, she had decided to conduct the ceremony indoors, using a fireplace instead of the usual outdoor fire ring. Yet due to the extreme conditions, she worried that even this precaution would not be sufficient. What if errant sparks flew up the chimney and out onto the land? She realized that the risk was too great and was prepared to give up the ceremony—unless she could receive a clear and unequivocal sign from the universe to proceed.

As a shaman, Sandra honored the elements of Nature and taught others to do so as well. This would not be the first or last time she would directly address her helping spirits and the spirits of Nature. On the morning of the ceremony, her prayer was to the point: "I need a sign in favor of the fire ceremony or I will cancel. If you give me rain for thirty seconds by 4:00 p.m., I'll take that as a 'yes.'" At that point in the day the sky was utterly clear—and dry. By afternoon a few clouds had appeared, and at precisely 4:00 p.m., it did rain, for thirty seconds, and then it stopped. The fire ceremony went off without a hitch.

Weather working is real and has been practiced in all of its manifestations from ancient times to this day. However, the work of influencing the weather spiritually is unknown to the majority of today's Western world. There is little room for it in our modern worldview, if we even think of it at all. What is more familiar to us, and a comfortable fit with our prevailing worldview, is the concept of *weather modification*—those activities designed to forcibly change the weather through mechanical means.

Today the arena of weather modification is one of aggressive pursuit. The interested parties range from government departments, such as the U.S. Department of Agriculture, to our military forces and those civilian sectors of the population involved in educational research, business, community services, and the like. The U.S. government has engaged in significant amounts of research and experiments with the aim of directly influencing weather outcomes, especially from the

1940s and continuing into the present. At least thirty other countries in the world, such as Thailand, with its Bureau of Royal Rainmaking, are also engaged in activities of weather modification.

In the United States, back in the 1800s, efforts to modify or alter weather events included burning forests, ringing church bells, firing cannons, and detonating dynamite or other explosives to deter hail and tornadoes. As it turns out, the methods of those times were not so far off compared to some used today. In 1891 the United States Congress allocated $9,000 for weather modification research—primarily for rainmaking under the Department of Agriculture.

In 1946, at the General Electric Research Laboratory in New York, Nobel Prize–winning chemist Irving Langmuir and researcher Vincent Schaefer were able to re-create a tiny "snowstorm" in a box. Out of this, through the additional expertise of fellow physical chemist and meteorologist Bernard Vonnegut, silver iodide cloud seeding was born. Langmuir and his colleagues continued their program of research and experiments, named Project Cirrus, and by the 1950s cloud seeding enjoyed a hopeful popularity in Western countries. "In those heady early days as much as 10 percent of the sky over the U.S. may have been under cultivation by cloud seeders, who claimed increases in rainfall of up to 15 percent or more."[1] In 1998 the National Oceanic and Atmospheric Administration reported that in ten states alone there were at least forty-eight civilian weather modification projects in the works. According to the World Meteorological Organization, in that same year a total of eighty-four efforts in twenty-six countries were in progress, mostly for rain enhancement and hail suppression.[2]

On October 13, 1947, Project Cirrus launched the first effort at large-scale weather modification through a collaboration of the U.S. Navy and Air Force to drain a hurricane of its energy with cloud seeding. The attempt to diminish the great storm, which had been spinning off the coast of Georgia and headed out to sea, may instead have caused it to suddenly veer around and directly strike Savannah, Georgia, with disastrous results. Similarly, in August 1952, off the coast of

England, the Royal Air Force conducted a cloud seeding experiment on an approaching storm, and this, too, resulted in a calamity for the resident coastal population. Despite these undesirable results, President Eisenhower appointed a committee to further investigate the possibility of storm abatement during the mid-1950s.

In 1962, U.S. researchers began another federally funded program, Project Stormfury, which targeted the hurricanes of the tropical and subtropical Atlantic, Caribbean, and Gulf of Mexico. However, the efforts of Project Stormfury brought a measure of international controversy to the issue of weather modification. In the late 1970s the government of Mexico protested the attempted interference, as the arid northern sectors of that country depend upon the rains that hurricanes and other tropical systems bring.[3] Even so, we continue to explore the idea of hurricane control to this day. In July 2001, for example, a private company, Dyn O Mat, dropped approximately 2,000 pounds of a gelatinous substance into a cloud and watched as the cloud immediately disappeared. However, the amount of material required to effectively treat a hurricane in this manner would be overwhelmingly huge and also would deposit a like amount of residue into the ocean.[4]

The tenor of weather modification took on a more warlike tone in the 1960s and '70s. In 1974 the U.S. Defense Department revealed that during the Vietnam War, between 1967 and 1972, it had engaged in an intensive program of cloud seeding over the skies of Vietnam, Laos, and Cambodia with the intention of creating enhanced rainfalls during the summer monsoon season so that the Ho Chi Minh Trail, the enemy's main supply line, would be rendered impassable.[5] Partly as a result of this program, the United Nations passed an agreement calling for a moratorium on efforts to change the weather for military purposes, or "the hostile use of environmental modification." It is questionable whether this agreement is fully honored by the nations of the world. For example, a 1996 U.S. Air Force report titled *Weather as a Force Multiplier: Owning the Weather in 2025* discusses the possibilities of weather modification for warfare.[6] Elsewhere, Pierre St. Amand of the U.S. Naval Weapons

Center reportedly stated, "We regard the weather as a weapon. Anything one can use to get his way is a weapon, and the weather is as good a one as any."[7] In light of this it is interesting to note that during the recent U.S.-led invasion of Iraq, the advance of the coalition ground troops was effectively curtailed for days due to a sandstorm of biblical proportions as it raged across the Iraqi countryside.

The 1960s and '70s were known as the "glory days" of weather modification as research projects expanded. Hopes ran high. Yet there are few undeniably clear success stories related to modern-day weather modification, at least so far. Statistically, the results of rain enhancement activities of the past forty years are more often than not frustratingly equivocal in their conclusions regarding their value. Articles about weather modification carry promise in their titles—"Cloud Dancers," for example, in the Spring 2000 issue of *Scientific American Presents* and "Squeezing Clouds" in the July 1999 issue of *Science News*—but it remains a field of dubious reliability to date. Nevertheless, a Science TV documentary entitled *Owning the Weather*, which aired in November 2004, generally portrays our corporate, scientific, and military sectors as hot on the trail of effective weather modification to the extent that the legal and moral questions of "leasing the rain" and "owning the weather" are no longer far-fetched.

Perhaps most disturbing of all is the High Frequency Active Auroral Research Program (HAARP). Created in 1993, HAARP is a jointly managed U.S. Air Force and Navy research program located in out-of-the-way Gakona, Alaska. Founded upon the work of the genius Nikola Tesla, who in 1886 invented the power and transmission system of alternating electrical current (AC), and who applied for many more patents for his inventions—including a "death ray" in 1940—HAARP is designed to manipulate the upper atmosphere, a layer beginning about 30 miles above our heads. The HAARP transmitter is a "phased array antenna system," in other words a large field of antennas designed to work together to focus radio-frequency energy capable of manipulating the ionosphere. The radio frequencies can be pulsed, shaped, and powered up in ways that supercede the capabilities of other existing transmitters.[8]

While HAARP is controversial for many people, there seems to be no last word on what it is ultimately about. One explanation is that it serves as an Arctic research station for purposes of greater understanding of the upper atmosphere, including solar-terrestrial research. What seems to disturb many is that HAARP is capable of beaming highly concentrated radio waves into the upper atmosphere, where its power can be utilized to superheat selected areas of our ionosphere. The stated purpose for this capacity is to enhance our communication and surveillance systems for civilian and defense purposes. There are several other atmospheric heaters in the world, but none so powerful as HAARP.

While there may be phenomenal research potential here, some fear that HAARP will lead to yet another hideous weapon of mass destruction, while others worry about its capacity to be misused regarding the weather. There is speculation that HAARP experiments may have deliberately shifted the jet stream above Gakona, Alaska, during the winter of 2000, pushing the colder air southward, which was followed by a rare tornado outbreak in Florida. It is a challenge to trust that we really know what we are doing with all this power and technological ability. HAARP and its potential to affect our atmosphere is yet another one of the major ethical and practical issues we face as a culture today, on par with nuclear and hydrogen power, genetically modified organisms, cloning, global warming, and so on.

Everything regarding the weather has a "downwind" effect, and a real potential for harm exists alongside the desired results. If a storm such as a hurricane is successfully turned, where does it then go? And what about its long- and short-term effects upon ecosystems, beyond issues of loss of life and property damage? Hugh, a rancher in southern Texas, told us he prays for the hurricanes to come so that the arid rangeland may be watered. We live on an extraordinarily complex planet and barely understand the subtleties of all the interwoven relationships and workings of our world.

When we approach weather modification as a confrontation,

we're less likely to care about possible secondary effects beyond the intended outcome. Disputes over cloud seeding are not uncommon, the main question being whether the practice gives to one area at the cost of another. In the winter of 2004, for example, a mountain town in Colorado budgeted hundreds of thousands of dollars to arrange for cloud seeding by cannon fire from the mountain's rim whenever there was a forecast for a promising snowstorm. Having endured extreme forest and range fires from two summer droughts, the town had decided to take action in this way to try to help themselves.

Downwind of the Colorado Rockies, however, in July 1999, the citizens of a dryland farming county in Kansas voted to discontinue a commercial cloud seeding program on the premise that regional hail suppression efforts were depriving them of rain. A local farmer, Keith Downing, argued that the Kansas Groundwater District #4 ought to be paying more attention to the issues of proper management and conservation of the invaluable groundwater rather than attempting to "Band-Aid" the problems through questionable weather modification practices.[9]

In the words of James Swan, author of *Nature as Teacher and Healer,*

> Weather modification is a dangerous business. A single thunderstorm can dump 125 million gallons of water. There is enough electrical energy in the average thunderstorm to meet the power needs of the United States for twenty minutes, the equivalent of a 120-kiloton nuclear bomb.[10]

From the eyes and heart of another worldview—a shamanic worldview—we can move beyond the limited activities of weather modification to consider the apparent miracles of weather working, the art of influencing the weather from a spiritually oriented perspective. Our ancestors regularly engaged in weather-working practices through their relationships with weather's spiritual side. There are those in the world today who remember the ancestral ways of honoring and working with the weather, and who still practice this art of relating.

According to the Koyukon peoples living today in the subarctic, boreal-forest realm of Alaska, Nature holds the power in their domain and cannot be conquered. Richard Nelson, who lived with the Koyukon, writes in *Make Prayers to the Raven,*

> Considering its power over people's lives and emotions, it is not surprising that weather is the most fully personified element in the Koyukon physical world. The interchange between people and these conscious entities is fairly elaborate and intense. Oncoming weather is announced by signs, it is received as a communion of awareness, and it is sometimes manipulated by people who have learned its few points of vulnerability.[11]

Similarly, in northern California, the Yurok tribe used a "rain stone" to help with their weather working. It was so potent in its abilities to manifest rain that the people buried it for safekeeping. The rain stone was accidentally unearthed by a road crew in 1959, and the next day 5 inches of rain fell. In 1966 the rain stone was inadvertently dug up once again, and this time there were floods.[12]

In the shamanic cultures of the past as well as the present, weather-working ability was and still is often part of the shaman's job description. This ability ideally is exercised for the survival and well-being of the community. Successful weather working also demonstrates the shaman's strong relationship with the spirits and the forces of Nature. Implicit in these demonstrations is an opportunity not for self-aggrandizement but to support the community in the certain knowledge that the spirits are really at work and that miracles can indeed be expected.

Wovoka, otherwise known as Jack Wilson, was a Paiute Ghost Dance prophet and shaman. On New Year's Day 1889, as he was chopping wood, Wovoka heard a "great noise." While on his way to investigate, he fell unconscious and experienced a profound vision in which the Creator instructed him to teach brotherhood among all Indian peoples, as well as between the Indian and the white man. Interestingly, this vision coincided with a total solar eclipse. From this experience Wovoka brought forth a new way, popularly known as the 1890 Ghost Dance Religion.[13]

These Ghost Dances, or Friendship Dances, came at a time of terrible suffering for the tribes of western North America: they faced the demise of their entire way of life as their lands and freedoms were appropriated by waves of immigrants moving west in search of homes and fortunes. Decimated by epidemic diseases and wars of resistance, the native peoples were ready to work—to dance—for the restoration of their world and lost loved ones. Along the way, as Wovoka's message traveled from tribe to tribe, it began to lose its teaching of brotherhood for *all,* and the dance, for some, became a way to restore the world and to eliminate the white man. The U.S. Army became aware of a growing power among the people of the plains, where the wars were still active, and the Ghost Dance religion was forbidden. It all ended tragically in a massacre of men, women, and children at Wounded Knee Creek, South Dakota, on the morning of December 29, 1890. Yet Wovoka and his teachings are not forgotten today. There are still Ghost, or Friendship, Dances conducted on behalf of the world, and a revival of this healing way may be emerging once again among Wovoka's people and others.

During his mystical experience, Wovoka was given power to work with the elements of Nature. He became well known for his healing and weather-working abilities, including his famous, or infamous (depending on your worldview), working to produce ice in the river on a sweltering day in July. He predicted that ice would be seen floating down the river on a certain day, and so it was. Some records chronicle that event as a genuine demonstration of Wovoka's ability to manifest a miracle of weather working, while others, who have no room for miracles, insist that Wovoka played a huge joke on gullible people. The ice event remains ambiguous as we attempt to look back to a time when none of us were present, yet numerous stories persist to this day from many individual accounts regarding Wovoka's exceptional abilities.

According to historical chronicles, Wovoka could accurately fore-tell storms and bring on drought-relieving rain and snow. And it is said that when his young son died, his intense grieving was accompanied by torrential rains and storms that threatened the homes and lives of his people, so much so that two other shamans had to approach him to ask him to calm the weather. In one account, remembered by many, Wovoka again demonstrated his powers when teased by some Numu men who were playing baseball (or pitching hay in another version). It was a hot, sunny day, and as he walked by, one of the men called him "rainmaker" and dared him to make it rain. "A cloud in that otherwise clear blue sky immediately appeared, and Wovoka had to be begged to 'call off his powers,' lest the baseball game or their crops be ruined."[14]

From our modern times, Dave, a longtime shamanic practitioner, told us of his memorable weather-related experience. We will never know what really happened here—whether Dave witnessed a genuine weather working or wonderful "coincidence." Either way, it stirs the imagination to think of the possibility of a responsive relationship with the weather.

What follows is an account of something I saw roughly ten years ago, and it is therefore probably inaccurate in some of the details. On the other hand, much of what I saw remains as clear as if it happened yesterday.

On Bainbridge Island, near Seattle, Washington, the city had commissioned a work of art that turned out to be a large wooden sculpture about 16 feet high. I remember it as somewhat abstract, but the subject was a thunderbird. I don't remember the title. I do remember that it had an inlaid section of bright metal reminiscent of a bolt of lightning. The sculpture was placed at a major intersection near the high school, and I happened to be driving by on the day of the dedication. I stopped to watch, along with a small crowd of perhaps one hundred people. City politicians made the typical speeches, and then a small, older Native American man was introduced. His name was Henry Seaweed. A helper accompanied him with a drum.

The helper sat off to the side and began drumming. Henry Seaweed, wearing a ceremonial head covering and a jacket with white ermine pelts, began to sing, dance slightly, and rattle. I remember his motions consisted primarily of pointing at the sky with one hand while rattling and pointing to the earth with the other. The drumming was soft and rather slow. This continued for several minutes. Suddenly, a few blocks to the west, there was a bright flash of lightning followed by a loud clap of thunder. I looked up to see a very dark cloud above us. Henry Seaweed ended his dance and prepared to leave. I don't remember that he said anything either before or after his work.

Thunder and lightning are very rare in that part of the country. I could not remember whether the dark cloud was there before Henry Seaweed began his dance. It was a typical Puget Sound day, cool and overcast, but not raining. The thunder and lightning were not followed by rain, as I remember.

The reaction of the crowd was interesting. I don't think they made any connection between Henry Seaweed's work and the thunder. Personally, I was so excited I was trembling. I felt that I had witnessed one of those occasions when shamanic work causes immediate and objective changes in the ordinary physical world in which we live. I will never forget it.

When practiced by indigenous tribal peoples, weather working has long enjoyed something of an exotic respectability in the eyes of the general public—especially when it is successful. In the 1970s a subsidiary company of Walt Disney, Calgary Productions, filmed a movie titled *Nomads of the North* in Banff, Alberta. At the beginning of the project everything was in place, from the constructed movie set to lodging for the crew to the one hundred extras. Yet the essential ingredient of snow was missing. Days passed without the expected snowfalls for that time of year, and the only thing accumulating was the growing financial cost. Finally someone came up with the idea of contacting Chief Johnny Bearspaw of the Stony Indian tribe. Chief Bearspaw and his tribal dancers had successfully weather-worked for the Calgary Rodeo Stampede a few years before, and at this point the movie people were desperate for help. Chief Bearspaw and thirty-one ceremonial dancers agreed to show up and perform a snow dance for the fee of $10 per dancer. They arrived the next morning in full regalia, and to the compelling beat of the large drums, they danced and chanted for snow. By the next morning at least 7 inches of snow had fallen, and the filming began.[15]

Among the Tibetan people there lived a Buddhist monk, Yeshe Dorje Rinpoche, who also worked with the weather. Born in 1926 in Tibet, he eventually moved to India in response to the Dalai Lama's request for him to come and establish a monastery for his particular sect of Tibetan Buddhism. Yeshe Dorje Rinpoche lived his long life intensely dedicated to his religious path. In addition to his other responsibilities, it was Yeshe Dorje's duty to work to avert hail from the Dalai Lama's ceremonies as well as to bring the timely blessing of rain at other ceremonies. Yeshe Dorje also successfully weather-worked for rain for communities suffering from prolonged droughts.[16]

In the United States lives another contemporary rainmaker, Matt Ryan. In recent years farmers from the drought-stricken areas of northern Montana, in the region known as the Hi-Line, pooled their money to hire Matt's services. A former New York City cab driver, Matt discovered he had a gift for relating to the weather. He attributes much of his success to his love for the clouds and his ability to "romance" them into giving up their life-giving rains or snows. A man with a deep spiritual connection to the natural world, he exhorts his clients to really look at the clouds and consider them as beings with feelings and desires for attention. Matt's weather working is often, though not always, dramatically successful. According to a *Los Angeles Times* article about

Matt's work with the struggling farmers, "None of the 250 Montanans who have paid Ryan more than $100,000 wants a refund. The man did what he promised, they say. He made it rain. He whipped up the sky as if beating a bowl of egg whites, turned the clouds frothy and produced a series of heartening storms."[17]

Regardless of the particular approach or method for weather working, underneath them all is a worldview that embraces all the earth's inhabitants, animate and inanimate, as alive and aware beings who are capable of responding to human desires, needs, and actions. Those who understand this relate to Nature as if they are truly a part of it, as if they are seen and, in turn, responded to by the natural world wherever they go. Our ancestors knew that their actions and even their thoughts mattered and could make a difference in the world around them. We can still find evidence of ancestral weather-working knowledge and practices in the Americas, Africa, Asia, Australia, Polynesia, Europe—just about anywhere there is weather and humans who know they depend upon it for life.

4

STEPPING THROUGH

WE FIND AND CROSS THE THRESHOLD

In the early days David and I could not immediately comprehend the potential that awaited us if we committed to a true collaboration with the spirits of weather. In our ignorance we assumed that relating to the weather would only raise the specter of controlling weather, with all its inherent issues of power and ethics.

We were looking for the promise of a spiritual relationship dedicated to healing and restoration of balance for the earth. We knew we were on the threshold of something vital, and as we evaluated the potential worth of this new direction in our shamanic practice we asked: Will this path be substantial? Creative? Of practical relevance to the needs of our world in these tricky times? Can it inspire spiritual growth? And finally, we wondered about our own ability to measure up; in other words, what would a collaboration with the spirits of weather ask of us?

I decided to consult a trusted and compassionate helping spirit:

I am just below the crest of the Continental Divide in the northern Rocky Mountains. The sky is an intense blue on this late autumn day. I make my way down a precipitous path from the uppermost hot-springs pool to the rim of the lowest and largest one. Ragged mountain peaks border the west side of a narrow valley far below, highlighted by the silver ribbon of a river coursing through. The drumbeat is insistent, and I refocus my intention to journey to the lower world for the help I seek.

I step into the pool of clear, warm water and immediately find the cleft in the rock wall that will send me on my shamanic journey down, down through a tunnel to another pool in an underground cave, where dark tree roots protrude from the ground above. I find an opening here also, and like water, I flow through a long tunnel that spirals down through the darkness until I finally feel the leafy branches of a great tree. I climb down into a junglelike clearing and follow the tree's taproot into the earth, where once again I rapidly descend in darkness, until I land on the sandy floor of a large and spacious grotto. I hear the roar of surf and smell the tang of sea air. Sunlight dances upon breaking waves just beyond the grotto's cavernous mouth. I emerge from the soft, still atmosphere and walk alongside the base of the cliff in a world filled with light, movement, and the sounds of life. In the distance is a small figure, backlit by the sun and perched upon a huge boulder facing the sea. I know this is Grandmother.

Her body and countenance speak of one who has spent many years living in the wild, and though she appears frail in her great age, I see her nimbly leap off the boulder to greet me. I am momentarily riveted by the power of her gaze, the piercing brightness of her eyes. The wind flutters the strands of seaweed and plants that make up her head and body ornaments, and dangling shells rhythmically clink together as Grandmother dances before me. I hear the drone of drums as I respectfully bow my head in salutation and wait for her invitation to speak. Then she smiles, and her face crinkles all over.

"Grandmother, please give me a teaching regarding the connection between humans and weather."

I watch as she raises her arms to invite and receive the elements of weather as they actively bless her with a wild procession of clouds, rain, wind, fog, and thunderous storm, finally breaking into sunshine, and ending with a vivid rainbow. Throughout it all she stands there, happily, at her ease . . .

Grandmother then turns to me and speaks of how the spirits of weather call to us and can use the forces of weather to get our attention. She says that weather affects us more deeply than we know. In our middle world, we may watch how rain brings on the beauty of flowers, yet we are not as aware of how the weather fashions us. She tells me that to be fully human, we must grow in to and stand in our power. As we do so, we'll learn to relate to the elements of weather as kin, for they are our relatives, and, when we respond to them as such, we share the gifts of our own aliveness.

As Grandmother speaks these last words, I hear the drums change their beat, calling me back. Though I am reluctant to leave her company, I respond to the insistent drumbeat and thank her for her willingness to help me. After taking a last look, I turn and retrace my steps back to the mountainside hot-spring pool and the sunshine and chill of our world on a late autumn day.

Grandmother's teaching inspired me to think about how I had responded to weather's elements in my life—by running indoors to escape drenching rain or blowing wind or an oncoming squall. Once in a while I welcomed rain and wind with my bare skin, reveling in the sensuality of weather's touch. And then there were those crackling times on a New Mexico mountaintop where I waited out thunderstorms perched inside a Forest Service fire lookout tower—a 90-foot lightning rod!

Today it's no longer easy to relate to the intensity of the feelings David and I stirred up—in ourselves and others—by approaching the threshold of this path. Yet it all turned out to be a necessary part of our learning curve. We were well aware that it was the shaman's duty to establish and maintain good relations between the human community and the spirits of the surrounding environs where the people lived, hunted, and traveled. Yet we had failed to make the deeper connection that was before us now—to a relationship with the spirits of weather that surround all of us, everywhere.

I like to think that my ignorance was more a matter of timeliness and readiness—both that of our culture and my own. I had to grow into my spiritual path to a certain degree, and I had to realize that I knew nothing. I was a blank slate in this realm, except for my lifelong passion and love for the weather. I had to repeatedly learn that to keep a "beginner's mind" alive in our consciousness, no matter how far we think we've come, is to keep an open door to the mysteries of life.

Additionally, in those earlier days David and I frequently encountered conflicted attitudes in other people who first heard of this work, obliging us to answer to misgivings regarding our personal ethics. Often we were met with an almost instantaneous "knee jerk" of misunderstanding, a reflexive reaction to any idea of intentionally relating to weather. Peoples' responses ranged from the incredulous "You can't be serious!" to reactions about issues of power—of controlling the weather. We found the latter response mostly among those who do accept that weather has a spirited nature. At first this was bewildering, though it should not have been, considering we are all brought up with more or less the same story of reality in our modern culture.

One afternoon while leading a five-day seminar in core shamanism at the Esalen Institute in Big Sur, California, we had just finished drumming for one of our favorite journey exercises, a group effort to meet with a spirit of weather and receive a teaching to bring back to our circle. There was a buzz in the room as small groups of participants compared and organized their journey findings in a summation for the entire circle. I watched curiously as one of the women, Pat, practically ran out of the room, and I was just about to go look for her when she returned, still visibly in an emotional state, though poised.

As usual, the group findings were strong. We all listened raptly to the wisdom coming forth, and few could miss that we were on the leading edge of discovery. When it was time for Pat's group, a volunteer gave the group's account and then turned to Pat, who apparently needed to speak for herself.

What followed was a forcefully worded, emotionally delivered diatribe as she recounted her journey and delivered the message from

her helping spirit. A strong woman, whom I had come to appreciate over our few days together, Pat looked directly at us and stated,
unequivocally, that we were outsiders, that we didn't know Father Sky
or Brother Wind, and that if we didn't understand seasons and mountains, then why were we asking about weather? We had no power . . .
we had no business seeking knowledge without relationship. Over and
over I heard the stinging words, "no power" and "outsiders."

Time stopped for me. I remember first being startled and then feeling a surge of adrenaline-stoked fires. My cheeks felt blazing hot, and
I wondered whether steam really could emerge from my ears like an
enraged dragon or overwrought teapot. Alongside me David was a calm
and steady presence. I remember how distant I felt, even through the
turmoil of temper and embarrassment. That distance offered me a profound stillness, a quiet place where I could just listen and not interrupt
in our defense, even as I took in the wide-eyed stares of all in the circle.
I knew in my heart that this wasn't about ego; it was either a great
teaching or a judgment from the spirits—or both.

As Pat spoke the harsh and contemptuous words of her helping
spirit, I had no idea how I would respond. All I could do was listen,
feel, and witness—and hope for inspiration. She finally finished, as
the quiet of twilight was upon us. The sounds of waves on an ebbing
tide drifted up from below, and, unnoticed, the sun had set behind a
horizon of clouds and fog.

I waited for what seemed like a long time as I breathed myself back
and then spoke the only reply I could offer: "You are absolutely right.
We have no power with the spirits of weather. And that is exactly why
we are here now asking them for teachings, for their guidance on how
to relate to them, to honor them. And if we are worthy, they may even
teach us how to work with them one day."

I reminded her that, as she had recounted in her journey, the weather
spirit teacher had, after all, given her a teaching for our circle beyond the
tongue-lashing—a brief description of a personal or community ceremony
to respectfully acknowledge and relate to weather's spiritual nature. In

the end David and I were able to point to this experience as a teaching that the spirits from which we seek help are compassionate in truth, yet compassion is not always expressed with tenderness.

Frustrated with what I felt was an adverse reaction to this work, I journeyed to my own weather spirit teacher, who immediately laughed and asked why I would expect anything different. The passion this sparks in people is a testament to the incredible powers of creation and destruction that weather holds and exercises in the world. It reaches right down into our soft spots, those vulnerable places of personal safety. Understandably, people will often react with emotion, and sometimes with anger.

I have come to thank Pat for that scathing moment. Her challenge turned out to be one of those rare gifts that can thrust you into a personal place of truth, of refined clarity. I realized that as I breathed myself back into the room for a response, I returned free of doubt, of any equivocation regarding the great worth of this path. It had done its job in refining my motives and intentions. I may or may not have spoken it aloud, but I knew where I stood with my helping spirits and trusted where they were leading me.

Next, David and I searched for any remaining legacies of indigenous wisdom as we looked toward our ancestors to learn how they conceived of weather. Naturally we had to step around our culture's standard judgments of the ancient world's relatedness to Nature as simple-minded, naive, and childish versions of reality. Few of us have not heard of the Greek god Zeus, with his thunderbolts, or the Norse god Thor, with his hammer, and others capable of hurling lightning toward the earth. A gigantic and powerful thunderbird—a great bird who flaps his wings and generates storms and lightning—figures for many peoples of North America as well as some parts of Africa.

The old deities were illustrious and mighty. There is Aeolus, the ancient Greek god of wind; Sila, the Inuit deity of sky and air; the Aztec gods Ehecatl of the winds and Tlaloc of the rain; Frigg, the Norse fertility goddess of the earth, sky, and clouds; Anu, the sky god of the Babylonians; Adad, the Mesopotamian rain and storm god; the Chinese Lei Kung, god of thunder, and Tien Mu, god of lightning; Tawhiri-Matea, the Maori god of the storm, winds, and elements; and Cuycha, rainbow deity of the Inca—to name just a few.

As David and I unearthed titles and descriptive sketches of barely remembered spirits, we learned that behind these venerable weather deities were still more powerful deities of even more ancient ages, who once preceded them in importance and relevance to human consciousness, while other spirits appeared to have been handed straight down through history, perhaps with a name change from time to time. What we found important in all of this is that these beings were conceived of as alive and sentient—and sometimes open to persuasion.

Martin Prechtel, initiated and trained in the Tzutujil Mayan tradition as a shaman, lived and practiced for many years in a Guatemalan village, and he speaks of an ancient spiritual contract between the village and the many deities known to its people: that the gods would keep the life force of the village alive, providing everything the villagers needed to thrive; and for their part, the humans must feed the gods "remembrance." The villagers offered remembrance in a variety of ways, which included many beautiful rituals, decorative objects, traditions of speech, and song and dance, as well as living life itself, so long as that remembrance was dedicated to the gods and flowed from a sense of gratitude for them and for life. The gods ate this remembrance; it kept them alive, and it had to be delicious. Martin writes, "A forgotten God was an angry God, or a dead God. In either case, the life sap would stop flowing, and all this life would be as if it had never existed. We would cease."[1] He also cautions us in a timely piece of advice:

Modern culture can ban gods, but they don't die or disappear; they simply go underground and get angry. Instead of being fed deliberately and ritually, they arbitrarily come and take their due. Old, alienated deities become enemies when you forget to invite them into your life.[2]

However, David and I sensed that there had to be more to our ancestral knowledge than a sacred assemblage of deities and magical animals. We suspected that this was only the surface layer left to us, that our modern worldview would not permit easy access to what might lie beneath those historical sketches. Time and again we faced unexpected limits in our capacity for vision as we encountered the power of the ordinary-reality perceptions we were raised with.

Eventually the doorway we were invited to step through grew more spacious and the path a bit easier to find, though always mysterious with its twists and blind corners. There were times when we felt thoroughly discouraged, yet I came to think of our search for knowledge and relatedness as somehow guided.

One day an incident occurred at just the right time to inspire me on. As I walked past the rare and used-book section of our local café, the Second Read, the title of an old children's book caught my eye. *Helping the Weatherman,* by Gertrude Alice Kay, tells the story of the adventures of a young girl and her little brother as they, assisted by Crow, try to take over for the old, tired weatherman. I was irresistibly drawn to this beautifully illustrated volume, until I saw the price. Too much, and so I reluctantly put it back. However, I couldn't shake off the feeling that this book was somehow important enough for me to pay the asking price. I finally did, and returned home with it to show David. Only this time when I opened the book I found an inscription, dated 1926, "To Ruth, from Big Nan." This was the sign I needed!

Another time when I felt disconnected from the work, David and I had to spend an unexpected night in Chicago, thanks to a blizzard and a missed train connection. It was bitterly cold, and once in our hotel room we stayed and ate travel food—crackers—for dinner. We turned on the TV for a weather report, and the program in progress happened to be *The X-Files.* Just before we flipped the channel, we realized the show was about a local weatherman whose repeated experiences of unrequited love conjured up episodes of inclement weather. The community suffered each time this man had to endure a harsh rejection. The situation grew more serious as the weatherman's mental and emotional stability worsened, until the town was faced with a life-threatening, tornadic storm. Somehow it all worked out, once the weatherman recognized his connection. What a teaching—and his love life improved, also!

The times of doubt and feelings of vulnerability that David and I endured softened the hardened edges of our worldview enough so that we could go forth wholeheartedly and continue to learn how to relate to the spirits of weather. We were ready to move on to the next level of our path—a closer look at the spiritual nature of this middle world and how it works, the key to any true understanding of the weather.

PART TWO

THE SPIRITUAL NATURE OF WEATHER

5

THE MIDDLE WORLD

HOME OF WEATHER

Creation is still going on . . . the creative forces are as great and as active today as they have ever been . . . tomorrow's morning will be as heroic as any of the world. Creation is here and now.

ROCKWELL KENT

Weather happens in the middle world. Here is where the dreams of weather play out—endless, relentless, and always unique. This is where the elements of weather figure and reconfigure into ever-changing expressions as they interact with the earth, our home in the middle world. In this realm the atmosphere and Earth unite in a dynamic dance of creation, destruction, and re-creation.

David's journey went like this:

I meet with Great Bird in the lower world, and we fly together, up, high into the sky, above the earth, above the clouds, until we can see the world as a beautiful ball, cloaked by a veil of shimmering atmosphere. Asking with my heart to meet one who can teach me about weather, I see the atmosphere begin to swirl, and from it appears the shape of a woman, whose gown is air and water, cloud and wind. I know that this is my weather teacher.

"What is weather?" I ask.

Feeling rather than hearing the answers, I know:

The weather is the circulation system of the earth. The weather is the elimination system of the earth. The weather is the immune system of the earth. The seasons are its respiration. As blood has red and white cells, so the earth has high- and low-pressure cells. As blood has immune cells, the earth has storms, hurricanes, and tornadoes.

Knowing that this lesson is over, I thank her and return to the middle world to watch the weather from above. I begin to merge with the weather, to become one with it; but the power is too great, and I have to pull back, to be only partially merged. In this partially merged state, I feel the weather in large populated areas, bringing in oxygen and removing the filth of civilization. Without weather we would suffocate in our own wastes. I feel great joy in the moving air, the mingling of hot and cold, dry and moist, as it brings freshness and life where it is needed.

I know, too, that the middle world is unique. The other worlds are outside of time and space, in perfect balance and harmony, forever. In this middle world, balance can be achieved only through movement, the rhythmic cyclic swing between dark and light, warm and cold, dry and moist. All these are needed in balance but must be experienced sequentially, mixing and moving so that a wide range of conditions will be experienced. Stagnation is death; weather is life.

◩

The middle world, particularly the earth and atmosphere—home of weather—is our source of nourishment, shelter, and our physical forms. We would lose consciousness and quickly die after only a few minutes of deprivation of the life force of air. We would be unable to thrive without the nourishing life force inherent in the plants and animals of the earth. And all life on earth as we know it would disappear entirely for lack of the life force of sunlight.

To gain a better understanding of weather and its relationships to this world, David and I searched for the underlying principles that could describe how things work in the middle world. Michael Harner teaches that "where others see disparate, unrelated parts, the shaman sees relationship where others only see contrast. The shaman sees unity and can draw upon this for healing and knowledge."[1] We turned to the teachings of our ancestors as well as those of our scientific world, where only the measurable is believed, and found that they seemed to corroborate one another. Shamanic practices of yesterday and today are based upon the shared knowledge of both our ancestors and modern physicists, who work with the possibilities of nonlocality, multiverses (otherwise known as parallel universes), and time out of time. Our culture is beginning to see that the mysteries and wonder of the spiritual realm also apply to what we think of today as the solid, "real" world.

For example, our concept of time as a linear experience is a definitive characteristic of the middle world. Ancestral wisdom, however, speaks of numinous worlds outside the constraints of time as we know them, worlds where time is elastic or can be suspended, worlds where there is no time but only the present moment, containing all there ever was or will be. Our scientific findings confirm the multifaceted nature of time. Einstein's theory of relativity states that "time elapses more slowly for an individual in motion than it does for a stationary individual."[2] This isn't what we would ordinarily think or feel, yet it demonstrates that the nature of time is plastic, something other than a relentless and constant progression of discrete units.

All over the world and for thousands of years, our ancestors have taught us that we are all related, that there is a great web of interconnectedness throughout the cosmos. Likewise, in quantum physics the concept of nonlocality shows that an event happening to one part of a system can instantly affect another, seemingly unconnected part.

Though separated by great distances, quantum systems "act like an intimately connected whole, regardless of whether their parts are far removed from each other."[3]

Additionally, in our culture the most well-received theory of how it all began is that great event we call the big bang. Our scientific origin myth, the big bang is the story of the birth of everything. The universe as we know it—every one of us, from a speck of dust to all the stars and galaxies—originated from this same event. Echoing the ancestral teachings of an original state of perfection that we all had to somehow leave, the big bang describes the dismemberment of that former state of oneness in the mightiest of explosions, thus catalyzing eternal rounds of creation and destruction of stars and worlds and all therein.

Ancestral knowledge also recognizes worlds and levels of existence beyond what we normally see, feel, hear, smell, taste, and touch. Today, through our scientific point of view, the possibility of multiple universes, as hinted at by the equations of string theory, becomes believable. It seems that the great truths are not to be denied access to our consciousness, be they the parables of myths or the theories of modern physics!

David and I began thinking of the workings of the world in terms of the principles of creation—the foundations of creative reality, or the fundamental laws, precepts, or truths—as well as their complex interrelationships. At the same time we soon realized that there is no such thing as a separate or discrete principle. We can talk about change, chaos, order, reciprocity, union, life force, power, form . . . yet there lie levels upon levels of meanings that overlap and entwine together, much like the subterranean roots of all the trees of a forest. Ancestral knowledge of this interconnected reality can be found in the famous Celtic knots carved and drawn on tombs, weapons, and personal ornaments throughout that ancient world.

We learned that no manifestation of weather visits us on its own; we have to come home to the middle world of Earth for our deepest understanding of its forces. A hurricane needs an ocean in order to form and grow and stay alive as a coherent storm. Clouds need the elements of dust and evaporated water from the earth's surface to form. Metaphors abound in Nature, showing us that what we really find when we scrutinize any one principle of creation is only a particular facet of the gem of the whole, like a single ray of light emanating from a star.

True enough, yet it is still worthwhile to consider discrete elements or principles, as each is a portal, an opening into the greater whole. A tornado, for instance, is an awesome and, to many, dreadful manifestation of a storm. More than simply whirling winds of extreme power, a tornado is composed of relationships between unstable air, temperature differentials, moisture, suitable terrain, a storm cell, and a front to go with it—to name just a few particulars. And there is more. The life of a tornado is a dramatic embodiment of principles of creativity at work. It is a primal dance of chaos and order, filled with the power of the middle world as it unleashes change wherever it goes.

So what is the nature of the middle world? Although it remains an unending mystery, we have learned that the middle world is the interface between worlds above and below that are located in the realms of nonordinary reality. These are known by various names, such as the otherworld, Dreamtime, the spirit world, the sacred, and the upper and lower worlds. The middle world itself is a miracle. It embodies the miracle of physicality. It is the duality within the one, time within no time, separateness where there is none, the tangible and intangible, seen and unseen—all here in this incredible crucible of the middle world. The middle world is a portal to the physical life experience and to the numinous realms as well.

The term *middle world* itself implies a larger picture, an expanse of time and space deep in the center of a reality of infinite timelessness and perfect union. It is upon this plane of physical existence that we are born out of that oneness, and from which we die back into. The Bible contains this passage:

And God said, let there be a firmament in the midst of the waters, and let it divide the waters from the waters. And God made the firmament, and divided the waters which were under the firmament from the waters which were above the firmament: and it was so. (Genesis 1:6–7)

Thus was born the middle world. Between the infinite oneness above and the infinite oneness below (the shaman's upper and lower worlds of pure compassion) springs the uniqueness that is our middle world of time and space, movement and change, birth and death.

The word *firmament* is built from the base of *firm,* that is, steady or stable. The *Shorter Oxford English Dictionary* defines *firmament* as "the arch or vault of heaven with its clouds and stars / anything which strengthens or supports / a substratum or foundation." In other words, firmament is a solid, steady foundation, somewhere in the middle of infinity, on which life can exist in all its physicality, with its joy and sorrow, fear and courage, truth and deception, birth and death . . .

Time rules here; here, one thing follows another, though not necessarily in a linear direction. More often we find movement in spirals and circles. Energy manifests as movement, and perfect balance is a fleeting moment in a rhythmic swing from one extreme to another. When we notice this movement, this dance between Chaos and Order in our bodies, we call it health. When we feel it in our hearts, we call it emotion. When we see it in the sky, we call it weather.

Significantly, the middle world contains both realms of reality. In our journeys we are taught that everything that happens in ordinary reality also happens in nonordinary reality. However, more things can happen in the greater, more fluid nonordinary-reality realms because those realms hold the possibilities of creation. We (not only humans) of the ordinary-reality realms are like filters or nets through which the creative potentials can manifest. Thus, it can be said that ordinary reality is created through us, and the middle world is what we make of it.

We, the inhabitants of this realm, are all related, all interconnected, and all collectively dreaming, manifesting our world.

What we think of as "reality" is not necessarily fixed—it can be altered. We can intentionally expand our "nets" or "filters" to accommodate other possibilities. The shaman understands that the nonordinary-reality worlds can feed our world with vitality and beauty and so actively works to encourage just this to foster a greater experience of well-being for the inhabitants of the middle world. The shaman knows how to access the extraordinary harmony of the nonordinary worlds and bring some of it back to the community. This is an advantage for people who wish to thrive and not just survive in the world. And so the shaman journeys and chants, dances, sings, and meditates to open her or his "net" to become a "hollow bone," a vehicle for the transmission of healing, harmonious energies to help transform ordinary reality. And it's not just about the shaman's ecstatic state; we are all capable of achieving this. We are all able, in one way or another, to open and expand, to harmonize and align with states of harmony. As we do so, we allow beauty to permeate more of our world.

One winter morning many years ago, as I trudged to a college class, I paused on a bridge over an irrigation ditch. An intricate and impossibly delicate ice crystal formation on the frozen stream caught my eye. Just in that moment the overcast sky shifted and shafts of sunlight broke out, highlighting the world. The startling beauty of that brilliant instant gifted me with an ecstatic moment, and a healing. A troubling weariness, a melancholic feeling that I hadn't been able to shake for days, evaporated, and I felt free to breathe again. In a flash I realized that though we suffer in life, we all have available to us—rich or poor, happy or sad—the incredible gift of Nature's beauty.

Somewhere in our evolution we were given the ability to appreciate this beauty and receive its life-enhancing gifts. It takes a real and alive relationship with Nature to live fully and know the joy of living on Earth that is our birthright. Otherwise, we risk creating lackluster, colorless lives, sadly devoid of the passion and abundance available to us. Though it seems that no one in life escapes suffering, if we have no heartfelt relationship with Nature, then we cut ourselves off from the most nourishing cord of life support that is always available to us. We lose touch with the very things and relationships that would balance suffering and bring peace to our minds, joy to our hearts, and provide balm for our souls. At these times, when beauty cannot be found, it is best to release and simply witness our state, knowing that this is more a reflection of our interior angst in the present moment than a condemnation of the true nature of the natural world. The renowned American poet Walt Whitman reminds us of this in one of his songs to the earth:

> I swear the earth shall surely be complete
> to him or her who shall be complete,
> The earth remains jagged and broken
> only to him or her who remains jagged and broken.

It's good to remember that a state of being can change for us at any moment. When our gates of perception open to the sacred in this middle world, we open also to the sacred within our interior world. Allowing ourselves the time and space to focus on a thing of beauty offers up a measure of harmony, of healing, to our world. From the cracks in city sidewalks where indomitable plants push through to pristine wilderness, our own backyards, and the skies above us, the gifts contained in the beauty of Nature in the middle world are everywhere, and they are a portal to the inherent grace of this world. It is this that nourishes our beings, inspires us, and helps us restore lost balance and well-being for ourselves and others. The more present or at home we are in our bodies, the more we are able to receive and to resonate with that beauty and reflect our own luminosity out into the world.

The shaman understands the creative nature of beauty and its power to heal wherever it is found. Not all of us, or even most of us, want to or can follow the path of shamanism with its attendant challenges and extraordinary gifts. Yet most if not all of us can avail ourselves of the beauty of Nature in uncomplicated ways, simply by being present with intention and desire, opening our hearts and thus our ability to appreciate and receive. Sometimes we have to look for these moments, and sometimes they find us . . .

Workshop participant Tom, the former Marine captain who shared the Odin story earlier, told of one such moment when he opened himself to the power of weather:

The first sergeant and I were sitting on the shores of Lake Belton, drinking a beer. The rain was traveling across the lake and driving people into shelter.

"What are you going to do, Captain?" he asked.

"I'm going to stay here and watch this," I replied.

Across the lake a large thunderhead had formed over the cliff face, the anvil rising up into the sky. Sunbeams bracketed the storm and we were in bright sunlight, warmed and comfortable. Out to the right a large flock of geese was flying along the cliff face, and as they flew under the thunderhead the updrafts caught them and they spiraled up through the vortex, completely at the mercy of the gargantuan forces there. The sun was shining through and reflecting off the cloud wisps in the vortex, and the geese seemed as tiny leaves swirling up to the heavens. The energy of the maelstrom easily carried them 5,000 to 7,000 feet into the air before they disappeared into the anvil. The first sergeant and I just sat in silent awe, and we agreed that we had been privileged to see a beautiful sight.

6

FORM

LIFE FORCE AND ITS TRANSFORMATIONS
IN THE MIDDLE WORLD

The earth, in all forms, is a constant source of life force . . .

I sit by a woodland stream,
On a rock ledge where I feel
A sense of sacred space.
A grandfather maple presides over this realm,
Scorched by lightning, and though hollow, very much alive.
Rocks, ferns, quiet pool, mounds of moss, small waterfall . . .
A beautiful configuring of life
Forms, as the stream weaves it together.
I close my eyes and sink
Into the sounds of rippling water.
The breeze brings to my ears snippets of birdsong
Punctuating the overlying hum of insects.
   The leaves of the old maple rustle their song . . .
   I ask for a message for our circle and wait . . .

We are essence of life.

once more . . .

We are essence of life.

The song beckons me down

Deeper into the earth, where I find this same place . . .

only more . . .

I open my eyes and see a shimmering world . . .

Surpassing the beauty of where I sit in body.

The song continues . . .

Life force is here

Life force is there . . .

It is source . . . We are source . . . Earth is source . . .

The Sun is source, and the Water, and the Air.

You contain it as well. It is everywhere.

It is universal energy . . .

Life force transfiguring

Into form.

The song sings through me . . .

We are Earth,

Earth is Sun,

Sun is Universe,

And so it goes . . .

Forever . . .

All within us.

I pull myself back to the "ordinary" world—which appears more extraordinary than ever—and make my way back to where our circle is forming. I have a message to share. We are form; we respond to form; we channel our creative energy into acts of form. Potters create new things from blobs of clay. Cooks transform distinct plant and animal parts into newly formed and edible creations. Writers bring into form new configurations of words and ideas. Mothers-to-be gestate and eventually birth fresh and unique humans into the world. The spirits in our journeys, dreams, and visions present many faces and many forms that we can relate to. We are spirits in human form.

Shamans know that form is sacred and contains great power. Form is a patterning, an ordering of energy, and it takes power to bond that energy into a particular order and shape. Shamans know, too, that form is not permanent or fixed. Ocean waves and elements of weather demonstrate that forms are ephemeral, some more so than others. Clouds continually transform as they travel around the globe, giving up one form for another, responding to the earth and sky in their changing ways and release of rain. Rocks also transform, yet so slowly according to our sense of time that we can barely perceive it. The sun appears constant, yet we know it fluctuates in radiant energy and will eventually become unrecognizable in its form as the life-giving star of our cosmic circle. Likewise our bodily forms change continuously throughout our lifetime. We swell and contract, ebb and flow.

Our forms, our bodies, are a gateway to the middle world and its offerings of beauty and life force. We receive the world through our bodies in many ways, yet most of the time we live our lives basically unaware of how much we are affected by the world around us, from the great seasonal cycles to the changing weathers to all the ebbs and flows of our natural environs. It is well documented but less well understood how the phases of the moon, changes in barometric pressures, and varieties of weather events affect our sense of balance and well-being—influences that range from the barely perceptible to the dramatic. We register effects somewhere in our beings whether we reside in urban, suburban, rural, or wilderness locations and whether we spend most of our time indoors or outdoors. We are intensely sensual beings who, for a multitude of reasons, mostly to do with lifestyle, worldview, and early conditioning, are disconnected and out of touch with most of our sensate abilities.

We know we exist in physical form, yet we lack an acute awareness of our more subtle, energetic forms and sensory capacities. Though we may not realize how we are or are not perceiving the world, it all still happens. We are surrounded by the activities of thousands of beings in Nature. This is what our ancestors tell us. And our modern scientists tell us about the continuous, unseen activities of subatomic particles and molecules that interweave everything, from the life changes of a mountain to the comings and goings of a thunderstorm to our own bodies and lifetimes.

Somewhere in our prehistory, thousands of years before the widespread use of written language, it is possible that ancestral humans could hear and see things that we aren't aware of now. They could see and feel *beings,* spirits of Nature, that we now think of as mythological. Our mainstream culture classifies these realms and their inhabitants as not "real"—a conclusion based upon our present inability to perceive a more "transparent" world. Since most of us cannot see, hear, or feel these beings, we think they do not exist. Many in our culture pronounce the notion of faeries, sprites, elementals, nature spirits, and a host of others as nonsense. This is an accurate word in that it aptly describes our perceptual state of "none sense," our habitual nonsensory way of life and, hence, lack of holistic understanding of our reality. In fact, we are all endowed with a multitude of innate sensory capacities beyond the five senses. Yet our culture's worldview tends to support and validate only our materially based senses, while the others are generally ignored.

David Abram, in his exceptional work *The Spell of the Sensuous,* writes,

> The deeply mysterious powers and entities with whom the shaman enters into a rapport are ultimately the same forces—the same plants, animals, forests, and winds—that to literate, "civilized" Europeans are just so much scenery.[1]

Any of us can develop our sensory abilities through intention and practice. If for no other reason, our experience of relatedness to the world and cosmos will be enhanced. Our ancestors lived successfully by intentionally working with their senses. They paid attention to the scents, sounds, sights, tastes, and feel of the world. So do we, both consciously and unconsciously. They took this to a deeper level, however, when they gleaned meaningful information from the shapes, patterns, and changing forms of Nature.

In other words, our ancestors and their shamans practiced the arts of divination and so were able to receive advice regarding their questions through *direct revelation*. They accomplished this in any number and variety of ways, such as observing and interpreting the dance of flames in a fire, the shapes and colorations on rocks, the random markings and patterns of fire-scorched scapulas of caribou, sheep, or beaver (the practice of "scapulamancy"), or the changing shapes and forms of the clouds above.

Ancestral knowledge teaches us that behind our ordinary states of awareness, there exists a far greater, more inclusive consciousness of this world through which all the animals, plants, stones, people, weathers, and so on are connected. Though our forms and sensate abilities may differ, we all have an ever-present, timeless connection with one another. In this we have union, one of the principles of creation that is essential to a deeper understanding of who we are and what weather is. Furthermore, this great middle-world consciousness is itself linked and energized by the vitality of the spirit world.

In the long-ago "Distant Time," say the Koyukon people, plants, animals, and humans could change their forms, and all were equal in worth. Similarly, ancestral knowledge of the Micmac peoples of the Canadian Maritimes teaches that form is not fixed in its shapes. Micmac cosmology recognizes the real world, a world different from our ordinary world, as inhabited by Persons. Ruth Holmes Whitehead of the Nova Scotia Museum writes,

> Persons are animate, living, whether or not they have a body of flesh and blood. Persons are conscious. One can have a relationship with any one of them. Persons include humans, but they may also

be animals or stars or thunders. They may be mountains or strange rocks or winds. They often have no one physical form. Their form is not fixed and they can appear as different things. It is their essential nature that is important, not their physical body.[2]

As humans around the world we may tell different creation stories, but our general understanding of the beginnings of the universe is essentially the same: at some sacred instance, it took a special kind of power, and an act of power, to create the world and then make it fit for habitation. This power is itself the power of the infinite transformations of energy into form and form into energy. It is an essence of nature that we humans as well as all life-forms depend upon for its generative vitality and cyclic patterns of energetic order.

One day during our residence as visiting teachers at the Esalen Institute, I learned something about a gift of energy, of vitality, when form releases its shape. I sat above the mouth of a narrow gorge where the cold waters of a stream meet sulfur waters from a hot spring and cascade together in a waterfall to the sea. I decided to try a simple rattle journey. I hoped to meet an ancestor of the Esselen people who once lived in this amazing place. As I rattled and focused my intention, the following scene gradually unfolded before me:

In my spirit body I descend the steep rock stairway for a closer look. It is a fair-weather day, with a fog bank lingering a ways off shore, typical for that time of year, and it's somewhat of a comfort to see that some things can be counted upon! I notice that there is more of a sandy beach than what I know "now," and I am surprised to see that the people have small boats that seem to be barely seaworthy, as water sloshes in and out with each wave. I watch as they bob up and down in the oncoming surf, just out of reach of where the waves break, like the otters I observe in our time.

The people in the boats are fishing, though for fish or abalone or kelp I can't tell for sure.

On the shore I see children and women involved in various tasks or games. Some look over in my direction and then turn back to their activities. Soon an older woman leaves the group and makes her way toward me along the ledge above tumbled rocks where the stream washes out from the canyon onto the beach. I can tell she knows I am here. She has a kind face and shows no fear of me. She looks somewhat familiar, and later I realize she would eventually, after her passing, evolve into the compassionate spiritual teacher that I sometimes visit in the lower world.

After polite greetings and expressions of goodwill, I ask this wisewoman for advice on how she and her people find well-being beyond the basics of food and shelter. She grins and proceeds to show me a profound teaching of a life enhanced by intentionality—by the deliberate act of absorbing the unlimited life force of the natural world. It is so simple. I see that each incoming ocean wave releases torrents of vital energy when it crashes upon the shore. The people simply reach out and "catch" this energy with their hands, and with focused intention they bring it close to their bodies so they can breathe the gift of it into their beings.

Later I tried it myself. Strangely, the real challenge for me, as one used to a complex and overstimulated way of life, was its very simplicity. I had to struggle to give myself the time to carry out this vital practice. But it worked.

There are many gifts of vitality and knowledge available to us through our experiences of form and its transformations. A grandmother spirit teacher once spoke to me of how everything has chosen a particular shape and that shape is simply a description, a form of being in this middle world; behind that form we are all one. She went on to teach that the middle world is the place where we can take a dense physical shape. This manifestation of form is special, and there is much to be learned from these shapes. She advised me to work with the ones who have no particular form and yet possess force or essence, such as wind and water; these formless beings manifest movement and power that we can experience and bring into our being. Furthermore, she said that it would be helpful for my efforts in relating to the weather spirits if I let them merge with me, by allowing them to merge into my form. This way I could learn to speak the same language—their language. Speaking the same language is a strong way to relate. Spirit Grandmother cautioned me, however, to remember that I do walk an edge here: learn to merge well and frequently, yet remember my own essence, my own being and form.

Unique teachings about form can occur during a *dismemberment* experience in a shamanic journey. David and I first learned about this from our original teacher and mentor, Michael Harner. Over the years we have seen that people who have never heard about dismemberment can spontaneously experience one. In shamanic cultures around the world this is known as a healing, and for some it is an initiation leading to a degree of readiness for the practice of shamanism. Typically in a dismemberment journey the body of the journeyer is destroyed. This can happen in any number and combination of ways, ranging from a gory tearing asunder to a gentle dissolution. In one way or another the spirit-body separates from its physical body counterpart, and the journeyer is ultimately left with only a sense of consciousness. At this point, with no definition of shape, the journeyer has a sense of freedom unlike any other. It is a rare pause, an instance of betwixt and between. Unless the spirits re-member or re-create our body immediately, we are able, in some way, to directly experience that sacred oneness—and formlessness—we all originally came from and are part of still, though we may struggle with the illusion of a sense of separation. It is an opportunity to "remember" ourselves in this greater, grander reality of true unity.

In some dismemberment journeys, when my body is shed, I initially experience an ecstasy of no form. Then I gradually become aware of a yearning for form—for any form. It is always a surprisingly deep and compelling attraction.

The earth is our anchor in the greater cosmos of this middle world.

We often speak of "grounding" ourselves, our energy, our ideas, our lives. We long for our ground, our home base, our roots, our nest. There are times in the lives of many of us when we feel cast adrift, directionless and disconnected from others and from ourselves. We may fear that we are hopelessly lost and can no longer recognize any form or structure to our lives. While this can bring us great suffering, it also holds the potential for the birth of something new.

Dismemberment experiences teach us—and heal us—but first comes the sacrifice. We must separate from our sense of form before we are able to receive, to learn, and to heal. If in our journeys, meditations, or dreams we experience our human form changing into a form of Nature, we know we have touched upon the great web of consciousness and the spirit world behind all things. We have managed to reach into that area of union, of oneness that is grace.

Origin stories of peoples from many different regions of the world recount the beginnings of all created things as birthed from a great dark void, a formless place of chaos, a primordial ocean that our ancestral beings somehow crawled or oozed from. The beginning was formlessness, within a chaos that holds the potential of everything. From this state of no-form somehow an energy of pattern, of order—a form—emerges.

Universal energy, or life force, is everywhere and in everything. It is constantly transfiguring into form and then into other forms, all in motion, all changing and exchanging. We are of the earth, and the earth is of the sun. We are elements of earth coalesced into form, as nebulous gases coalesce into stars and stars gather into galaxies. Plants are literally earth and water elements and sunlight transmuted into form; and through them, so are we. We are all elements of the source, unique expressions of creative life force, and our forms constantly change—and always are sacred.

7

WHAT IS WEATHER?

EMOTION, RECIPROCITY, AND CHANGE

As our middle-world teachings and explorations deepened, David and I eventually spiraled back around to where we could look more meaningfully at the subject of weather's spiritual nature. Once again I turned to my compassionate helping spirits:

◤◢

I visit my spiritual weather teacher, who lives under an open sky in an upper-world realm of windswept tundra. My guardian animal spirits and I travel through the sun and several layers of weather and over a shimmering rainbow to get to his domain. As I journey, I carry my yearning to learn more about weather's true nature. Grandfather is waiting for me. His features are sharply molded, and his intense eyes pierce me with their luminosity. He says:

"Weather is a vital life force of Earth. Planets that have Weather are dynamic and physically alive. The moon has no Weather. Long ago, Earth and Weather created each other and made an agreement to forever exist in intimate relationship with one another—on behalf of life."

I ask for clarification, and he replies:

"Weather comes from the place of creative potential and manifests

as individual spirits of Weather in a multitude of outward expressions mirroring Earth. Weather is always changing and therefore highly responsive to the thoughts, feelings, and physical nature of Earth. Thus Weather also responds to the needs of Earth in terms of aliveness and balance. The spirits of Weather express their emotions in a continual dance of relatedness with those of Earth."

Grandfather pauses, and when he sees that I am ready for more, he continues:

"Because of the malleable and reciprocal nature of Weather, humans affect it and help determine its expressions more than we realize. Weather is emotion and responds to our emotions and focused thoughts. This is one way humans can influence the forms Weather takes. But that is for later. Now go and practice what you have been given."

Our aim of learning how to relate harmoniously and effectively with the weather spirits required of us an understanding of the forces behind the weather we experience in this world—the dramatic and the subtle, the commonplace, and the rare. Earlier explorations focused on form and formlessness in the middle world through the interactions of the principles of chaos and order. Now we were able to look more closely at Grandfather's teachings of weather's spiritual nature in terms of the creative principles of emotion, reciprocity, and change.

David and I continued journeying to all the worlds we could find for help in understanding at least some small part of this great mystery. Knowing that this search for knowledge couldn't be limited to our efforts alone, we welcomed the contributions of numerous people who joined in with their own journeys over the following seven years. The generosity of the helping spirits seemed to increase as we demonstrated our willingness to show up and learn from them. Indeed, compassionate spirits we had not met before joined our circle.

Though we couldn't meet and relate to every embodied kind of weather, we had the tools of our shamanic path and the good sense to turn to our helping spirits for their wisdom to discover what is important and useful for all of us to know now. We focused our sights on understanding weather's spiritual nature and its role in this world. We trusted that eventually this would lead us to a friendly familiarity with the entity we were attempting to relate to. As shamanic practitioners we are always obligated to find out just who it is we're courting and possibly about to enter into an alliance with. As with any helping spirit or potential friend, we want to know something of this being's nature, wisdom, level of compassion, and power. Above all, does this being exhibit a willingness to ally with us for the greater good?

During the winter of 2001, in one of our workshops at the Esalen Institute, a young woman, Madeleina, journeyed to learn something about the nature of weather. Madeleina and her power animal flew up on a magic carpet until they broke through a "thick, sticky membrane" and encountered a dynamic and volatile goddess figure who she thought she had met before in another guise:

I was wary of her as an authentic spirit of Nature. . . . I asked her if indeed she was and she became very fierce and nearly offended. She flashed lightning bolts from her eyes and the wind picked up around me. She had constant breezes around her and was wearing many colors. When I asked the question, "What is weather?" she softened and became very explanatory, filling my head with images and phrases, almost more information than I could hold. She said, "Weather is the emanation of the conscious life force of the void. The void produces waves, constantly flowing. These waves of energy enter our world to become, each one, an individual spirit of weather, shaping into form to guide the wave to materialization for this physical plane. The luminous field of pure being has a central pulse, like our bodies, that sends the waves. Once the weather has manifested in form it acts like the lymph does. It flows throughout, its function to clean, clear, and recycle energy."

She continued, "Also, weather is the poetry of the Great Mystery. Even more, it is theater. It's an expression in the material plane for the Great Mystery, and for all the helping weather spirits to play, dance, and manifest their essence in form."

She would have given me more, but this was enough for now. She became fierce again, and then called me her daughter and kissed my head and said I could call on her for strength.

Madeleina's journey affirmed teachings from our earlier journeys. We were beginning to see that the experiences of others could corroborate what we were learning, and we welcomed any new insights other contributors might bring to our work.

During my own second journey to the volatile cloud spirit I was given a teaching that has echoed in so many other journeys since then, and we began to understand why this cloud being responds so forcefully: it is filled with passion! The cloud spirit told me that weather is an emotional expression. We all have our individual "weather events." The spirit went on to explain, "A vital principle of universal creation is emotion. Emotion is everywhere. Look to your emotions. Look to the emotions of weather."

Bill Brunton, anthropologist, college professor emeritus, and field associate for the Foundation for Shamanic Studies (FSS), journeyed for a weather teaching during the January 2000 FSS council meeting and offered us an account of his experience:

Eagle took me on a flight into and through the clouds. I saw a cloud being and thought this might be the spirit I would learn from. We continued to ascend. We flew into space and saw the earth—saw the moon, the stars, and the cosmic radiation.

The teaching was that the weather is not a local phenomenon. Each aspect of weather is a result of the whole—everything makes a contribution.

That weather should therefore be approached holistically. Also, weather is the emotion of the planet—not the logic.

〰

As Stephen Rosen observes in Weathering, when standing upright we touch the earth with our feet while the rest of our bodies extend into the atmosphere, the physical domain of weather. Our bond with the sky is multifaceted and permeates our lives beyond our normal awareness. Some peoples, however, formally recognize the weathers within us. This knowledge figures prominently in traditional Chinese medicine as well as in the healing lore of the Tzutujil Mayans, who speak of weather patterns in our bodies and say that "the weather outside is the emotion of the Earth."[1]

Weather, like the rest of us, is filled with individual expressions and manifestations of personality and mood. As mentioned earlier, we often use language that speaks to our emotional kinship with weather: "they have a stormy relationship"; "my thinking is foggy"; "she has a sunny disposition"; "we took a whirlwind tour of the city"; "he thundered his reply"; "in a flash they got it"; "she runs like the wind"; "he beamed with happiness." From our literary and historical research, we found many references to weather as emotional beings, who when honored are pleased but can also be offended or angered, and who may deliver all manner of storms, howling winds, gentle breezes, healing rains, floods, droughts, glowing rainbows, mists and fogs, fair skies . . .

These are but a few examples describing weather in terms of what David and I think of as one of the creative principles of the middle world: emotion. We also continued our investigation into the spiritual nature of weather and its capacity to shape our world in terms of the other two principles mentioned above: reciprocity and change.

To help us shed more light on these principles, John, a shamanic practitioner and adventurer, journeyed to a helpful spirit with the question, "What is weather?"

"What you call weather is simply, or at the most basic, energy moving through a more or less fluid system—air, water, molten rock, even 'solid' rock, or the earth and her elements. Energy moving through the earth's mass produces change. The earth's rocks and their millions of years of circulation in the form you call tectonic plates is the rollicking, roiling boil of energy moving."

Feeling like I was being given more of a basic geology lesson than a journey, I asked the weather spirit, "What does this have to do with me? What can I learn from what I have been shown?" The weather spirit answered,

"Your thoughts are your weather system adjusting and moving and changing as energy moves through you. Stand back and watch your thoughts and feelings, as they are the clouds ever moving and reshaping, bringing precipitation and shade to you, your own weather system. You are a part of weather—it is a part of you as your thoughts. Thoughts are your weather."

John's experience offered us the teaching of an underlying energy, a substratum of life force with creative movements through all things, be they rocks or elements of weather or our own thoughts. Thanks to the unified nature of existence, the principles of change and reciprocity, continuously interwoven throughout all the doings and beings of this middle world, profoundly shape our inner and outer worlds.

Another practitioner, Neil, was shown how essential the principle of reciprocity is to the creation of weather. He first observed a boulder rolling across the surface of the earth, gathering up plants, sticks, and other matter as it grew to an enormous size. Then his helping spirits carried him to an overlook, where he gazed upon a body of water and received:

≈

. . . the understanding that weather is an interface. Just as what is going on at the surface of the sea is an expression of all the conditions above and below it, so weather is an ongoing interface of conditions. It was a very profound understanding of weather as something that exists in its changing ways only because it is an expression of the interface of all the conditions "above and below."

≈

John and Neil's journeys, as well as those of many others, showed us how the principle of reciprocity is key to any understanding of intentional relationship with the spirits of weather. Their journeys also speak to the creative principle of change and its manifestations of weather. As David and I looked at change as another grand theme or creative principle of this middle world, we could see how easily it relates to weather and emotion, for what excites, addles, irritates, inspires, and terrifies us more than change in our lives and world? It is the rare individual who can remain unmoved before the face of change, especially whilst caught in the throes of its more dramatic workings.

Early on, my spiritual teacher in nonordinary reality had described weather to me as "a moving and changing expression of life force." In our weather-dancing workshops, where participants journeyed to gain some understanding about the spiritual nature of weather, Cynthi was taught that "weather is like breathing, and any change creates weather, both macrocosmically and microcosmically." Linda asked the weather spirits whether our world was experiencing aberrant weather conditions, and she was advised that "Earth is a whole living organism, and these weather conditions represent stressors—changes, imbalances, obstructions, and energy surges in Earth's field, just like the etheric field of an individual." Linda R.'s question of "What is weather?" was elegantly answered in this succinct statement: "It is a circle of never-ending change without which we could not sustain our existence on Earth."

The climate and the weather have been master teachers of the principle of change in our world. It is no surprise that here we are today, our modern world faced with an eternal mandate of change. We are continually called upon to evolve, to refashion and create anew our responses to the state of the world. Our survival as a species, and as beings fully aware of ourselves and our interdependence with all other beings, depends upon a willingness to consciously participate in our evolution, to intentionally change for the purpose of restoring lost harmony to our lives and world. Our relationship with the forces and spirits of the weather we experience every day provides a potent calling and opportunity to learn to live gracefully and successfully with the challenges and gifts of change.

I return to the realm of the cloud spirit. I find myself hovering, with my power animal, before a gigantic and glowering cloud face. My attention is riveted by its continually shifting features within the dark and darker gray cloud mass, sometimes smooth and soft, sometimes craggy and sharp. Its expressions range from jovial and inviting to fierce grimaces of pursed lips and narrowing eyes. In other moments the cloud spirit's face is bland and inscrutable. What is constant are its glowing eyes. I can almost feel the fires of corralled lightning bolts behind its stare. I half expect to be swiped by one at any second. Respectfully, yet determinedly, I hail the cloud spirit and ask for another teaching about weather that would be useful for all.

"I am change!" *it bellows.* "Spirit of Change I am. You have turned away from me because your world seeks to control, to hold to things, to resist change.* You are not in control! *And not in control of your lives. You may be in control of what you wear for the weather, but not what is the weather.* Embrace change—*align with the forces of change. Embrace weather. Open to the changes it brings. Open to the teachings of those changes. Open to your lack of control.* Celebrate that!"

I ask whether we are supposed to worship weather.

"No! *But open to it, align with it, receive its teachings.* Love the weather!"

I thank this impressive spirit and prepare to take my leave. As we turn away, I hear this last utterance, a warning perhaps:

"Watch what happens when weather doesn't change . . ."

8

CHAOS, ORDER, AND POWER AT WORK

WEATHER IN THE MIDDLE WORLD

It takes a certain kind of magic . . . to set a hurricane in motion. First, you have to make the thunderstorms, and then "you have to get the thunderstorms dancing," as Florida State University climatologist James O'Brien puts it. "You have to get them dancing in a big circle dance."

J. MADELINE NASH, "WAIT TILL NEXT TIME"

The principle of change in the middle world is enfolded within the dance of chaos and order. Within acts of change, of the creation and destruction that are weather's movements and effects, we find power—power gained and power lost. Wrapping back on itself, power incites change, and it takes an act of power to wrest order from chaos. Throughout it all, there is the rule of reciprocity, an active mirroring that teases apart the union, the oneness of all things. Chaos, in turn, births it all, and the dance goes on.

The creative principles of chaos and order rule everywhere, in our bodies and in the world outside our bodies. A storm such as a hurricane, when in order, possesses a defined form and thus is strong and alive. David Schoen, author of Divine Tempest, describes a hurricane:

> The whole storm revolves around the eye as its center and source of power. It is a chimney of complete calm in the middle of some of the most violent, destructive energy there is, a paradox of stillness in the center of whirling wind and water.[1]

Eventually the hurricane's order must break down and the storm's powerful energy weakens. It returns to a state of chaos once again as it dissipates into the atmosphere. Without its intrinsic order, what once riveted our attention with its potential for widespread destruction, as well as wondrous beauty, is no longer considered a coherent system or weather entity, save by memory and tasks of cleanup and repair.

Everything comes and goes. The grandest civilizations of times past have realized a destiny of rising to a state of ordered power and definition, possessing hierarchy, politics, socioeconomic organization, and material wealth and then, invariably, falling out of form, out of order. At this stage the remaining people, with their remnants of the embedded culture, either revert back to a former epoch of land-based tribal, peasant, small-community living or are absorbed into the new paradigm of conquering peoples. This lasts for a while, until it cycles round again, if conditions are favorable for expansion. Like waves— or hurricanes—sometimes these civilizations grow into magnificent entities, and sometimes they cannot live up to their potential and just fizzle.

Historians may or may not bemoan this rise and fall, this attainment and loss of glory, but like the perfection of the curling wave, the mighty swirling of the whirlwind, the striking figure in a cloud, or the circle dance of winds and thunderstorms around the calm eye of the hurricane, there comes the time to release, to give over and return to the original source from whence we all emerged. Shamans and other mystics know about this becoming and unbecoming and seek to literally embody the power and knowledge it holds through the numinous experiences of shape-shifting, transfiguration, and dismemberment.

When I need renewal, I have learned to visit those places where ocean and land meet. Anchored to the solid and stable edge of the great North American continent, I can allow myself to relax. There is something primal to absorb here, something that our modern world hasn't changed. Waves form out of the formless ocean, sculpted by winds, currents, lunar cycles, and features of underwater terrain; they rise in height, motion, and power, each one unique. Sometimes traveling for thousands of miles, the waves eventually crest and, in their fullness and glory, crash upon the shores, to once again meld back into the watery depths. One thing I watch for, and sometimes think I see, is a moment "on hold," a pause, once the wave has reached its pinnacle, before it lets it all go. How many of us are willing to release when we've reached our peak? Does a storm hold on to its pent-up force, or is the true power found in the release? This is a story and metaphor for life itself.

There are profound mysteries inherent in the order of cycles, such as life cycles of birth to death, annual seasonal cycles, solar cycles, monthly lunar cycles, diurnal tidal cycles, and the daily biological rhythms of our own bodies. Our very cells continually undergo cycles of birth, growth, death, birth . . . we are re-creating ourselves all the time! The universe is a continual spiraling of evolution, cycling as we do in our soul's evolution, in our bodies, in our culture, and in our world and times.

A cycle, in which one form changes into another in an overall predictable pattern, is a way of order. For eons spiritual leaders around the world, from the shamans of hunter-gatherer bands to imperial leaders of vast kingdoms, have valued and sought alignment with the power of cosmic and earthly cycles. It was their sacred duty and one of their most important responsibilities to work to maintain this order and to align the life of their community within this greater order.

Many origin myths speak of an original primal state of chaos—a dark place with no form, order, or definition, a place of pure potential with no direction or focus. Out of this state a creator deity or force emerges and introduces order to the cosmos, often with a great fight or sacrifice. Out of darkness flares a point of light, that point defined by and defining darkness. From the womb of silence resounds song, from chaos emerges order, and formlessness ultimately begets form.

In the Enuma Elish, the Babylonian creation story, we find Tiamat, the formidable, terrible "chaos dragon." Marduk, the storm god, in an unimaginable act of power, trapped and slew Tiamat and created the features of the earth through the pieces of her dismembered body. He fashioned the sky from half of her great body and the earth and features of terrain from the other. As Tiamat's waters spilled out, Marduk used them to fertilize the earth. Destruction begat creation as Marduk, a weather deity, wrested order from chaos and made a new world.[2]

Throughout the ancient Celtic lands of Europe, there is a tradition whereby the shaman voluntarily enters into the affairs of chaos and purposefully engages in battle with the dangerous and destructive forces of chaos that are afoot in the world, especially during late fall and winter. In old Irish lore, these minions of chaos are known as the Formorians. Tom Cowan describes them as

> those powers that cause harm, destroy life, disrupt the natural order and fitness of things. Certainly the Formorians, in their disordered and grotesque aspects, are those very forces. And yet their role as parents and spouses of Irish gods and heroes implies that they play a necessary role in the natural order, that their destructive natures are important in maintaining the balance between life and death that makes existence possible.[3]

True to the calling of the Celtic shaman, every autumn Cowan leads shamanic practitioners on an inspired and challenging Wild Hunt, an intentional engagement with the formidable Formorians with the mission of reclaiming enough order to restore and maintain harmony and balance in the world for another year. Although no degree of success can ever be assured (for the battle may be "won" for only a time), the shamans must carefully prepare for the Wild Hunt, for it is a risky, though worthwhile, endeavor. The stakes couldn't be higher.

According to Richard Nelson, author of *Make Prayers to the Raven*, who once lived with a band of Koyukon people in Alaska, Koyukon elders have noticed signs of disorder, both obvious and subtle, even in their wilderness environment. Animals are behaving abnormally, such as ravens coming into the villages begging for food "like orphans with no self-respect." The Koyukon attribute this apparent imbalance partly to the loss of medicine people, those willing and able to work with the spirits of the animals and the elemental forces of Nature.[4]

During the winter of 2000, while living and working at the Esalen Institute, I faltered in my ability to write and attend to this work. My responsibilities to the community were weighing on me, and during my free time I could not bring myself to pay attention to volumes of notes or rough drafts or even the books I longed to read. I could pay attention only to the outdoors—the many and changing moods of ocean and sky, the monarch butterflies floating overhead or clumping by the hundreds in a particular tree. I felt chaotic, like a butterfly who is buffeted hither and thither by random gusts of wind. I had lost my sense of order.

Distracted and cranky, I journeyed to the upper world to my spiritual weather teacher in the hope of renewing my focus and motivation. As he obligingly tossed a few snippets of advice my way, I realized that I was being pulled energetically to the left—my eyes kept glimpsing a tree beyond where we were standing. A tree? This made no sense—how could there be a good-sized tree in my teacher's realm of wind-scoured tundra? A tree in this place was not in order! Laughing, my teacher paused and released me from the requirements of polite attention. I turned toward this tree. That was when I realized there was another individual with us, a man relaxing on the ground under the tree, one whom I thought I recognized, but I wasn't sure—he seemed too big. I approached him respectfully and introduced myself. I will never forget the kindness I saw in his eyes as he smiled at me and introduced himself as Wovoka.

Surprised and honored to be in the presence of this individual's spirit, I took a deep breath, expressed my appreciation, and asked for his teaching.

Wovoka's message to me was about the importance of order, describing the shaman's work as restoring order when chaos moves in. He added emphatically, "It is important to do this work without blame."

As I heard this I understood how his original vision of a renewed world could include all people, as there were none deserving of damnation. To my knowledge Wovoka's inspired message back in the 1800s called for all peoples to join together in the Friendship Dance (better known today as the Ghost Dance), a sacred community ceremony to align with the ancestors to restore lost beauty, lost harmony, and lost order to a ravaged world. I have long admired Wovoka's courage and compassion, which must have been exceptional, since he, a mortal and fallible human, was able to detach from the grip of judgment and vengeance, especially at a peak time of devastating loss of order for the Native American peoples of the western United States—loss of homelands, ways of life, sovereignty, and loved ones.

In the same heartfelt manner, Wovoka's spirit explained that all of us, today, need to "work to restore order from a place of compassion."

Our time together was ending, yet I had one more question I wanted to ask: "Why did you make ice in the river in July? Why that kind of weather working?"

He said, "Because it got people's attention—something out of order."

As we continued to explore the weather through our journeys and those of others, its spiritual nature was most often presented in terms of change engendered by the dance of chaos and order. Change inspires the dance, and its movements beget power, as chaos and order reciprocally ebb and flow. The forces of weather are moving expressions of formlessness becoming forms and forms changing. We learned that the spiritual forces of weather nurture, purify, and entertain the earth. Weather constantly shape-shifts, changing and flowing like a symphony or dance, expressing the harmony inherent in chaos.

One of our most fruitful journey directions was to witness the creation of weather. For many people this journey experience was the hardest to put into words, as it brought them to deep states of feeling, both emotional and physical. Fortunately, a few could talk about it. Here is Joan's account:

※

As I came through the lower-world tunnel I noticed it became darker and darker. I could not tell where the tunnel ended and the lower world began. I could only feel the space. Out of that blackness, Eagle swooped down and lifted me up through the broiling, charcoal gray clouds up to the sun. The sun was sending off huge explosions, and we were very close to this primal intensity of fire, within which there were darker spots.

As I followed the radiance and scorching heat (I was feeling it physically), I could see that radiance streaming out into the void—the cold, black void. When that radiance hit the void it seemed like a war, and sometimes like a dance—always changing, always dynamic. At times a spark was created and that spark was their child. This spark was the seed of lightning and the winds.

When the polarity had reached a certain balance, it created high-pressure systems, but I sensed that each had its own balance that was appropriate for each quality of weather.

I was really physically and mentally charged after this!

※

Heather's experience shows us more about the beauty and balance found in the powerful cycles of chaos and order, and how all are intertwined and interdependent, as expressed through the elements of weather:

⠶

Jesus took me way, way up and held my hands as the spirits of weather blew and blew. He held me very tightly so I did not get blown away. Suddenly, a beautiful organization of chaos appeared—all set out in order and evenly like a gyroscope containing the perfect balance. Jesus showed me that it was all very delicate, and an intrinsic balance is needed to keep everything from tipping. Before it had been easy to maintain the balance, but now, with all the pollutants and gases tipping the scales, the balance of the whole delicate web is disrupted. Because of this:

The moon is saddened by the effects of her cycles: floods, droughts.

The water's spirit is heavy, as her job to carry water is more complex with the entire imbalance.

Wind, needed to carry out her task in Nature, is truly distraught to be dispersing pollutants that further disturb the intrinsic and delicate web and balance.

Fire feels saddened to be blamed as incendiary—but fire is essential to the cycle. However, the chemicals make fire rage out of the fire spirit's control.

As one cycle gets affected all elements are affected, and the gyroscope/ hologram tips and shifts violently like a seesaw—no longer the gentle dances of imperceptible changes and counterbalances.

⠶

Heather's journey experience addresses what many indigenous elders and shamanic practitioners see: a growing state of imbalance, a distressing lack of order or harmony, in our world's ecology. Fortunately, thanks to the principle of change, nothing stays the same, so there is room for optimism in our ability to participate in a rectification, a restoration of balance and vitality to the world.

Carol's journey to learn about the creation of weather led her on another kind of dance, one that asks us to suspend judgment about what is "bad" and what is "good"—a necessary willingness on our part if we are to begin to understand and make friends with weather. Her journey also has a galactic reach:

I went to a lakeshore in the lower world, where I was met by two sea turtles. They guided my canoe back into the middle world somewhere in the Pacific Ocean. They showed me how an impulse comes up from the molten core of the earth, inspiring a single drop of water and a single bit of breeze to play together. As they play they call other droplets and breezes, and spirit emerges to dance with them. The dance gets bigger and stronger as more wind and water join in.

I was sucked up into the middle of a waterspout that moved onshore and tugged at grasses, trees, houses, et cetera. [It was] very forceful and, from our human perspective, very destructive, but from inside it was an exhilarating game, a dance of exchange of energies. The uprooted tree or shattered house was as delighted with the dance as the wind that pulled it in. Then the energy subsided into a lazy, tropical time of ease.

So we followed this wave or dance impulse around the globe for a while. Then we went out into space, where the sea turtles showed me a grid of interconnection between Earth, moon, sun, planets, and galaxy. Then they took me back into the molten lead/crystalline center of the earth to sense the upwelling of ripples of energy that begin the dance. Full circle!

These journeys, besides describing the process of chaos and order, also witnessed the *power* in the creation of weather. Each time weather changes its face, or its form in the world, power is released— sometimes in enormous amounts. In the world of physics, power can be simply defined as the ability to move or transform energy. Through the principles of change and the interactions of chaos and order, we experience weather's power and its effects upon the earth, which ultimately create a temporary state of balance in certain places or regions. Power may be the most compelling, misunderstood, and, potentially, dangerous of all the principles of creation.

What is power in the middle world? What is the nature of power, and what do we need to know about right use of power? What is spiritual power, and how does it differ from other kinds of power? Where does power come from? How do we obtain power?

Worldwide, the weather deities of our ancestors embody or personify power. True to the essence of power, most of these deities carry a dual nature and inspire both love and fear from the human world. The Aztec rain and storm god Tlaloc was revered and feared by the people of Mexico, who well knew the beneficent gifts of rain and rainstorms but also suffered from the ravages of floods. Yet it is said that the Aztec cult of Tlaloc was one of the bloodiest, including ritual sacrifices of babies and young children, the tears of their crying mothers an additional enticement for rain to fall.[5]

In the biblical Old Testament, Yahweh, also a supreme sky deity, was both feared and loved. In the well-known story of Noah and his ark, Yahweh visited upon the world an enormously destructive flood out of his disgust with mankind and, in the end, gave us the rainbow as a sign of his promise to never do that again.

The Skidi Pawnee of the central plains worshipped Tirawahat, a true sky deity who lived above the clouds. As an omnipotent and creative sky father, Tirawahat was responsible for the cyclic order of the sun, moon, and stars. Tamra Andrews, author of *Legends of the Earth, Sea, and Sky,* describes him thus: "As a sky god, he was impersonal and invisible, yet his people recognized him in the lightning that flashed, in the wind that rustled the branches, and in the light that filtered through the wafting clouds." The individual elements of weather were Tirawahat's messengers and intermediaries between his realm and the people. As such, they were capable of transmitting his creative and fearsome power to earth.[6]

The Inuit recognize the divine power of Sila, the supreme spirit of air and atmosphere, who supports "the world and the weather and all life on earth," and who speaks with all the voices of Nature, including those of storm and sea and sunlight and children's play, in infinite variations.[7] Sila also possesses a dual nature of gentleness and ferocity. As the engendering spiritual force of rain, snow, wind, and storm, Sila commands respect as a creative and moral guardian for the natural world and its animals.[8]

In our language the word *power* comes from the Latin *potere,* "to be powerful" or "to be potent," and the Old French *poeir,* "to be able." According to *Webster's Ninth Collegiate Dictionary, power* means "possession of control, authority, or influence over others." This is the first definition. In Webster's second definition, *power* is defined as "the ability to act or produce an effect." Then comes "physical might," followed by "an order of angels," followed by "a source or means of supplying energy." Last are definitions of "magnification" and "scope or comprehensiveness." Among the words *Webster's* lists as synonyms for *power* defined as "the right to govern or rule or determine" we encounter *authority, jurisdiction, control, command, sway,* and *dominion.* Finally, when *power* is defined as "ability to exert effort," we are directed to the synonyms *force, energy, strength,* and *might;* in this usage, *Webster's* states, "*power* may imply latent or exerted physical, mental, or spiritual ability to act or be acted upon."

Webster's first definition of *power* as the possession of control and authority over others aptly describes our culture's predominant understanding and relationship with power. For indigenous traditions, however, the concept of power embodies all the elements of the natural world. A primal world force or energy exists everywhere and enlivens all things and beings of the universe. In the languages of these traditions the essence of power carries a quality of sacredness. It is *orenda* for the Haudenosaunee or Iroquois, *wakan* for the Lakota, *manitou* for the Algonquin, and *shakti* for Hindus. The Hawaiians speak of *mana,* and the Chinese work with *chi.* In Australia the Aboriginal peoples know of the power of *djang,* the sacred, creative energy that originally formed the world. This energy, this primal power of the Dreamtime, is stored in certain sacred features of the landscape and is accessible to those who know how to use it for a variety of needs, including the need for rain or sunshine.[9]

Anthropologist Lowell John Bean looked at the subject of power in California Indian belief systems. Their understanding of power that he describes is similar to that of other traditions around the world. Power is what makes things happen, but it is not a mindless, inanimate force—it is conscious. Power can be found more easily in some places than in others. There is a prevailing balance (a dance) of power in the universe, though in the world we live in, many compete for power and attempt to hoard it. It is the role of human beings to learn how to appropriately interact with power so that the cosmic order and harmony of the universe may be served.[10]

Tom Cowan describes the all-inclusive Celtic view of spiritual power:

> The natural world is alive with power, information, counsel, and wisdom. The Divine Power behind can, and does, communicate to us through natural phenomena such as animals, weather patterns, plants, landscapes, and the spirits of these things. The faces carved in the rotting trunks of ancient trees were the Celts' attempts to portray and honor this intelligence behind and within creation.[11]

We cannot satisfactorily remove indigenous names for power from their cultural contexts and confine them to a definition that rests easily alongside our modernistic worldview. The deepest understanding requires an intimacy of life experience in any particular culture. One would have to be raised within the language and traditions of a particular people to fully *know* the meaning of their word for power. What we can do, though, is receive these words and their implied concepts as crosscultural teachings of a worldwide recognition and knowledge of true power, the life force of the universe that exists in all things and is sacred. Perhaps in our own Western culture we can once again find our sense of the sacred inherent in all things and, in so doing, recover a relationship with power that is far less conflicted and more balanced with life-sustaining ways.

A strong wind blows through the night and well into the next day. We spend a good part of that day reveling in the power of wind, the way it stirs up the sea and keeps the clouds scudding across the sky. We breathe salt spray and our ears are filled with a host of wind songs. Sometimes it is a cacophony when trees, plants, and tent walls shudder and creak as they two-step with the wind. I finally grow tired of eating my hair every time I try to speak. I am dizzy and off balance and feel like a wildly swinging weather vane. I want to get indoors for a respite, and it seems like a good opportunity to journey for a teaching about the nature of power:

I am with my weather teacher in the upper world, and I find his realm predictably windy. He tells me that one important aspect of relating to power is clarity of purpose. We walk through a fog and come to an opening where we can look outward. All I can see is a brief glimpse of ruined buildings. My teacher merely comments that "there is a lot of confusion to clear up." He advises me to visit my ancestress today for an additional teaching about power.

I thank him and fly off in the direction that will lead me to the realm of my long-ago Celtic ancestress. She lives along a northern shore, apparently on her own. Just as my power animal and I arrive, I see her pulling what looks like a log or the body of a seal from the sea and up the shore past the high-tide line. She has strong, defined muscles, dark brown hair, and darker eyes. She is lean, beautiful, physically powerful. I can also see that she has a little girl baby—another ancestress for our family! As mothers so often do, she intuits why I am here. We visit awhile so she can nurse the baby, and then she puts her down in an outdoor enclosure to sleep. She walks with a purposeful stride and leads me to the top of the cliff overlook. It is still windy . . .

She looks directly and intently at me as she says, "It is important for you to intentionally align yourself with power and with a strong clarity of purpose. People assign incorrect purposes to the powers of Nature. They think of wind as destructive. This is a mistaken and limiting judgment. Powers of Nature are expressions. They are expressions of a purpose."

She then shows me how she relates to this wind:

She stands facing the wind, her long hair streaming behind her, and her garment flattened against the front of her erect body. She calls out in a loud and clear voice, "Hey you! Hey you! There is someone here who wants to talk to you—to meet you! Hey you! You are blowing strong and fine—you are powerful and beautiful! What is your business?"

We pause and listen to hear the spirit of this wind tell us that it is needed to move a large storm system from the ocean over to the land. The land calls for rain, and the clouds need the work of wind for this. We thank the wind for its efforts. My ancestress starts spinning around and around and the wind blows through her hair and garments, and she falls to the earth laughing. I am dizzy again. I thank her and leave.

When I return from this journey, the wind's volume has noticeably increased. The glass doors and windows are shaking; the sounds of their vibrations add to wind's high-pitched shriek. I quickly move deeper into the room, as a climax of some sort seems imminent. Moments later, the wind lets up as the leading edge of a rainstorm moves in off the ocean. Once ashore, the storm gentles as it settles in for a good soaking. The overdue rainy season has finally begun.

THE FACES OF WEATHER

There is no such thing as bad weather.
There's only many different types of good weather.

COLONEL SANDERS

E very weather event, each storm, breeze, or drop of rain, is a manifestation in the middle world of the power of the weather spirits. The creative force behind all acts and manifestations of weather's power does not, itself, have a specific form. What it has is *potential,* the potential of unformed energy. Furthermore, this energy of potential has spirit and gives birth to spirited forms or elements of weather. We can perceive a particular form when this energy is ordered into a state of coherency, when energetic particles or waves are in alignment. The form of a rainbow is an alignment of raindrops suspended in waves of sunlight. Its spirit holds the template of rainbow, and when the necessary elements are present, we can see a luminous, ephemeral arc as it coalesces into form. In the words of David's spiritual teacher, "Weather is power taking on the cloak of the elements available to it."

Weather, as with any alive and creative thing, continually offers up unique and ever-changing moments all over the earth. A frown or smile or gesture or breeze or storm or cloud can give us important information of the moment, yet it is only the outer layer, the presenting facade of the nature of its being—and it always changes. If we are awake, any particular element of weather can usher us in through its portal to the deeper story. All we have to remember is that we aren't looking at the whole story, that the answer both is and isn't there.

We may never have experienced a tornado and perhaps don't worry about the threat of one. Nonetheless, this entity of conjoined elements of weather taps into our subconscious realms. Without understanding anything of the physics of weather, the very face of a tornado or whirlwind can draw us toward its mysteries as it beckons us through our own portals of fascination.

Why is this? There are other images that don't reach in as readily or as deeply. Perhaps it has something to do with the shape, the very form of the spinning vortex of a funnel cloud. My spiritual weather teacher calls the word *symbol* "an empowered essence of form." The spiral is one of humankind's oldest and most widespread original symbols, and it figures prominently in our present-day designs. We find spirals on ancient rock art, Neolithic pottery shards, and old and new architecture and ornament. It may well be that we still respond to the *spirit* of whirlwind. After all, we have eons of experience with the spiral as a symbol of evolution—that which is coming into form and then spiraling back out into the void that gave it birth. Tornadoes, whirlwinds, and water spouts all show us this.

We can also reflect on the snowflake. No two are identical. Each is an art form created by a snowstorm that, in turn, is engendered by a grand orchestration of chaotic and orderly foundational forces of creation. The potential of snow, born of a pregnant promise held in the chaos of atmosphere, finds its way into a form of weather, perhaps a blizzard. As an intricate, unique crystal of water, the snowflake falls to earth and melts down into the rocks and soils, joins the great waters, or is taken into living beings, or all of the above. Eventually what was once snow, born of air, now water, through the fire of the sun, becomes vapor and rises back up into the atmosphere through what we call the "water cycle"—all in this middle world.

This is true shape-shifting! In the practice of shape-shifting we intentionally exchange one form for another. There are great teachings inherent in this act. When we speak of "walking in another's shoes," we're in touch with a remnant of that old knowledge. As we can see from the Micmac people's stories, they knew that power held the world together and that each and every form was a manifestation of a unique order of power. All conscious manifestations of power, with or without a form, were regarded and respected as Persons, and some Persons could intentionally use power according to their will. The shamans were recognized as Persons able to effectively use power for the good of the community as well as for their own benefit. They could change their own patterns of power, and their own forms, at will.[1]

David and I went through a period of a few years in which nearly every time we journeyed for a teaching about the nature of weather, we shape-shifted into one or more of weather's many faces or forms. I asked one of my spirit teachers about the continual emphasis on shape-shifting. In reply, he advised me to follow the path of form:

Weather is a master teacher of form and of form changing. The force of weather is a moving expression of its form. Weather takes on many forms, expresses many forms. By exploring form, you will find teachings of metamorphosis.

Your form, your body, is sacred. Being of form, you are far more able to relate to form than you are to concepts and words alone. Through the vehicle of a form, you are better able to identify and receive, to bring a concept home to yourself. This is why symbols are so useful for you.

Form is your portal to understanding the weathers of the middle world—and why you were given "only" experiences of weather's changing forms.

To learn about weather from its various personas, we need to cultivate and access a certain level of awareness. We need to know about boundaries—especially our own. We need to know that deception or illusion is all too possible as we look at the world. Too often we gaze at clouds and just see "clouds"; if we have studied about them in our school years, we may just identify them as "cumulus," "stratus," "cirrus," or "cumulonimbus" and stop there. Our life experience may be such that we can sometimes accurately predict coming weather by our scientific knowledge of cloud types and behavior. None of this is wrong, yet it is limited in scope and perception.

Elaine, a shamanic practitioner in New Jersey, gets another picture from the clouds she gazes upon almost daily. She is able to recognize and relate to the clouds as sentient beings, as spirits manifest, and she divines accurate information from them regarding matters in her life, as well as for the people who come to her healing sessions. Most often Elaine works with metaphorical understandings of the cloud shapes she observes, though sometimes the cloud spirits give her useful literal messages.

All the forms, or faces, of weather carry a story for those who notice them and can understand their meaning. In the language of the Inuit, it is said that there are many words for snow, each describing a different kind of snow as well as the local weather conditions that create it. But what about all the different winds in the world? Some peoples have named them—chinook, foehn, mistral, jet stream, trade winds—and then there are countless other breezes and winds of the moment, wafting or screeching by in varying intensities and directions. Other peoples recognize a variety of rains—male rain, female rain, soft rain, hard rain, sky milk, tears, and so forth.

For some years I studied plants, mostly through books and various herbal workshops, and eventually I was ready for an understanding of the herbs beyond their physical appearances and properties. I wanted a spiritual connection with these powerful and generous beings. On one of my shamanic journeys to the lower world, a helpful spirit appeared to me in the form of a two-legged plant being who offered the advice that if I wanted to go more deeply to a place of understanding and relationship with the plant people, I needed to surrender, for a year at least, my habit of naming a plant by its common or folk name. Instead, I was instructed to respectfully ask the spirit of each plant for a name of the plant's choosing. I immediately understood that this simple change in my approach would help me penetrate the veil of what I thought I knew and reach beyond the boundary of the stereotype. This way I could more authentically engage in a relationship with a plant, and vice versa. *For who among us is willing to be friends with one who cannot see or know us for who we are?*

David and I looked for what would represent a more or less consensual understanding of weather's personalities yet at the same time honor the validity of the unique teachings we all are capable of receiving and bringing forth into the world. Though the many world creation stories remind us that no one has the only "right" or entire answer, we can each bring forth pieces of the grand puzzle to see the greater pattern as it takes shape—or form.

Once again I consulted with my weather teacher. This time I found him on a mountaintop in the upper world at play with weather, and laughing heartily. He waved his arms around in a manner that reminded me of an orchestra conductor. A host of different elements of weather were about, and I felt I had happened by during the tune-up exercises before the symphony is performed. Not wishing to intrude, I waited. Suddenly my weather teacher turned toward me, holding a bundle of lightning bolts in a rather classic godlike pose. I asked him for a teaching about weather spirits. He described a weather spirit as the alive, sentient essence of any force of weather. A weather spirit, he said, is capable of relating with humans and other beings. I asked, "Then how does a spirit of weather manifest its force in ordinary reality?" He replied, "Reciprocally. The spirit, the alive essence, takes it all in, all the cues and messages from Earth, and gives it back. There is a constant flow back and forth."

Thinking the lesson finished, I was about to thank my teacher when he held up his hand, cocked his head to the side, and listened. I became aware of lightning flickering around us as the clouds started roiling over and under and around one another. He turned to me and sighed, saying, "They have so many faces." I understood that he was now speaking of weather spirits of the middle world, in ordinary reality. He described them as capricious, changeable, ephemeral, playful, and childish. Their emotions are affected by what is going on in the world (as above, so below). They can be moved to pity and are also capable of anger. His advice to me was to be alert and in the moment with them. Additionally, I would do well to seek out their spiritual essences in the reliably compassionate realms of the upper and lower worlds for the help I need to safely and effectively work with the weathers of the middle world. He finished our session with a reminder: "It is an old relationship—humans and weather."

Our research of historical literature revealed that ancestral portrayals of the spirits of weather were diverse, unique, and many. Most seemed to represent deities—gods, goddesses, demigods—who, despite their extraordinary powers, exhibited human characteristics, especially those of passion. They often were born of supreme and aloof nonhuman deities, yet they were more accessible than those deities and apt to be involved in the affairs of humans. They could and did mete out both punishments and gifts to humankind.

Not all weather spirits present in human form—or any particular form at all. Today, perhaps the most well-known spirit of weather is a magical and immensely powerful animal, the thunderbird. Knowledge of thunderbirds exists among peoples of several continents. Hindu mythology describes Garuda, the great demigod eagle associated with sky, wind, and lightning.[2] Chinese mythology identifies certain birds as wind deities and also as personifications of fire, sun, clouds, and thunderbolts. Cultures of South Africa describe a giant thunderbird that stirs up weather and is an instigator of storms, particularly those with lightning.

Thunderbirds figure prominently among many peoples of North

America, usually in relation to eagles and hawks. The Ojibwa knew them well and recognized that they, too, are capable of shape-shifting, sometimes into human form. In addition to their abilities to create and bring on winds and thunderstorms, thunderbirds were known to metamorphose enough to occasionally enter the world of humans to mate and produce "human" offspring.[3]

When I first heard of the thunderbirds human aspect, I was especially excited, as it corroborated an earlier, experiential weather journey where I faced a giant, dark bird reminiscent of a golden eagle. Immobilized with awe, I suddenly flashed on a man—a god?—then in the next instant merged with thunderbird, feeling its wildness and passion, but only for a moment, as I clearly could not absorb a full dose. I remember thinking that it is true, after all, that lightning bolts from the Thunderers (spiritual beings of Iroquois tradition) change and wake up the earth. They energize the earth when their searing, brilliant flashes of lightning discharge power both to and between the earth and sky, especially in those places where release is needed. I watched the thunderbird's great talons turn into sinuous lightning bolts and heard the thunderous sound of its beating wings. Once again, only for an instant, the thunderbird's face looked human. Back to myself and on my way home from this journey, I was cautioned to take care in relating with this element, this force of weather.

Marguerite, a shamanic practitioner and teacher for her community, journeyed to learn more about the faces or personas of weather and how we are all related. She first met two beings, a "long, bearded, slender man" and a "woodsy fairy lady" who identified themselves as "archetypal weather spirits." As soon as Marguerite voiced her request to learn more about the nature of weather, they laughingly faded away and she found herself surrounded by a mist:

◿◺

. . . *and then there was this question in the mist, "Do you know where weather comes from?"*

I replied, "From our earth." The mist praised me for my answer: "Yes, the weather is part of the earth. . . . The earth's weather is part of the earth. Other weather is part of other things."

I focused my intent and asked for more. The mist moved me and I saw and felt: cold, hot, windy, calm, rain, snow, sleet, hail, howling winds . . . the weather has many faces, many moods . . . all created in relationship to and as part of the earth. The faces of weather are the faces of earth, air, water, and fire relationships. Particular weather is the outside of what is inside.

I was floating in clouds, fluffy and light; I became fluffy light clouds. . . . It was intoxicating. . . . Then I became gray, heavy clouds, [with] lots of water and pressure, then I was on a lightning arc . . . and I became the lightning arc . . . I was hot and crackly . . . I hit a tall Douglas fir . . . it burst into flames and began to burn . . . I was hot wind, blowing the fire around, eating up trees and all else . . . then I felt wet and was a pounding rain . . . the fire left . . .

I heard, "These are the faces of weather, they are to be studied, to be enjoyed, to be feared and to be loved . . . but most of all, these faces are your faces, these conditions are your conditions. You make the weather as surely as you walk each day."

I asked, "Do you mean that how we humans live on the earth is part of how the weather is formed?"

"You got it." A large chuckle, and I saw my power spirits dancing and encouraging. "You are the origin of harmony and weather; you are within the space of time; you are the many faces of being; you are the weather in all forms and all seasons . . . you are yours to discover."

───

In our first weather-dancing workshop, organized by Linda Crane, some of the journey teachings for our circle described the spirits of weather this way: "The weather spirits can be found in each one of us. Like us, their faces vary from harsh to gentle. They can reflect the state of society's consciousness, and we can call upon them to help humanity." This was intriguing information for our purpose of discovering whether and how we can intentionally relate to the forces of weather for the overall good. Linda's journeys that day brought more clarity to the developing scenario. In one of our follow-up conversations during the last few months of her life, we turned once again to our mutual fascination, the spirituality of weather and what it means for us in this world. I asked her to summarize what she had learned from her journeys about the faces of weather and whether she had any particular advice or caution that she wanted to leave us with:

> There is a weather spirit for every element of weather that interacts with the earth in this middle world. Spirits and beings of this middle world are mirrored by [those in] other worlds, so there are spirits of weather in the upper world as well.
>
> We must be aware that *when the sky deity is seen as that which is all good, then the earth becomes the shadow.* When humans don't want to acknowledge their own shadow they perceive the earth and the serpent as negative—evil—and only God (the sky deity) as good. The gods are "good" and "bad" only because we are in a dream of duality. The reality is there are no "good" or "bad" spirits—they are only real!

10

THE SACRED NATURE
OF STORM

When a vision comes from the thunderbeings of the west,
it comes with terror like a thunderstorm;
but when the storm of vision has passed,
the world is greener and happier;
for wherever the truth of vision comes upon the world,
it is like a rain.
The world, you see, is happier after the terror of the storm.

BLACK ELK

No one element of weather arouses more passion in us than a storm. Not only do we dread storms because of our own learned experience, but we may also be influenced by our heredity. Biologist and author Loren Eisley writes that "at the deepest level of the subconscious mind of all those descended from ice age people, there swirls the genetic memory of an unending snowstorm."[1]

Our human psyches also have a fascination for disasters. At this time in our culture, books and television programs abound with natural calamities such as earthquakes, wildfires, volcanic eruptions, tsunamis, and an entire supercharged class of storms known as megastorms: category 5 tornadoes, class 5 hurricanes, typhoons, and "hundred-year" floods, ice storms, blizzards, or worse. Yet following these natural disasters, with their sorrowful losses of life and habitat, people often speak of blessings—gifts that seem to come forth amid all the destruction and pain. An old and well-known proverb bids us look for the silver lining in the dark clouds. Is this proverbial advice simply a testament to the undaunted human spirit, or is it something more? Joseph, an artist and dowser spoke to us of another side of storm: "The darker, the more ominous the weather is, the more brilliant the light becomes and the greater an illumination of awareness can occur within the observer."

The citizens of Hamtramck, Michigan, suffered major damage to their town when multiple tornadoes swept through a few years ago. The unwelcome twisters, however, left them with something to ponder. As Connie, Michigan resident and workshop participant, relates: "Hamtramck is predominately Polish Catholic with several large churches. Though the destruction was bad enough that the National Guard had to cordon off the city for weeks, none of the churches—even the tallest—were touched. Another amazement was that a life-sized, solid stone statue of Jesus with his arms extended was lifted and turned and set back down on its pedestal, now facing a different direction."

We have it in our power to cultivate a perspective that is spacious, allowing for a necessary role as well as a sacred persona for storms. Storms can shake us, threaten our foundations, and, if we're lucky, wake us up. They can wound us and they can heal us. Any willingness on our part to transcend our survival fears and soften our attitudes toward storms will foster beneficial change for our own hearts. If we can accomplish this with weather that we fear and that is capable of harming us, then we'll surely grow in our ability to love and live fearlessly.

As a child Jerry Dennis witnessed a scene of great distress when he stood with others on the shore of Lake Michigan during a sudden, calamitous storm and watched the wind-driven waves drown people. Nearly all attempts to help failed, though the people trapped in the thrashing waters were barely more than an arm's reach away. The would-be rescuers could only stand by, powerless and horrified, as they watched people roll under the waves for the last time. Stunned, Jerry emerged from this tragic event with a teaching that informs his life to this day:

> The world is there to be seen in its entirety—the whole, astonishing, complex wonder of it at once—but we catch glimpses only. It is our curse. We are not equipped to see the whole picture or to understand it if we could. That is why storms excite us—they force a larger awareness. We're not accustomed to having sudden, massive perceptions thrust upon us. It makes a big impression. We never forget.[2]

Our friend Petra related to us how stormy weather drove her to a major insight of her life, provided the setting for a healing of her heart when she was losing heart, and ultimately transformed the spiritual and practical focus of her life. It occurred when she was on a great adventure hiking the Santiago de Compostela pilgrimage trail, a famous trek through Spain beginning in the Pyrenees Mountains and ending at a shrine by the seashore, 540 miles away.

Petra (whose name means "rock" in German) is a strong, vital woman who feels a passionate love for the natural world. She is also an experienced hiker and climber and had successfully hiked alone from her home in Germany to the beginning of the great walk. Halfway through the trek Petra was forced to walk in stormy weather for an entire day, through a flat and treeless plain. For a span of at least 17 kilometers, wind-driven rain relentlessly lashed her face, without a moment's reprieve. Wet, tired, cold, and getting colder, Petra longed for shelter—any sort of shelter—but there was none.

By late afternoon the situation had worsened, as the water-soaked dirt and clay road became nearly impassable. Petra felt that with each step her boots were growing heavier with ponderous globs of mud, while at the same time, the road's surface turned dangerously slick. Carrying a full backpack, she could not afford to be clumsy, yet she was rapidly losing her ability to continue, to take even one more step.

Exhausted and anxious, Petra suddenly realized that all along she had been engaged in a battle solely with the external world—with the weather and her circumstances. With this insight, she surrendered to a deep sense of acceptance of her situation and the present moment. "I gave up the fight with Nature," she says. From this new place of internal spaciousness, Petra was able to see what she couldn't see before. She stepped off the muddy path and into a stony field. Not only was it possible for her to walk on the rocks as stepping-stones, but as she looked at them glistening in the rain, she noticed green shoots of new wheat growing up and around their edges. At first sight, the wheat's ability to thrive in a stony field surprised Petra, but then, she explains, "I saw how the wheat loves the stones, and that the wheat could deal with it. This was a big gift from the storm: the calling of my life is to *love the stones.* If the day had been sunny this would never had happened for me." Petra added that a second metaphor for her life is that sometimes we have to go off the beaten or normal path.

For many peoples in the world, storms have sacred origins. From the Tibetan Bon tradition, one creation story honors Klu-mo, a female spirit of the primal waters who spontaneously emerged as a sacred being whose body is intimately connected with earth and sky. She has the eyes of sun and moon that bring on the new day as they open and the night when they close. The crown of her head is the sky realm. Klu-mo's shining teeth are the stars. The oceans are her blood and the rivers her veins. Storms rush out of her mouth as lightning darts from her tongue. Clouds take their shape from the exhalations of her breath as winds blow out of her nostrils. Her tears give rain to the earth.[3]

The story of Klu-mo is but one example of many origin stories where storms are interwoven into the fabric of creation of cosmos and earth, including primary deities. The Hindu tradition honors the storm god Indra, who once held the highest place in the hierarchy of the Vedic pantheon, and who was responsible for all the activities of the atmosphere. Time and again, from the very beginning, Indra has saved the land from drought. Horses and elephants worked with Indra, and various elements of weather served as his tools, such as Vajra, the thunderbolt, and a rainbow as his bow. It is said that Indra had a violent—stormy—nature and fought many heroic battles with demons and other deities on behalf of the world below.[4]

The sacred and creative power of storm is also recognized by the Skidi Pawnee, who say the world was created during the first thunderstorm.[5] Tribal peoples of the Great Plains give thanks for the thunderstorms of spring, knowing that lightning awakens and charges the earth with its vital energy after the long winter. Likewise the Russian storm god, Perun, frees the sun from its winter prison each year and liberates the rains that are locked up in cloud castles. For the Dinka of Sudan the primary deity is Deng, who is associated with thunderstorms and whose name means "rain." Deng is honored both as an ancestral deity and as a creative force that brings fertility to the land as well as destruction.[6]

Despite their tremendous, and seemingly capricious, capacity for destruction, storms have another side, a spiritual role that peoples in the world have recognized for a long while. The traditional teachings of the Iroquois nation portray the Thunderers "as powerful beings guarding the earth from evil."[7] The Iroquois honor a thunder deity, Hino, who lives in the clouds with his rainbow wife and serves as a sky guardian, protecting his people from natural forces of harm.[8] One of the annual ceremonies of Thanksgiving offered by the Seneca is dedicated to the Thunderers.

Among the most powerful of the Lakota shamans are those who have been called by the thunder beings. According to Lame Deer, a

Lakota medicine man, "If the thunder-beings want to put their power on earth, among the people, they send a dream to a man, a vision about thunder and lightning. By this dream they appoint him to work his power for them in a human way."[9] Lame Deer makes it clear that though the power of the thunder beings, the Wakinyan, is considered beneficial, the thunder beings are nonetheless a fearsome and dangerous facet of the Great Spirit, Wakan Tanka.

The traditions of the Dakota peoples of Portage la Prairie in Manitoba teach that before birth many shamans-to-be travel around the earth with the Wakia, the Thunderers, in every thunderstorm, seeking a place to be born. Then, when it is time for a person to become a shaman, the Wakia send a sign so that the community will know and can support the individual's calling.

In addition to heralding the profound events of birth and visioning, thunderstorms and rainbows are known to present at the moment of death or during a memorial service, particularly when the individual has lived a spiritually oriented life—such as that of a shaman. David and I had the rare good fortune to enjoy a friendship and working relationship with such a person. On the eve before her sunrise memorial service, we gathered with some of her close friends and family members at her home near the waterfront in Gloucester, Massachusetts. After plans for the ceremony were in place, we drove toward the inn for the night. It was near dusk when an otherwise sunny, breezy, and partly cloudy day abruptly transformed into something else. We watched as the fair-weather clouds coalesced into a large circular shape suggesting a pretornadic wall cloud—just above our heads. The breeze turned into a wind as the sky rapidly darkened into a luminous greenish gray wash. The circle cloud began revolving and small, sinuous cloud nipples or protuberances formed, looking like they might snake all the way down to the treetops or ground. A woman from Kansas later told me that she had started looking for a ditch to jump in as she walked under the metamorphosing sky. Soon after a thunderstorm erupted, and at storm's end the sky shimmered with an enormous double rainbow that remained suspended for at least half an hour—long enough to make the front page of the next morning's local newspaper.

Knowing our friend as we did, we felt certain she was part of this event, and for many of us this was confirmed on the afternoon of the following day, which was another partly sunny, breezy day in that area with no reported storms. Yet a fishing boat with children aboard was treated to the sight of a vertical rainbow, hanging in the air directly above the rocky headland where her service took place that morning. Reportedly the captain, who knew of her, told the kids that he heard that a real shaman had passed away and that there was a memorial in her honor that day, in that very place, marked by the rainbow.

We heard another unusual story about weather and a memorial service from Kim, of Alice Springs, Australia. In the year 2000, she told us, an Aboriginal traditional elder and well-known social activist for Aboriginal rights had passed away. His funeral was being held that day just outside of town. He had been beloved by many, and everyone was very sad. It was a day of almost continuous storms and rain, a rare event in that arid part of the world. People huddled in a tin-roofed building while storm rains poured down, and it was said that these were tears of sympathy joining in with the human grief. Finally, late that afternoon, the rain stopped as an enormous rainbow appeared over the funeral proceedings.

I have loved storms since childhood, and though I still get frightened during especially charged thunderstorms, I can now focus my attention on a storm's spirit in an attempt to greet and honor this unique being of weather. Once in a while a helping spirit journeys with me into the storm and I am able to briefly merge with its power, as one of its elements of cloud, wind, rain, or lightning. I began collecting storm waters from each that passed over, from thunderstorms, snowfalls, tropical storms, nor'easters. We drink a little of the essence from such storms and use the rest in ceremony. Afterward we often place the bowl of ceremonially charged storm waters outside on an altar to evaporate and infuse the atmosphere with our appreciation and intentions for offering healing to the sky. This is one way we can work spiritually to help balance the toxins that are routinely pumped into the very air and atmosphere we depend upon for life.

David and I solicited journeys about storms from others in addition to our own. Knowing that we all have our individual filters of perception, this allowed us to include a variety of journey experiences so that the spirits could have a voice with a broad range of notes, a wide carrying capacity, and clarity. We had learned that cross-culturally, even peoples who routinely display vengeful and hostile acts toward storms see them as serving essential roles in the continuance of life and fertility in our world. We wondered whether people in our culture would receive this same wisdom through their journeys. In the end we found no contradictions and a lot of commonality in the teachings about the spiritual nature and roles of storms. Most journeys provided teachings on topics of cleansing, with storm as the restoration and maintenance of balance, a wake-up call, a fresh start, and a reflection of us humans—mostly collectively, but sometimes individually.

Robert, an early contributor to our work, sent us this journey in answer to a question we were working with: "What is the role of storms?" The compassionate being he consulted, Red Spirit, answered with one word: "Balance."

Robert then asked the real question he wanted to address: "What is a storm?" The spirit answered Robert in the following dialogue:

"In the desert, there can be a wind spout that can last just a minute. But if you were an insect living in that sand, wouldn't you be in a storm? A tornado is a storm, but what of the wind that pushes the butterflies away? Is that not a storm to them? The question 'What is the role of storms?' cannot be answered in the way it was said. But what I can tell you is this: Spirit is never ending and never stopping. Something that is created by spirit, by Nature, is created to fill a need."

I say, "I am not sure I understand." Red Spirit stands up and opens his hand, palm up, and says, "Come."

I am standing with him on the edge of an erupting volcano. The lava is covering the land, moving toward the water, where it will make the island larger. It is an island—I see water in the distance. Red Spirit says, "There is a need for the land to be renewed and to grow. The storm that was created inside the earth fills the need."

We are on a mountain, in the winter, in front of a huge bank of snow. As the bottom layer gives way, there is a large avalanche. The wall of snow comes down, covering trees and houses. "A storm of snow," says the spirit, "reminds people they are not in harmony. What they do to their world has created the extraordinary amount of snow. They need to remember."

We move and are now standing on the plains. I see in the distance a funnel of a tornado that is forming. Red Spirit says, "There is a release. There must be a release of all energy, for energy cannot remain confined. It cannot build and build without release. This storm releases the energy that is trapped within Nature. If it were not for that, the weather might be different in many places. Though the tornado can be powerful and destructive, it is also brief and local. The damage on a worldwide scale is minimal."

We are now standing in a forest. I see the lightning light up the sky. The wind is blowing. Lightning strikes and the first sign of smoke is in the sky. Red Spirit says, "Sometimes things must be destroyed in order for things to be born, whether trees or animals. All are part of the scheme of spirit. The role of this storm is not to bring destruction, but to bring rebirth."

Red Spirit touches my hand. "There is no one answer because different storms are for different purposes."

Robin's journey corroborates the teachings of Red Spirit and further introduces the human element of causality to the role of storms:

I went to the lower world and was taken along a shoreline during a storm, and the waves came up and molded the land, sculpted it, deposited materials. I went farther up on the land and the wind came up and blew hard. It blew parts of the land away, exposing new rock and land. The particles that it blew rained down like tiny seeds and then took root as seedlings, fields of them.

I was shown that weather is what shapes the earth. It renews the earth by moving its parts and elements around to start up again. It is ever changing. Even droughts have a purpose: to let the land and elements relax and rest.

I asked for another teaching and was told that the weather (and storm) cannot do its job, or is having a hard time doing its job, because of interference. Much of the interference comes from toxins and pollutants, which weigh down the air and wind and rain. I asked what could be done to help and was told, "Heal the heart." I understood this to mean that we must "heal our hearts" in order to see the weather and its role and honor the weather."

Continuing with the message of human interference, Elaine's journey teaching brought her face to face with a tornado ripping through buildings, clearing a path. She heard, "Too many buildings, there is no place for us to go," and related how Nature spirits under the earth were working furiously as the earth listed from side to side, chanting, "We must create balance." Elaine understood that their work is much harder because humans do not strive to keep balance on the earth. She saw extreme weather and was told, "You humans work well together in crisis, well in chaos, so go and work well together—here is your crisis."

Sinead also journeyed for storm teachings, and her experience gave us another angle to the human connection with violent weather and natural disasters, one that revisited the issue of our emotions:

❧

I was led up a mountain to the top. We were in this thick fog. At the top was this Zeus-like character, and he was directing things. These little people were coming up the mountain with these tightly coiled objects that were in the shape of sausages. They would hand them to this Zeus-like guy, and he would toss them into the air, where they would uncoil and form storms. I was told that the coils contained all the repressed emotions that humans carry around with them.

I was given one of the coils to hold, and my whole body vibrated and shook. I was also told that sometimes there are so many of these that natural disasters are created. Because of the loss the humans experience in these situations, their self-erected walls go down, and they're able to release some of their pent-up emotions along with the sorrow they feel about their immediate situation, so it sort of clears the air.

❧

As David and I received journey contributions from others we saw that many spoke to the powerful blessings that storms can bring us through their power, beauty, and even destructive force. Furthermore, these teachings came from people who not only feel compassion for those who suffer but themselves have experienced fear and genuine hardship from the effects of storms. These individuals, and others like them, are a testament to the greater harmony of the shamanic worldview.

In one of our classes at the Esalen Insitute, Katie learned in her journey that storms are about change, transitions, and shifts—letting go to make way for something new. Storms are a reminder to humans of Nature's power and strength. And that is not all. They bring another gift to us: the possibility of inner peace, an experience of tranquillity for both the outer world and our inner being once the storm moves on.

During what was an exhilarating journey experience for Iam, he, too, saw the changes that storms can evoke in us: they teach us about another side to conflict as they sweep in with their power of turmoil and destruction—and when they pass, they often leave behind a sense of rage spent. We can feel it in cleansed air and a feeling of peaceful relief. Storms teach us of our smallness and the greatness of All Being, and that we humans are all part of the balance. As the spirit of storm told Iam, "It is the tempest that brings forth the nectar of the wildflower."

At a Nova Scotia workshop, a year before the Halifax region was struck by Hurricane Juan, Steve met the spirit of a tornado, who told him about the need for the movement of change:

> We are similar in spirit [to you], which is why we have come to each other. We are still at the core. Around that core is a controlled chaos, and we must remain in motion, for if we become still we cease to exist. Many may see us as arbitrary or destructive, but we have a creative function. We clear the field and rearrange the elements so that new forms may arise.

Steve's teaching from the spirit of tornado brought us back, full circle, to the spiritual nature of weather, where there is always something else to learn and another way to understand what storms are up to. A workshop participant met Stormy Man:

He was huge and had the presence of a stone person. Out of his mouth was a cool breath of mist as he spoke.

"Weather is the breath of the universe. The Great Mother exhales to teach, to cleanse. She teaches by atmospheric disturbance. She teaches how to protect ourselves from the elements—the way to make way for the forces that are great and powerful, and how to live in harmony with them."

Once again we had spiraled around in our bid for knowledge, and we were now ready for the next level: the matter of relationship, of intentionally living with the forces and beings of weather. To Paul the storm spirits forthrightly communicated that they work for the balance and health of the earth, and that "we should stop bitching when it isn't always sunny. If humankind lived in harmony with the earth, [the weather spirits] wouldn't do so much damage." At the end of Paul's journey, the spirit of storm left him with a parting reminder for us all: "Like you, we are walking on the altar that is the earth."

PART THREE

WEATHER
SHAMANISM

11

ENLIVENED RELATIONSHIP WITH NATURE

THE WAY IN

*There is a great wisdom in personalizing the
    physical world.
Relationship requires a sense of respect
and equality for the other,
and to cultivate a relationship with the Divine
demands that we treat with respect and equality
the natural world that contains the Divine.
This is one of the shaman's great insights;
we can approach the Divine Mystery of the Universe
    through Nature,
and our relationship with the Divine
evolves from our partnership with Nature.*

TOM COWAN, *FIRE IN THE HEAD*

The weather offers us a portal, a way in, to Nature. Once we set
our intention to engage in a conscious relationship with Nature,
we are inspired to expand our focus beyond personal boundaries of self-

interest. This is not to say that we are asked to abandon ourselves, for we are Nature, and therefore we stand to gain not only an expanded sense of self, but also a better understanding of our place within the workings of this world.

As Tom Cowan writes, "Shamans also demonstrate that we cannot launch an undifferentiated relationship with 'Nature as a whole.' We must begin on a smaller, more personal level."[1] We can begin by looking for an opening where our hearts are already touched by an element of Nature—some place in us that shimmers with resonance—be it the caress of a mild breeze or wind blustering through our hair, the warmth of spring sunlight, or the way a sunbeam reveals a secluded spot in the forest. The aroma of aromatic sagebrush after a rainstorm may awaken us, or perhaps the deepening rumbles of an approaching storm with the brilliance of its lightning strikes will quicken our imaginations. The magnetic presence of an "elder" tree may call to us; likewise the deep quiet of snowfall on a winter's night. Allow that element to serve as teacher, as a guide through a doorway most of us may not have approached since we were children.

We might be inspired by the shape-shifting interplay of clouds . . .

During the summer and fall of 2003 David and I became deeply involved in an intensive study of clouds, which culminated in a creative effort we named cloud dancing. While I have watched and admired clouds all my life—from lawns and fields of childhood to fire lookout towers to just about everywhere I could see the sky—I never saw them as intently and passionately as then. From thinking of them as "clouds," I learned to know them as Cloud People. I had already experienced shamanic journeys to cloud beings and had repeatedly shape-shifted into clouds, but that summer carried me to new levels of attention and respect for the Cloud People. I became a hunter of clouds, of their forms, beauty, and wisdom, and I was a lover of them as well. As my intensity of focus and appreciation grew, so did a feeling of relatedness. I felt the joy of accordance; I felt that the Cloud People supported what I was up to and perhaps even loved me back. Inspired and humbled by that feeling of responsiveness, I was able to maintain my interest throughout the many hours and days of our project, which manifested in a set of divinatory cloud portraits and a booklet that we called *CloudDancing: Wisdom from the Sky*.

For *CloudDancing* we needed a wide variety of photographic images of the clouds that would be suitable for the purposes of divination. David and I wanted to bring forth a tool, through the images, to enhance visual awareness, to get across the message that the weather is alive and connected to us, and to support the ancestral wisdom of gaining useful, practical, and inspiring information directly from Nature. We wanted to help awaken and encourage our ability to receive insights and information from the images and symbols, feelings, actions, and sounds of Nature through what is known as direct revelation, the most ancient method of learning other than hands-on experience.

What was most exciting to us was the seeming responsiveness of the Cloud People once we had sincerely engaged with our project, as they offered us a generosity of shapes and colors such as I had not seen before. In fact, I had often complained that the clouds where we live were generally rather flat and less than dramatic. Yet as soon as we began our project, day after day unusual and interesting cloud formations sailed by overhead in a seemingly endless variety of images. At the point where I had only four days left to complete our collection of one hundred portraits for publication, I realized I was missing a particular kind of cloud I have always enjoyed and mostly observed in mountain country: lenticular clouds. I felt sad about this but resigned myself to its absence, as in the seven years I had lived by the shore this intriguing formation has shown up only a few times. Yet, "magically," lenticular clouds appeared in the sky as I drove home after a hike, when I just happened to have a camera!

David describes the uniqueness of the cloud portraits this way:

> The power of each image is in its reflection of the spirit and power
> of the sky at that moment. A particular cloud exists only for a short

time in ordinary reality, yet in nonordinary reality, the spirits of this and every cloud are always there—every cloud that has existed or will ever exist. Clouds, by nature, are ephemeral. These clouds, however, have chosen to stay with us.[2]

My appreciation for the clouds does not diminish even though that summer of dancing with the Cloud People has passed. I know they will always offer me a portal, a pathway to my internal soul and to those places of wonderment and abiding love for the natural world. I feel a jolt of gratitude whenever people who divine with the *CloudDancing* cards or who simply admire the portraits tell me they no longer look at the sky in the same way as before—that the Cloud People have touched their hearts, too.

Our willingness to open our hearts to any particular expression of Nature will lead us unerringly back to our real home in this middle world, home to ourselves and our place in all of creation. "Opening your heart" implies a certain willingness to love and be loved, and it takes an *intention* for this to be so. If our intention is to establish an openhearted relationship with weather, then we can begin by offering any element of weather the gift of our attention. Relating to the weather also requires of us a certain awareness and sensibility—an alert and sympathetic responsiveness—so that we may "approach the Divine Mystery of the Universe through Nature."

We all have the ability to experience different states of consciousness; it's part of our internal structure. This is an asset for us when we want to meditate or undergo a shamanic journey. In the course of our normal lives we spend much of our time weaving in and out of states of alert awareness and those of trance as our brain waves and attention shift repeatedly. Most of our awake trance states are momentary and light and occur as our brain waves move back and forth from "normal" experiences of lucid attentiveness, which lie within the beta brain-wave range, where we are awake and functioning normally, to the lighter trances of the alpha range. In contrast, we also experience episodes of deep and deeper brain-wave shifts into the delta and theta ranges when we sleep and dream.

How do we know if we are in trance or not? The easiest way to know is when we have just emerged from one. Telltale signs are that we can't remember how we got where we are (for example, driving past the highway landmark we were looking for), or somewhere in the course of a conversation we realize we stopped listening, or we have to reread the last paragraph or page we just finished. These trance states are so light as to be barely noticeable. However, the uncommon, open-eyed, awake state of trance is recognizable as something unique and nonordinary. It usually involves a feeling of expansiveness of the self, as if our boundaries suddenly became permeable or were suspended. Those who experience these states often describe them as moments of enhanced awareness when they unequivocally know that they are one with the universe or Nature, and that all is well after all. Such experiences can inspire a lasting and welcome opening of the heart along with an abiding sense of trust in life.

Furthermore, we all live within a consensual agreement (some would say *collective trance*) of a worldview that defines—and creates—our experience of ordinary reality. It takes a dedicated practice of mindful attention to reveal the pervasiveness of the ordinary-reality trance as it directs and shapes our lives, and to discover how we may be living on "automatic" from day to day. With intention and focused effort, we have a real opportunity to learn how a lack of awareness restricts our abilities to "see," to know there is an unseen, vital world all around us.

Indeed, David and I have found that in those times when we were able to deeply relax and momentarily suspend our normal perceptual parameters and definitions of the world, we were nearly overwhelmed by a melee of signals, signs, and information. We soon learned that without a selective focus to our seeing or listening, feeling, or intuiting, we risked becoming easily confused, even dizzy!

Nature's elements can teach us to develop an attentive awareness of how we routinely encounter the beings, seen and unseen, with whom we share the earth. If we just walk past a rock or plant or human without giving more than a superficial glance, limiting our mental notes to gender or species, big or little, animate or inanimate, threatening or pleasant, then we relinquish an opportunity for relatedness. How many times do we step outdoors and pause long enough to survey the sky? Realistically, in our rushed adult lives, we can't take the time to stop and closely observe everything within our reach—though little children avidly do so. But at least we can be conscious of our choices and aware that we may be passing up the possibility of valuable teachings and help when we don't pause.

The rural Scottish Highlanders of the nineteenth century, and their ancestors before them, understood their relatedness—and dependency—upon the forces and elements of Nature. The ancestral Highlanders have been characterized as a people who freely and lovingly expressed their kinship with the sun, moon, wind, storms, air, sea, and mountains. From the work *Carmina Gadelica* by Alexander Carmichael, we have a large collection of old Scottish blessings, hymns, and prayers, many of which dwell on the elements of Nature. Cowan writes that these elders "neither romanticized nor demonized these forces of nature. They lived with them physically and spiritually."[3] They honored the rising of the sun and moon, and their own rising each day. They saw the earth and sky as filled with spirited beings, elements of Nature who noticed and responded to them, and who could receive the peoples' blessings and expressions of love—and, in return, could bestow blessings and love. It was a reciprocal world, filled with an intimacy of the divine and the familiar.

Many of what we would think of as mundane activities— "smooring," or banking the hearth fire at night, milking the cows, collecting eggs from the hens, planting gardens—also deserved appropriate blessings, thus adding a divine element to the work of the day. These were *daily* blessings. The Highlanders lived with the sure knowledge of the support and protection of the sacred. When storms threatened they blessed them as well, despite their potential for destruction, with hope that proper recognition and honoring would ensure at least some measure of protection.

It would be a mistake to consider the blessings of the Highlanders as superstitiously self-serving. Those who blessed were aware that we are a part of it all and could see the divine everywhere. What an enlivened sense of the world they must have had—it begs Einstein's famous wondering, "Is the universe a friendly place?"

Cowan joins his voice with the many pleas of indigenous peoples around the planet in encouraging all of us to find our own sense of love for the natural world and to offer blessings from our hearts for the beauty, the power, and the sacredness we live within. We are asked to carry on the ancient earth-honoring customs of our ancestors. "Even though it jangles every scientific, rational nerve in your body, try to think of the storm and the whirlwind as somehow deserving of your blessing. If we don't do these things, who will?"[4]

Time and again David and I were encouraged by our helping spirits to learn how to more sincerely love the weather—all weather—and to focus our attentions and honoring on every kind of weather, regardless of personal preference. The weather spirits themselves made it clear that our appreciation of all of weather's expressions is absolutely necessary for an enlivened relationship with them.

Though we both carry an innate love for the natural world and weather, this task of overall appreciation regardless of personal preference was, and remains, challenging. Over the years we have worked hard to monitor our thoughts and attitudes about particular weather events. Complaints about the weather, as we know, are a common feature in the conversations of our culture. Yet even as we diligently refrained from habitually complaining about the weather, we eventually recognized that we also needed to admit to our true feelings, for how else can we be authentic in our relationships? We were learning that all weathers could be genuinely honored, no matter what our emotional and physiological responses.

Early on I toppled off my own pedestal of a nearly self-righteous practice of never allowing a single utterance of dislike of any weather to leave my lips. It was our first summer on the coast of Maine. It was an unusually wet summer, and though I require a lot of sunlight for my sense of well-being, I was proudly hanging in there—until the fog moved in. I had expected to experience fog along the Maine coast and knew it well from my days along the Pacific shores of the Northwest. But I did not know fog from this realm.

Day after day after day, and night after night after night, the fog stayed with us. I had never seen anything like it. At first I thought it beautiful, mysterious, soft, captivating—so "Maine!" As my defenses eroded away, my ideas of this fog eventually sank from "beautiful" to just "so Maine." From this point I struggled to think only that and not snarl out some other description. Relentlessly the fog persisted, and as it continued to dominate the outdoors I gave up going anywhere—it felt more claustrophobic outside than in. I grew sleepy, irritable, depressed, and hungry. This was more like winter than late June.

On the morning of the seventh or eighth or ninth day of the cloying dampness, I settled with a book and cup of coffee in a large chair in the living room. I started to read, but I couldn't concentrate. The words wouldn't stick; nothing made sense. The horrifying thought abruptly came to me that the fog had finally entered my brain, invading my sacrosanct interior realm, and would now rule me as well as the outdoors. Flinging my book aside, I leapt from the chair and tore through the door out onto the porch. I jumped up and down and, shaking my fist, shouted to Fog that I couldn't—wouldn't—take this anymore. I turned my back on Fog and stomped inside to plop on the chair once more. I felt silly but relieved, as if a damp weight had lifted off my shoulders.

And then it was Fog's turn. Five minutes later, there was a stirring. A fresh breeze blew through, the first since Fog's arrival so long ago. A quick burst of rain followed the breeze, and suddenly I could see a little more outside, and then farther as the trees at the end of the meadow came into view. Patches of blue sky appeared overhead—and sunlight! Now I could see to the far side of the river. I ran out just in time to see the last of Fog's tendrils gracefully swirl away. In that moment, I knew without a doubt that weather is alive and hears us.

Our trusted helping spirits introduced David and I to new tutelary spirits, those willing to usher us to the threshold of weather's spiritual world. We knew that at any point along the way, the portal to the weather spirits, and their readiness to be in relationship with us, could close. We suspected that some portals would take a long time to open, if ever they did. We learned to appreciate each step and to value every demonstration of weather's notice of our efforts, no matter how small or ambiguous, for each carried a gift of relatedness.

I was advised to spend at least ten minutes a day outside, paying attention to the sky, the earth, and especially the weather of the moment. This simple practice would not only help me learn more about weather's nature and workings in this world but would also allow the elements of weather to get to know me. Attentiveness to the weather is as important an opportunity for learning and relating as the seemingly more spectacular shamanic journey work.

Before long it began to look like our efforts of attention were adding up to a noticeable effect. The helping spirits seemed to take our inquiries seriously, and we knew that we risked a breach of trust if we were to ignore their teachings. The sustained focus served to place the weather, and its many personas, at the forefront of our consciousness so that a strong foundation for relationship could evolve.

David and I also discovered, as is natural for people of dissimilar personalities, that we each hold an affinity for different kinds of weather, even opposite types. For David, prolonged sunny weather of about four days' duration leaves him longing for cloud cover. I, on the other hand, cave in sooner: after only two overcast or fogbound days, I crave the return of the sun's brilliance. This is when I try to remember that we have a good balance in this effort together.

Martin Prechtel writes, in his account of his shamanic development under the tutelage of the renowned Tzutujil Mayan village shaman, Chiv, that each had their own affinity for various elements of Nature, and that while he could call and relate to wind, his teacher did better with rain. According to Prechtel's experience, "calling" an element of weather or any other being of Nature does not mean chasing it. He speaks more of understanding the particular element so well that you can become an object of that being's desire—you become fascinating, irresistible to whom you wish to call to you.[5]

What makes this connection possible, according to the knowledge of the Tzutujil Mayan shamans, is that the entire world and our human bodies reside within one another, and that our nature is the imagination of the gods, as is all of the natural world. Prechtel learned that a shaman has to intentionally seek to become Nature—as thoroughly as possible—and not be satisfied to simply observe Nature. In this way the soul of the shaman would reveal itself, little by little, and would thrive. To change weather, Prechtel learned that the shaman could call with the "unspoken voice" of his nature, expressed through the heart rather than with human words.[6]

Within the worldview of the Ojibwa of Canada, there is, behind and through all, a sacred spiritual essence that is responsible for thought and speech that finds its way into the forms of humans as well as rocks, animals, winds, and clouds. People of power, those consciously in touch with this truth of unity within diversity, such as Ojibwa shamans, have been known to change their forms at will and thus are sometimes able to influence the behavior of other forms or beings. These shamans know the common language of Nature.[7]

To relate spiritually to the forces of weather is to better our lives and the world of our present and our future. To relate effectively requires a special kind of attention from us, a willingness to extend beyond the confines of the ordinary perceptual ways we are taught to see and live with. It can be a lot of work, and it takes sustained effort to free ourselves and enter, at will, into heightened states of conscious awareness—yet the results are worth it.

> *I am the one, I am the other.*
> *I am the way in, I am the way out.*
> *I am the portal, I am the womb.*
> *I am the potential, I am the manifest.*
> *I am the changer, I am the changed.*
> *Come with your heart,*
> *and leave with your soul.*
>
> THE CLOUD PEOPLE

12

THE DANCE OF POWER

FIRST STEPS

So firm was the belief of the Maori in mana *that those who were held to possess it in high degree were credited with amazing powers, such as control over, or power to influence, natural phenomena. For instance, such highly endowed men could . . . cause the sun to shine, mist to disappear, and many other things equally marvelous.*

E. BEST, *MAORI RELIGION AND MYTHOLOGY*

Our car radio suddenly blared an emergency signal as the country western station in Oklahoma interrupted its program. Startled out of a light doze (David was driving), I heard the announcer warn the public about an approaching storm front with severe thunderstorms, high winds, hail, heavy rains, and tornadoes. It was leaving Texas on its way east and was predicted to sweep through Oklahoma that afternoon and evening. Thoroughly awake now, I checked the map and saw that it wouldn't be too much longer before the front entered Tennessee, where we were driving on Interstate 40, headed west toward the front. Despite the clear skies and January sunshine, the news of an imminent change in the weather was not entirely unexpected—two nights before the Weather Channel had described yet another Pacific storm ramming into the California coast, causing flooding, landslides, and snowfalls with attendant avalanche danger—and heading east. I had hoped that by the time we met up with this storm it would be spent. Instead, the energy intensified as it reconfigured into an enormously long front, razing the countryside in its advance. The possible strategy of driving around the thing was impossible, as the radio announcer said the front stretched from the Gulf of Mexico all the way north to the Great Lakes region.

David was nervous and I was scared. Few situations can make me feel more vulnerable than being caught in the path of a tornado during the nighttime hours in a flimsy motel where I am a stranger. I felt trapped, and though I knew my emotions were disproportionate to the real threat, I couldn't shake off a feeling of impending doom. A day earlier or a day later in our departure from home would have made a difference. How ironic that we had pushed our way through the beginnings of a snowstorm so we could experience clear roads the rest of the way. How ironic that I am a lover of weather and now was biting my nails over a weather experience still hundreds of miles away!

We continued driving west, resigned to our lack of control, and stopped for the night in the Tennessee countryside hamlet of Hurricane Mills. The motel was up on a hillside with woods behind us, and that felt good. We unpacked our car and flipped on the TV. There were several tornadoes reported on the ground in Oklahoma, in a direct line with our location, and severe weather reports of damage north and south. The front was predicted to pass over us in the predawn hours. The only thing left to do was to get in touch with the weather spirits.

I stood up and rattled for myself while David journeyed with our drumming CD. While David visited his teacher in the lower world, I headed to the upper world to my weather teacher for advice:

Grandfather's first comment to me is that this is the time of water and water's power on Earth to create change and to cleanse. Thus the tragic tsunami disaster, the flooding rivers in Ohio, Utah, Arizona, and elsewhere, and the heavy rains and snows leading to avalanches and lethal mudslides in California. He points out that it often takes big storms and earthquakes to unleash the waters, and we are in that process now.

I admit to him that I am afraid of the oncoming storm front. He gently reproaches me with a reminder that I know storms are creative beings as well, and that I am obsessing with their destructive side only. I ask Grandfather how to deal with this frightening storm, and he answers, "All that you can do is to honor it and communicate . . ."

His words trail off as we abruptly fly up into the air and directly back to this middle world to meet with the storm front itself! I can no longer perceive my teacher, but I know he is around and I clearly feel the presence of my power animal. I rattle harder and call out a greeting to the storm, requesting a meeting with its spirit. At first I can feel only the life of this storm front and the intense sense of purpose it carries to make way for the waters, to usher in the heavy rains to follow. It has little time for me. I honor the storm spirit anyway—compliment it and thank it for its sacred role. No response. I persist, and I state that I, along with other people, am learning to honor the weather spirits and to open our hearts to them, that David and I are presently traveling out to the coast of California, to where this storm first came ashore, to work to open the hearts of more people regarding the spirits of weather.

I keep on rattling and talking and let the storm know that we two-legged creatures are fragile and suffering from the ill effects of ignorance, and of too much chaos and disasters in our world. I ask the storm whether it can please accomplish its work and at the same time be gentle with us on the earth as it passes through. I ask the storm spirit whether its fingers of lightning and tornadoes could not come all the way down to earth—or if so, could they touch where the least harm would be done to two-legged creatures, plants, and animals? I cannot tell if the storm *spirit agrees, and I feel funny asking it to behave in a certain way . . .*

At this point Grandfather pulls me back to his realm, where I find myself shape-shifted into the storm itself. My intention had been to transfigure into Storm's divinity—maybe I have and maybe I haven't— but I can feel Storm Spirit's energy and personality. Its power is dazzling, and I am moved by the beauty of its lightning and tornadic fingers. As part of the storm, I can feel an intense desire to contact the earth. I feel a sense of searching for where to touch ground, for those places where energy is lacking or where there is too much power locked up. I realize how the intense rains connect the storm to the earth. I revel in the storm's ecstasy of carrying out its purpose for being. At last I fully return to myself, still in Grandfather's domain. As I thank him, he repeats, "All you can do is to honor . . ."

At dusk David and I walked down the hill to a small restaurant for dinner. The weather still felt calm, though high clouds were moving in. When we returned to the motel for the night, I unpacked some tobacco and ceremonial water and we went to each of the four corners of the motel property, offering prayers and some of our dinner food along with the tobacco and water to the directions and spirits of the place for the protection and well-being of all. I noticed I no longer had that sweaty-palm feeling of overwhelming fear. Back in the room, we had a last look at the Weather Channel; the damage reports and predictions were even more threatening, but surprisingly, I felt peaceful—worried, but no longer afraid. I fell into a restful sleep and did not awaken until just before dawn, when a warm gust of moist air blew in through the open window.

Fully awake, I stayed quiet and listened. All I could hear was a gentle rain. Feeling peaceful, I dozed until it was time to get on with another travel day. As we packed our car the rain fell harder and the wind gusted, but nothing alarming in intensity. We drove that entire morning through heavy rain without mishap. The radio reports had another story, however—the storm front had indeed been fierce, as damaging hail, winds, and lightning were reported just north of us, and a tornado touched down south of us, in Alabama. As far as we could tell, there were no reports of significant injuries. We drove on west into the clear skies of Oklahoma, feeling grateful for our experience and the teaching.

This encounter reminded me that to consciously relate to weather is to dance with weather. It is an act of focused intention, with clarity of purpose and presence in the moment. When inspired and energized by love it can become an ecstatic act of power. Our spirit teachers repeatedly speak to us about the power of strength that is enlivened and intensified by compassion. We align ourselves with the power of compassion when we spend energy and time on behalf of another. Shamans well know that to successfully call upon the assistance of their helping spirits is to work with a power that is infused with unlimited compassion.

Mystical, esoteric traditions understand the individual human's power to influence manifestations in this world. Eckhart Tolle, a contemporary mystic and philosopher, teaches that we are all part of one divine organism. As such, when we focus our attention on anything in Nature—a cloud, a breeze, or the plant that waves in the wind—we complete a circuit of awareness. When we admire the beauty of the sky, the attention we offer becomes a catalyst for the sky's awareness of itself, which, in turn, sparks our own self-awareness. Tolle asserts that Nature is waiting for us to wake up to this, and the beings of Nature are calling us to draw closer to them through our hearts and attention.

Ancestral traditions were well aware of this relationship of humans and the natural world and took great responsibility for their cocreative role. In the eyes of indigenous peoples, we are not really human until we understand this. According to Calvin Luther Martin, the Navajo people "see man and woman intertwined, yin and yang, between them accomplishing the purposes of the earth, housing the powerful events of the landscape and firmament surrounding them. They have no choice but to perform: humans are the earth and sky aware of themselves."[1]

Once again, we find the creative principles of unity (we are all part of the world and each other) and reciprocity (we and the world affect and mirror one other).

To date, quantum physics would seem to confirm this indigenous knowledge through its own findings, gleaned from experiments with atomic particles and waves. Simply put, quantum theorists discovered that the human in the lab coat, the one watching over an ongoing experiment, inadvertently affects its process and/or results. In these experiments the individual is the observer, and the observer is more than an onlooker. The observer, by observing, is actually a participant—an integral part of the action and part of the manifestation.

Furthermore, on the quantum level, the form that something takes is defined by the observer. Whether an electron exhibits as a particle or a wave depends upon how you look at it—upon the intention of the observer. Similarly, there are many choices available to biological stem cells for their eventual formation, and the particular form that any one of them takes is but one possibility of many, though they all come from the same original matrix. This is the creative principle of unity, the sacred union that lies behind all differentiation.

But who is the "participant-observer"? In the shamanic, ancestral worldview, everything in Nature is alive and has consciousness and is therefore capable of observing and participating in the creation of ordinary reality. Everything or everyone has a part in calling something into being, into a form or an expression. We can see that this is so through the lens of the physics of weather as well as in the spiritual nature of weather. Measurable factors such as temperature, moisture, terrain, air pressure, available sunlight, and levels of air pollution all help determine the appearances of weather, as do our emotions, thoughts, yearnings, and activities of living. The spirited, sacred potential of weather—the power that lies behind the outer facades or faces of its elements—is responsive in its nature. Weather manifests its particular forms in response to how it is *called down,* which is key to any active relationship with weather.

The Bushmen of southern Africa, the Pomo of California, the Aborigines of Australia, and many other ancestral and indigenous peoples knew that in the time of long ago, in the Dreamtime of creation, all supernatural beings and animals and other life forces could talk, and they had power. Of course, humans could talk with these beings as well, though they may have required training and sacrifice to do so. Today, it may be harder to communicate with these other forms of creation, but it is still possible, if we can find a common language and heartfelt feelings. Through our efforts to respectfully communicate and partner together with them on behalf of well-being and beauty in the world, we can still possibly influence their behavior—as they will influence ours.

My Nature-spirit grandmother of the lower world offered me the metaphor of a river and its power. The river, when wide, often exhibits a placid nature. Running smoothly and slowly, it can be sluggish in places, with eddies and stagnant backwaters. When squeezed into a narrow gorge or canyon, however, the river abruptly intensifies into a tumbling, rushing, tumultuous torrent. The energized, enlivened river is forceful in its power and not easily deterred from its course. We humans use our technological abilities to avail ourselves of this enhanced energy. We transform some of it to other forms of power that we use daily for our needs, such as hydroelectricity.

Grandmother took the metaphor a little further and showed me that when a significant rainstorm occurs, the river is even more energized and focused, and its flow becomes immensely powerful, so much so that the river can barely be contained within its banks, sometimes flooding the surrounding countryside. And so it is with us when we focus our intentions with clarity of purpose, and when our actions are in alignment with the unlimited compassion of the helping spirits, our own power becomes strong, focused, and transformative.

However, in developing a relationship of this kind with power, we have to understand more about the nature of power and where we stand with power. We need to gain clarity about the hidden nature of our personal need for power before we can reliably relate with the weather in a clean, effective, and safe way; otherwise we are only courting trouble. (The word for *power* among the Esselen and other California tribes is synonymous with the word *poison*.[2]) This kind of knowledge doesn't come easily, and the learning of it is an ongoing task. Depending upon our individual perspectives and intentions, our understanding of power varies widely, and wildly. We recognize physical power, political power, economic power, military power, the power of individual charisma, the power to make decisions and carry them forth, the power of a ruler to rule benevolently, as well as the hurtful power of intimidation when exercised by those unconcerned with anything beyond personal desires or fear. We are all capable of wielding the power to destroy and, in turn, of suffering the destructive effects of powerful acts motivated by fear. Likely we have always lived with the power of fear, which when in balance motivates us to exercise caution in the risks we take, yet when out of balance profoundly inhibits our ability to live life fully.

One night I received a significant teaching about power and my relationship to it. The sinuous image of an inexorably oncoming tornado has been a recurrent nightmare for me since childhood. In the past, in those dreams, I spotted the tornado from afar and watched it hurtling toward me; I always felt helpless and terrified. Sometimes I was with a loved one or two, but most often I was outside, alone in a vast landscape. At times I'd run from it, other times I'd find a place to hide and cower. Then there were those instances where I was responsible for the safety of others and was further tormented by the worry of making the right decision, the one that would save us all. I always woke up before it arrived, never knowing if we would have made it.

Over the past decade or so, however, these scenes have changed. This seems to have occurred some years after I embarked upon my spiritual path of shamanism. At first the difference was subtle: The tornado whirled along a path parallel to mine, and I felt less fear. Once

I successfully herded a group of children into a rural schoolhouse and to safety. I noticed that the dreams were no longer terrifying, and I started to relax. And then there came one more memorable than all the rest:

⌗

I am in my mother's house, the way it was when I was a child, but I am grown, as I know myself now. My mother is no longer here. A sister and her partner, my son, and David—none of whom grew up in my mother's house—are with me. My attention is drawn to the window of the kitchen door. I look out into the backyard and there is a tornado forming behind the tall pine trees across the way. It looms above everything, even the old oak where my rope swing dangles. Just as I freeze in fear, a sacred being, a man-bird, arises from the top of the charcoal gray twister. He is magnificent, with outstretched giant arm-wings. He slowly pirouettes in one direction and then the opposite. I can see his striking profile and long, swinging braids. I forget my fear as I admire him and thrill to his powerful, proud beauty. Suddenly he disappears into the tornado, while out from its middle emerges another being. Only this one is immediately terrifying. It is a face, like an ancient, giant cave bear—and it is angry, or hungry. The instant I think I cannot let its brilliant eyes find me, they do. Our eyes lock together and his fierce gaze pierces my defenses. I know he is coming for me.

I yell for everyone to run to the hallway, and we huddle at the bottom of the stairway. Desperately I review my options. I can wait for it to strike in the next minute or somehow find a way to change the situation. I realize that I can change it, yet I have to be careful, for there are traps. I can't just will the tornado to skirt around us and pass the danger on to someone else in the neighborhood. Instead, I have to find a way to convince it to withdraw or rein in its fearsome and wondrous power—to express its beauty in a place where none will be harmed.

I awake with this thought. My heart is pounding, and I am considerably energized and relieved to be finished, for now, with this big dream.

⌗

We so often have confused ideas and emotions about the nature of power. We appreciate power; we love it and desire it; we bemoan lack of it. Yet today we more commonly understand and experience power in the manner of strength and control, and only in a limited way with divinity. We tend to mistrust power, and with good reason, since for too long, too many humans, animals, forests, rivers, and indeed most of Nature here on Earth has been subjugated to abuses of power. Few of us are raised and educated to see and appreciate the divine, the sacred, everywhere in the world around us, including ourselves.

We are drawn to power like moths to a flame, and for good reason, for who among us could survive in this physical world without some amount of personal power? At the same time we fear power because we know what fire can do to moths that don't respect its essence and power enough to maintain a proper distance. But do we have it right? What if those moths knew it was time to give up their forms and so in ecstasy fly "too close" to the compellingly attractive flame?

Love is another manifestation of power, and we sing of the power of love, and through acts of love we celebrate its matchless ability to heal, uplift, and sustain our lives. We also marvel at the power of sexuality—both its light and shadow sides—a power that directly aligns us with the mystery of creativity or, when misused, can unhinge us from our life force. Through our religious observances and spiritual practices we reach out to divine power by practices of prayer, meditation, song, dance, and the shamanic journey.

There are stories of miraculous feats of shamans in the olden days—tales of power. In contrast to the lot of modern shamans, those individuals were supported by a community worldview that gave them an extra advantage, so to speak—though they still had to mount the horse and ride it, they enjoyed a spirited perspective of reality that helped boost them up onto the horse's back. We can see that while the ancestral community had a definite need for spiritual help—power—to assist with living, with healing, and with remote viewing and communicating, our modern need for power has not lessened, and it may actually have increased. It may be that our spiritual muscles are weakened due to our reliance upon modern technology, but they aren't gone, and they will respond to the proper types and amounts of exercise.

Native American peoples such as the Salish traditionally sent their children out into Nature, into the weather and the terrain of the forests, mountains, and valleys, to seek out spiritual allies and to ask for gifts of power in order to live a good life. This quest for spiritual help and guidance can invoke significant physical and emotional suffering on the part of the supplicant and may be repeated as needed during the course of an individual's lifetime. For the Lakota people, "crying for a vision" is a sacred rite that involves a period of fasting from food, water, and human contact in a place of power such as a mountain or hilltop. Other peoples in North America seek their visions within the utter darkness of caves. Such a quest is a practice found worldwide in one variation or another, with the common ground of being a solitary experience in Nature, with some amount of suffering.

Well-known spiritual and religious leaders have turned to the practice of experiencing Nature in solitude as they sought spiritual power and its sustenance. The story of Buddha speaks of him spending years fasting and meditating in solitude in Nature, culminating with his experience of enlightenment after enduring mighty and horrible temptations of illusion while sitting under the bodhi tree. The prophet Muhammad underwent a time of solitude in a cave. John the Baptist, of the Old Testament, was a wilderness wanderer and mystic. And Jesus of Nazareth spent at least one period of fasting and solitude in the wild, it is said, for forty days and nights.

The Arctic explorer Knud Rasmussen sat with Igjugarjuk, a Caribou Inuit shaman of the Hudson Bay environs, and later wrote of how Igjugarjuk found shamanic power. Igjugarjuk's bid for power required that he endure privations that would easily have killed most people. "When I was to be a shaman," he said, "I chose suffering through the two things that are most dangerous to us humans, suffering through hunger and suffering through cold."

Igjugarjuk's story is one of sitting still in a small snow hut for almost thirty days without food and with only a few mouthfuls of water. All of this with no blanket and in the middle of winter. Igjugarjuk relates that he was instructed to think only one thing: that he wanted to be a shaman and was appealing to a powerful spirit to take pity on him. He said he "died" a little, and only after collapsing was he aided by the spirit he sought help from.

Afterward, in his role of shaman for the community, when asked to work with something difficult, Igjugarjuk returned alone to the wild places for three days and two nights or two days and three nights, to wander and listen for the information he needed to be of assistance. He advised that it is not enough to simply want to be a shaman. A "certain mysterious power" in the universe must be involved. To his people this power is *sila,* personified as the deity Sila, and is known as a "force that is at the same time the universe, the weather, and a mixture of common sense, intelligence, and wisdom. *It is a power that can be evoked and applied.*"[3]

Though these are stories of shamans of times past gaining their powers to shamanize, there is a valuable teaching in them for those of us who want to live our lives awake and aware of our true nature and of our true place and relationship with all inhabitants of this middle world. What emerges from these stories and many others is the necessity of physical, emotional, and spiritual connection with the natural world. We may not choose to give ourselves up to the wilderness in solitude and fasting, but we must find ways to establish and nurture an alive, vital relationship with Nature. Otherwise, in the eyes of many who hold ancestral wisdom, we will never be able to become fully human and thus will continue to foul that which gives us life.

Few of us are fortunate enough to have a close relationship with living examples of such individuals, those who could model a way of life with an inspirited orientation. However, it is not too late to regain a holistic, sacred perspective, since the spirits of weather and the powerful beauty of weather's expressions can bring us just what we need. Weather calls us to align ourselves with the direction and expression of natural power, and to do so possessing a clarity of purpose to restore and foster harmony and balance in our lives and world.

On what turned out to be a seminal visit to my spiritual weather teacher, I asked for advice on what to communicate to people about relating to weather. In answer, he showed me that any attempt to wield "power-over" with weather in our efforts to influence weather yields unpredictable, possibly undesirable, or even regrettable results.

I watch as my teacher reaches up to grab and squeeze a cloud in his fist; what emerges is dust mixed with some rain. He has me try this, and I feel a bit squeamish as I squeeze this being. Once again, out comes rain, changing to dust as it falls to the earth. I now see him ask and cajole another cloud— he even tickles it!—and immediately rain gushes out in what feels like a downpour of cloud laughter and delight. I understand that my teacher has honored the cloud and given pleasure to it, and it released rain because it wanted to—and because it had rain to give.

Next he speaks to me of reciprocity and lets me know that this is what it is all about. The cloud received, was moved, and wanted to give back. When it was squeezed, things worked differently. My teacher emphatically states:

"Power-over is not predictable in its results."

Thinking this journey lesson complete, I start to thank my teacher, but he abruptly steps forward, and now we are standing toe to toe. His bold eyes stare intently into mine, riveting my attention, and I hear, "Relationship is the key."

I ask, "Why have a relationship with weather?"

And he answers, "Because it promotes harmony for your lives and your world. This is what really matters."

He goes on to say that weather will play a prominent role in the cleansing to come—and in the healing. Once again, I hear drumbeats calling me back to our world, and as I turn to leave my teacher adds, "To start relating to weather, give thanks for all of it—for the rains, for the winds, for the fair weather. Love the weather and let it love you. Give to the spirits of weather—offer your love, your honoring, and your attention. Remember to give before asking—always asking, never demanding."

13

TO HONOR HURRICANE

A DIVINE TEMPEST

As humans we are not accustomed to
"thanking" the hurricane for our existence,
but perhaps we should.
None of us would be here today
without the hurricane's creative contributions
to the evolution of life itself.

DAVID SCHOEN, *DIVINE TEMPEST*

From the earth's earliest epochs, hurricanes have served as a primary force of creation, as well as destruction, for our world. They embody most elements of weather: rain, wind, fog, thunderstorms, tornadoes, water spouts, and, not the least, fair weather within their great eyes. They also contribute to additional weathers such as snowstorms and blizzards. No one really understands how hurricanes form, yet when they do, their massive spirals arouse our emotions and inspire us to action—if only the action of meticulous attention and tracking.

As far back as three to four billion years ago, hurricanes were a prominent creative force in the development of the earth and atmosphere.

Not only did they contribute to the atmosphere as we know it, but the unparalleled power and electricity of those primal storms exerted a profound energizing effect upon various inert elements and chemicals so that organic compounds eventually formed to create the earliest life-forms on our planet. We also have hurricanes to thank for the distribution—and redistribution—of life, as they stir up and churn the surface of the earth wherever they sweep through, absorbing and depositing nutrients, seeds, and other life-forms in their great wakes.[1]

In the fall of 2003, still hurricane season, thirty-five experienced shamanic practitioners gathered together in New York for a reunion. David and I were invited to present our two-day weather-dancing workshop. A week earlier a tropical storm, previously a hurricane, had brushed by us in Maine. At that time there were four named tropical storms—some with hurricane status—spinning around in the Atlantic, each in a different stage of its life span. I felt inspired to dedicate the final ceremony of the workshop to hurricanes, and so I painted a large, spiral symbol for our altar centerpiece, mixing the tropical rainwaters into the work.

On the afternoon of the ceremony our large group of weather dancers worked together to create a stunning altar. People had traveled in from different parts of the country, each with some weather-related object and jars of water collected from various sources such as rain, the Great Lakes, rivers, springs, and the oceans. Others brought pieces of wood from lightning-struck trees, as well as rocks, jewels, tools, shells, and pictures. We even had glow-in-the-dark lightning rods as well as a toy "thunder tube" sent by a friend in Canada. Working with focused intention, we created an altar of unique beauty that, once complete, seemed to come alive and infuse the ceremonial space with a pulsing life force that emanated outward in all directions.

We formally dedicated the evening ceremony to the spirit of hurricanes, and all its weathers, for the purpose of redressing any "wrongs" in our individual and collective past relationships with the weather. Once begun, the ceremony took on a life of its own—dynamic, beautiful, and healing. We each drummed, rattled, sang, and danced with the intention to shape-shift or transfigure[2] into an element of weather. For some this was an event of initiation and commitment to a path of weather shamanism, while for others it brought spontaneous personal healing (in shamanic traditions a healing for one can be a healing for all). For most it was an experience of pure joy, the ecstasy inherent in a shamanic working to honor and to heal.

A few days later, as David and I were driving home, we heard on the radio that Hurricane Lily, headed for the Gulf Coast and nearly class 5 in power, had suddenly and inexplicably ratcheted down to a class 1 by the time she came ashore. The announcer quoted a National Oceanic and Atmospheric Administration (NOAA) official as saying that he expected to see a rash of Ph.D. dissertations on that one, as no one could thus far explain what had happened; a class 5 hurricane that could diminish so quickly defied rational explanation. David and I looked at each other and grinned, knowing that there must have been other weather workings around Lily, and our circle's big-hearted ceremony was a part of it, too.

The hurricane season of 2004, when Florida was hit by no less than four of the mighty storms, was remarkable for its high numbers, including fifteen named storms, three thousand deaths, and about $42 billion in damages. The infamy of the 2005 hurricane season, however, surpasses that of 2004, which at the time had been considered a record season not likely to be repeated in the near future. During the 2005 season, however, Florida was hit again, and Hurricane Katrina's knockout blow to the eastern Gulf Coast led to the destructive flooding and cascade of crises for New Orleans and her thousands of resident humans and animals. Shortly after, Hurricane Rita also struck the Gulf Coast, this time threatening Houston. Though not as devastating as Katrina, Rita added to the travails of the region, necessitating an enormous evacuation effort on the part of the residents of Houston, including those who had just moved there as refugees from New Orleans. As late as mid-October in 2005, meteorologists used the last name from their list for the newest tropical storm, Wilma—a record in itself. By October 19, barely three days after her naming, Hurricane Wilma had been classified as a class 5 "monster," the strongest, most intense Atlantic storm ever recorded, with wind speeds clocked at 175 miles per hour and a record low pressure of 882 millibars. Paul, a resident of southern Florida, shares his perspective:

> The power of Nature. Man plans and God laughs. So here comes Hurricane Wilma. It is one of the worst hurricanes in history. It barreled into Miami at 6:00 a.m. Monday morning and lasted a mere four hours, yet its wrath was of biblical proportions. We have a home in Miami and Sanibel and an office in Miami. Sanibel Island was supposed to be the center. I prayed and meditated and put a white light around the properties. The storm changed course and came in fifty miles south of Sanibel. We were spared. It then crossed into Miami and the news showed my office building torn apart, but for a few unscathed offices. Mine was unscathed. Finally it came a little north and just missed our home. We lost electricity but nothing more.
>
> And so, lessons. Hard to say, but once again Nature in all its splendor and glory lives. It is alive. It is conscious. It is one with us. We are all part of Nature. We are not separate from it. We are not adversaries. Rather we are respectful companions living in harmony.

Before it ended at the late date of December 30, the 2005 hurricane season counted six additional tropical storms and hurricanes: Alpha, Beta, Gamma, Delta, Epsilon, and Zeta—all named from the Greek alphabet, and another new record. This season offered up the most named storms ever (twenty-eight), the most hurricanes (fourteen), and the most category 5 hurricanes (three). Meteorologists are beginning to say that we may be in for a cycle of ten to twenty years' duration of severe tropical tempests.

Michele, a gifted astrologer and shamanic practitioner from Florida, shared her insights and experiences with the hurricanes that struck her home area during the 2004 season. Following a warning from her helping spirits that there would be a crisis involving wind and water by the end of August, she "refreshed" her family's hurricane supplies and bought a new generator a week before Hurricane Frances became a threat. As an astrologer, Michele's perspective on the Florida hurricanes is this:

> To me, Florida is a Piscean state—watery and spiritual. Like Andrew in 1992, the hurricanes came and hit land in the least populated parts of the state, which is a blessing. Jupiter is the planetary force of expansion, and every twelve years he moves through Virgo. In August of 1992, Jupiter was in Virgo and Andrew hit the state. This time around Jupiter was in Virgo again, except this time opposing Uranus in Pisces. Uranus rules lightning; Uranus wakes us up. Uranus is the higher octave of Mercury, and Mercury rules weather. Mercury in Virgo was just coming out of retrograde and opposed Uranus.
>
> Each storm has its own distinct flavor [or] energy. Frances was clear and bright, the winds distinct. Blue sky was visible through the feeder bands. Looking up at the sky, it was beautiful to watch the clouds swirl by in distinct bands. While Frances did the most damage to our area, her presence felt the gentlest. Ivan was just blustery. We got whipping rain even though he was out in the Gulf. Jeanne was gray and murky. I couldn't see the sky; her energy was like gray, thick soup. The clouds hardly swirled, but her wind howled like a Halloween horror movie. She was a night storm. Frances came in the light of day.

As a shamanic practitioner, Michele met with the spirit of Hurricane Frances as the storm approached her area:

◩

I met my teacher and traveled to the storm. . . . I was in the eye and then in the bands. . . . I moved in both directions. I merged in love. I asked, "What is the hurricane's message?" I heard, "What looks like chaos is really control." Control and management of energy, of wind and water, of thoughts and emotions. The spirits of weather are managing energy in a systematic way. They said Florida is being dismembered so new energy can manifest. The earth is waiting for it because of the stagnation present. The air literally changes after a hurricane. Ions shift. The spirit of the hurricane was glad I approached her with love.

I was told that we as a people don't know how to dream or work in partnership with weather, the spirits of Nature. This is an imbalance within us and around us. The storm talked to me about fear and what negative intent does and creates. I was shown why the storms are so fierce this season. One reason is the planetary alignments (Mercury/Uranus opposition), which magnifies the other two reasons: 1) Our thoughts are energy, and because of the presidential elections there is residual hatred and distrust that continue to be projected at the state of Florida from around the country, especially during the week of the Republican convention. . . . And 2) TV stations, in a self-promoting fashion, are feeding fear and panic to boost their ratings. I saw this energy of fear like a band reaching out, magnetizing the storm's direction.

Then I was sent to the high-pressure zone to talk to the wind: "All is in divine order."

◩

Others in Michele's circle of shamanic practitioners also journeyed to Hurricane Frances. One participant wrote that she approached Frances with love and respect and found the hurricane's spirit to be a very willful being, with immense strength and focused intent. This person felt that Frances was about anger and transformation, especially regarding human materialism and denial of the damage we create through our lifestyles. The practitioner's suggestion to Frances that there were more peaceful ways to bring forth transformation met with only moderate success. She says,

> This hurricane was not really a hurricane. She was a universal wake-up call. . . . Frances represented the union of the divine feminine with the divine masculine . . . the being was more feminine and her action more masculine, like a hit-over-the-head—Get this!—kind of energy. However, I also understood that Frances was more than my ability or place to negotiate. So I transfigured into my divinity and became one with Frances.

Another shamanic practitioner, Priscilla, living in Naples, Florida, who was not in contact with Michele's circle, journeyed to Frances as she drew near and came back with a somewhat similar portrayal of the great storm:

I met Frances as a "pirate queen" and captain of a pirate ship on her way to Florida to plunder. I asked Frances to change course; she laughed gruffly and answered, "What is a pirate if a pirate doesn't plunder? And there is a lot to plunder in Florida!" Frances challenged me to a duel of swordplay.

We fought until exhausted. She laughed heartily again and said I was a good challenge, and would I drink and parlay with her for a while? Which we did. She was a hearty woman, full of life. Frances liked to show her strength, so we fought another sword battle. No winner, of course. Then she challenged me to a game of chess. Stalemate. She said Fort Lauderdale and Palm Beach would provide good plundering. Then she looked at me and said, laughing, that the plundering would be good in Naples, too . . . and gave me a wink!

Priscilla went ahead with her own hurricane preparations, yet again, for she had faced Hurricane Charley in 2004 and Hurricane Isabel in 2003. She shared this point of view:

The day following Hurricane Charley's visit to southwest Florida, I was dismayed to see a news program titled "The Wrath of Charley." A hurricane does not have a sense of right or wrong, good or evil, wrath or mercy. It is simply living its life the way it was meant to do. The dictionary states the meaning of wrath to be "intense anger, rage, fury" and "any action of vengeance." What revenge would a hurricane seek?

As a shamanic practitioner, I have journeyed to storms to learn about them and with a desire to "reason" with them. When you journey to an aspect of the weather such as a hurricane, you can get a new perspective on the world we are a part of. Whereas some people will rail against the weather, the shamanic practitioner realizes that nothing in Nature is good or evil—it just is. Nature exists because it yearns to be what it is.

Journeying to the weather can change your outlook on why things happen in life and can give new perspectives about our natural world. Journeying to the weather will help you realize that although you may not understand why an event has occurred, you know the event has occurred for a reason. Hurricane Charley did not rain wrath down upon us; no, Charley was a big, powerful force reminding us that Nature still rules our world.

Paul, who also encountered Hurricane Charley, had worked with us some years before in a workshop. He wrote to us:

Ever since our journey at Esalen I believe that we have an intimate connection with weather. There is just one source of energy, and it flows through all of us and through all of Nature. The key is to realize the connection, try to understand it, and respect the fact that we are one. During this storm season we were hit with four major hurricanes within a month. It was unprecedented. But then again the state of this planet is unprecedented.

As Charley bore down upon Paul's home on Sanibel Island, he envisioned his home in a bubble of protection and then worked to deflect the full force of the hurricane. In fact, Charley did veer away northward, and though Sanibel was hit, it did not suffer a direct one. Astonished, Paul saw in the aftermath that his house had been spared. Though he lost a number of large trees, all fell parallel to the house. His home was the only one on the street without damage. Paul used this same strategy with the other three hurricanes that hit the area around that time. He wrote:

So what are the lessons here? We were lucky. We were in a state of grace. We were one with the storms, respected them, and realized they meant no harm. They can have tragic results, but they don't intend good or bad. They just are. You learn to cope. You learn to respect energy. You learn that it is not personal. You learn that you are part of that energy and you too can do anything with the power you have.

One individual received through a shamanic journey the message that it was not only humans who would be affected by a hurricane but also all the insects, birds, and beasts of the land, sea, and air. However, it was only humans who dreaded it. Another teaching was that there is nothing anyone can do to prevent the natural order, and humans have the free will to take flight and return to rebuild or stay and suffer any destruction. Another person met the spirit "in charge of all hurricanes," who reveled in the changes he was about to make and, during the journey, showed people bulldozing landscape for their "creative" work. "If they can clean away the homes of others to do their work, why are they troubled if I do the same?" asked this spirit. The "spirit-in-charge-of-all-hurricanes" viewed his hurricanes as gifts to the world, capable of forming new combinations and relationships.

A few years earlier in the province of Nova Scotia, Marguerite and a group of novice shamanic journeyers under her tutelage worked to understand more about Hurricane Juan, who was churning his way to a predicted direct hit on the city of Halifax the next night. Marguerite wrote to us to describe the experience:

> One woman saw the hurricane as an agent of clearing; another experienced the calm eye of the hurricane; while yet another saw the hurricane as the tangible connection of earth and people and atmosphere. One shamanic student reported the hurricane as a cleansing gift to our land and people, which several years before had been the site of the crash of a large Swiss Air jetliner that had left people with a lot of trauma, expressed as depression and sorrow.

Marguerite went on to describe something of her own experience with Hurricane Juan. She portrayed her city and province in general as relatively unconcerned about the approaching storm: "We have many storms and are outdoor people; we Nova Scotians are used to weather and in love with the ocean." As she went to bed on the evening of Juan's imminent arrival, Marguerite asked her helping spirits to connect her to the storm.

> I left the windows in my room open. At about midnight I wakened to a sort of calm and then heard the wind. I went out to my deck and felt rather than saw the movement of the storm. I went back to my room and sat on my bed between the east- and south-facing windows and asked to be with the storm. I was inside a calm, yellow-gray space. I gradually understood it as the eye.
>
> My spirits had a lot to say, but I really could only just feel the movement of the storm. I asked to go to the outer edges, and there I could feel power, movement, and direction. I asked for the trees to bow in the wind, and I could hear the movement of our trees in the ravine behind my house. In the wind I could hear the water of our little brook and then the movement of water on our lake. The wind

increased and I asked for it to take care. The cleansing force seen earlier by the shamanic students was present.

Then it was just gone. I could hear the winds, but they were not present; the clouds could be seen and yet not seen. My trees and the area around us sighed as the lights went out and it was calm. I was calm and cleansed and felt entirely at one.

I slept and wakened to rain, torrential rain. I put out some basins to gather hurricane water and then called Nan. It was hard to tell her what had happened. It seemed magical and yet real, wondrous and yet ordinary, cleansing and yet lingering. The rains were extraordinary. Sheets of rain coming down, water bouncing off the pavement and later running in torrents down the street. There was no power. I read and talked to my spirits. Later in the day neighbors came to the door to be certain I was all right. I was fine! We had only four trees down on our two streets; my neighbors who listen to the drumming from my house regularly joked that my spirits protected the neighborhood.

This last statement is not bragging and certainly not a guarantee—rather it is an aftermath often reported by people who work with these storms, who attempt to engage with them in a responsible and respectful manner.

Marguerite and her neighbors found numerous ways to support each other in the days following that destructive storm. It took a week or more to restore electrical power to many neighborhoods, and the main road was closed for days due to many fallen trees. The provincial authorities asked people to stay home; thus few except emergency workers could leave for their jobs or to do errands. The piercing buzz of chainsaws permeated the atmosphere during daylight hours. People helped one another with cleanup chores and with sharing of resources such as candles, propane, and food. Numerous neighborhood barbecues and feasts were held, as defrosting freezers had to be emptied. By candlelight, neighbors stayed together in the evenings to sing or play bridge or board games. Because everyone had to stay home there was an uncommon amount of "free" time, with interesting results. Marguerite describes one day:

> I lay out on my lawn looking up at the sky, divining clouds. My neighbor came over to ask what I was doing. When I told him he asked if he could join me. In a short while there were eleven of us on the front lawn in turn saying: oh, there is a swan . . . deer . . . rabbit . . . bear; look at that wagon; and on and on. I think they all saw their power animals!

Marguerite acknowledges both sides of the visit from Hurricane Juan, who imposed and gifted lasting change on her and many others of her province:

> It is now two years later. There are lots of disaster stories. You can still see windfall from Juan. The city has changed and there are fewer trees. People have complained about the insurance companies. The emergency-measures people are at work improving our responsiveness. It would be easy to emphasize disaster.
>
> I think back to the journeys those shamanic students did and think of the knowledge and insight they carried. Juan did destroy and cleanse. As weather, it brought change. As spirit, Juan is with me. I live with the experience of a break in the business of modern life; the enjoyment of my students and neighbors; the night sky; the discovery of what is important in the basics of living. I go away a lot to be "in Nature," but during this time we had the experience of being present to one another in our very neighborhood, and being present to our houses, gardens, and land. Juan brought gifts; those gifts live in my heart and changed my perspective. The week that followed Juan was clear and warm and loving in weather and in relationships.

Many people in North America learned about the nature and role of hurricanes that season, both through first-hand experience and through shamanic journeying. Even though threatened with the real possibility of injury or property damage, those who could work with their predicaments and challenges from a shamanic worldview found opportunities for valuable lessons and personal growth. They were the ones who could step beyond their fears and find a place of acceptance and grace. They did not forget that we have the option of relating to that which could otherwise victimize us, and so they were able to claim their own stance of strength and endurance.

An e-mail message from Wendyne to her circle shows us how this can work:

I am in great awe of the power of intention as a result of my process of moving through the experience of Hurricane Frances. These last two weeks have been a time of death and rebirth for me and for our center, Solutions Center for Personal Growth, incorporated in 1991. When we lost the center during the storm due to water pouring into the building, many came to our rescue and assisted us in taking out our personal and professional possessions—files, computers, sound computers, instruments, art, books, et cetera—all our sacred stuff! Several of you offered us a place to rest, to store our stuff, to come in from the heat. I thank you all.

Suddenly everything has changed. I have not forgotten that all year I had been writing about creating a new space. I have not forgotten that every morning I meditated about the land and the things we want to build: the sound temple, the art building and gallery, the bodywork space, the theater, the bookstore, the cafeteria, the nature trails. I ask myself, "Did Hurricane Frances come for me?"

My study of the Universal Law says *yes*, it did, as it did for all of us. For some reason many were ready for a major shift—a little death and rebirth. The question now is: Are we willing to understand Mother Nature in this way? Are we willing to remember that all things are in order, that everything is part of our bigger process? I believe that the consciousness of our part of Florida brought Frances to us. It is up to each of us to know why we needed it and what we learned.

I myself have become so grateful for all I have. I have become much closer with all my extended family members and I learned that I love them all very much. I have learned that *intention* is a *force,* like gravity and other laws of physics. I have learned that it is time for me to slow down!

Two weeks later Wendyne's area was hit again, this time by Hurricane Jeanne.

After Frances passed through her area, Michele wrote this to her friends:

Well, the winds from Frances have died down and the cleanup has begun. Trees down, traffic lights out. Our house never lost power, but many homes throughout south Florida are without. I-95 is closed north of us because of the damage and south Florida can't get restocked with food supplies. Our grocery stores are out of bread, butter, eggs, and milk. Schools are closed again tomorrow. People seem to be shell-shocked from the whole experience. There is deep soul loss and trauma.

I know that our shamanic journeys made a difference, because Frances stalled and went slowly through the state after dropping her winds from 140 to 160 mph to 105 mph! A big thank you! This was more of a wind system than rain. It was awesome connecting with the wind energy.

Please keep Florida in your journeys to transmute the fear energy. Thanks for all your wishes, prayers, and journeys.

What all of these shamanic practitioners have shown us through their experiences, and similarly to our hurricane ceremony, is that a primary and effective way to work with the weather is to *honor* it. This refers to the kind of honoring that combines respect with love for the storm, or any other element of weather, as another living being, and that recognizes that, no matter how we may feel about its effects, it is a being with a purpose—a divine purpose, if you will. Honoring allows for the role that we each must play and creates a space for true collaboration.

It is never as simple as "if we do this, then that is what will happen." That's the catch. That is the challenge in all instances of relating to and working with weather. As shamanic practitioners, we may each have our own individual ways of addressing and working with the spirit of a storm and its potential to harm; yet if we infuse our relating with respect and with love, then we comport ourselves as real human beings.

14

WEATHER WORKING

A CLOSER LOOK

*Shall tomorrow's weather be fair or foul? Blow wind—
blow mostly from the south, for I go afishing. "Nay, good
friend," exclaims the golfer, "the day must be dry and
the wind in the west." The farmer moistens his finger
and points it toward the sky. "Rain, come, quickly, for
my crops," is his prayer. But the maiden's voice is full of
pleading: "Let the sun shine tomorrow that my heart may
be light on my wedding day."*

"THE WEATHER," BY CHARLES F. TALMAN

Once we began teaching our introductory workshop on weather shamanism, David and I noticed that people began showing up whose main focus was to learn how to influence the weather—to weather-work. Indeed, our own fascination for this potentially useful, though tricky, application of weather shamanism escalated as our basic understanding of weather's spiritual nature deepened, along with our maturing abilities to love and relate to the weather spirits themselves.

Through our research we had discovered a bewildering variety of attitudes and styles of weather working in the world. For our own clarification in relating to the weather, and so that we could more effectively help others in their understanding, I journeyed to my weather teacher in the upper world to find a useful and more inclusive way to look at what it means to "influence the weather."

My teacher gave me a look that asked "what took you so long?" He then offered me a basic model that embodies three discrete levels or categories, nested together in a series of concentric circles—much like the pictographs etched on stone in ancient cave dwellings or rock outcroppings in the wild. He cautioned me to avoid grasping this model too tightly; as with everything else in the universe, we're all connected behind many facades, and so our multilevel theory is useful only if we understand that the distinctions can overlap and meld into one another.

In the model of the concentric circles, the innermost circle is the heart, the central core to all the outer circles. This is the place of *weather dancing,* the harmony in relationship that permeates and enlivens all the other circles. At the outermost circle, the farthest removed from the heart place, is *weather modification,* more about power-over than relatedness. In between the innermost and outermost circles we have the place of *weather working,* consisting of practices that may lean either way: inward toward the heart-core of weather dancing or outward to the realm of power and control of weather modification.

Additionally, my weather teacher told me that weather modification is still a kind of relating to weather, an attempt to align with the weather, yet it is more like an eagle breaking in on an osprey's flight, a power-over kind of alignment. Sometimes the eagle may achieve the intended result, yet through reinforcing a relationship of enmity and competition. To shoot crystals into passing clouds of a storm front is an attempt to break in, to get them to release their rain or fish. Fish? I realized that my teacher was referring to a confrontation I witnessed during the week of the 9/11 attack. I was working in my front yard when a movement caught my attention, and I looked up just in time to see an osprey flying toward me with a fish in its talons. Just behind the osprey flew a bald eagle about to intercept. Right before my eyes, the eagle dove toward the osprey, who immediately dropped the fish, which the eagle adroitly caught in midair. Then the eagle flew off with the fish in its talons and the osprey in hot pursuit. They flew out of my sight, so I couldn't tell what happened in the end.

My teacher went on to explain that cloud seeding itself doesn't have to be strictly an act of power-over. "Seeding" implies an attempt to work with creative forces to engender rain. But it falls short in the realm of relationship. We cannot know the hearts of those who fly into the clouds for this purpose, but the language of the written and oral accounts of weather modification indicates it is primarily about scientific and technological know-how, and not about a sense of a collaborative relationship with the forces of weather and their spirits, of honoring and feeling grateful for the desired results. More often than not, weather modification is fueled by the attitudes of entitlement and hubris that our culture normally directs toward the natural world.

There are other approaches to influencing the weather that, similarly to weather modification, are also goal oriented. We think of these approaches as weather working, where the tenor of practitioners' attitudes regarding their relationship to the weather spirits can range from loving or matter-of-fact to fearful or angry. This leads to a variety of weather-working methods that include the harmonious and friendly as well as acts of intimidation from a desire for power-over. We could say that weather modification overlaps here—especially with regard to the desire for power over the weather. Yet weather working differs significantly from weather modification in that its approaches are always spiritually oriented. In its highest sense, weather working is performed on behalf of something—a place, a community, a situation—for which real healing is needed, and not based on what we may personally desire.

Finally, my teacher described how weather dancing is about harmony, respect, and love in relationship with the spirits and forces of weather. It is about how we can live and dance together at the highest spiritual level. The possibilities that weather workings strive for lie here, and yet the weather dancer may never actively seek a particular kind of weather. So it is not goal oriented in that sense. Rather, from this place we find the dance that engenders a spiritual alignment of allowing and honoring the uniqueness and sacredness of the other, of even occasionally becoming the other. Positioned at the core of the entire model, the essence of weather dancing is capable of radiating outward and through the other layers, infusing them with its harmony—just like our great and brilliant sun radiates its shine throughout our solar system.

Around the world, there are significant stylistic differences in weather-working practices, as might be expected when differing worldviews and approaches to life are considered. Despite their differences, all of these cultures acknowledge that the forces of weather are spiritually alive and sentient. Among peoples with this knowledge, ways of weather working are determined by their culture and locality: the particular needs of a community within the context of the overall qualities and features of the home terrain that sustains them. We live in a world of vastly different bioregions and climates, and local indigenous peoples have developed unique cultural responses suitable for their particular environments.

Some peoples relate to the weather out of fear and even loathing. The Guajiro of South America, for example, work with methods of threat and intimidation to achieve the desired result; for example, they shoot arrows at promising clouds to pierce them and force the release of rain for their parched lands. Other tribes in wet regions may fire shotguns or shoot or brandish arrows at unwanted storms to dispel or frighten them away. These actions may be accompanied by incantations and angry gestures of defiance or vengefulness toward the storm spirit that could destroy their homes, gardens, and fruit trees or even bring sicknesses to the people. The Jivaro treat oncoming storms as if they were fighting their enemies. The shaman and others may jump up and down, shaking their lances, using the same shouted expressions that they would use to taunt and daunt their human enemies. In a similarly warlike fashion, the Cayapo shoot arrows into clouds, shake their fists, strike the ground with their war clubs, and, more recently, fire guns "to have revenge on thunder."[1]

Deliberate attempts to evoke the pity of weather spirits are also employed. Among the North American Koyukon, to help avert a storm, sometimes a female dog is pinched until she yelps. Other accounts maintain that on occasion of dire need, some of the Aymara and Quechua peoples of South America may beat their children or tie up large numbers of black sheep in a city plaza and starve them in hopes that suffering will bring rain—the tears of spirits of weather.[2]

According to the records of the Mayan codices, the ancient Mayans honored Chac, a primary deity of creation and a patron of agriculture who was especially associated with lightning, storms, and rain. A late summer ritual for invoking rain utilized four boys, one tied to each of the four corners of the altar. They had to croak like frogs to help summon rain, as frog callings often announce imminent rains. We can imagine that this ritual could have been physically demanding and stressful to those boys, while an honor to serve their people.[3]

Such practices may sound unappealing, and it is tempting to judge them as dysfunctional and hurtful. However, we are looking at this picture through our culturally biased eyes, and not through the eyes and experience of people whose lives are immediately threatened by too much or lack of rain and storms. It can be said that these South American peoples are more warlike than others, hence their seemingly adversarial approaches to weather working. Yet in our own culture, where many decry the high level of violence and militarism, we too have bombed clouds.

More frequently we find evidence of harmonious weather workings. In general, these methods employ the ritual or ceremonial use of song and chant, dance, prayer, food or drink or herbal offerings such as tobacco, and more. Weather workings can be as simple as when many of us as children chanted (and maybe danced as we sang) the ditty "Rain, rain go away! Come again another day!" At the other end of the spectrum, we have the example of the Hopi people of the Southwest, who are well known for their successful rainmaking not only by virtue of their beautiful and elaborate ceremonies but also because these ceremonies come from a matrix of a people traditionally dedicated to living spiritually oriented and intentionally nonmaterialistic lives. As such they are able to continue to live and "dry-farm" corn in a notably arid region as they have done for hundreds of years.

Perhaps closer to home is the story of young Taylor Newton, age nine, of Connecticut, who in September 1995 performed a weather working of his own. Distressed over the severe, summer-long drought and consequent suffering of the gardens, trees, animals, and people of his hometown, one evening he donned his moccasins, painted his face and chest, took his mother's drum, and proceeded alone to the backyard, where he danced and drummed in an effort to bring much-needed rain. According to Taylor, "Once I was done, the wind started blowing and trees were rustling. I thought, 'Wow, this is neat.' I never got spooked." Taylor performed his weather working from the heart. When asked why he chose to do it, he replied that he danced for rain because "I wanted to help the people of the town." It rained several times during the remainder of that week.[4]

In another story, our friend Peggy found a different way to work harmoniously with the weather spirits on behalf of her local environs. She lives in the Big Sur region of California, which had endured a drought of nearly seven years' duration. Finally Peggy, who has lived on her small farm for twenty-five years, could no longer tolerate what she felt were unacceptable levels of suffering on the part of the plants and animals. From a profound sense of relatedness and compassionate empathy, Peggy spontaneously began to weather-work on behalf of the world around her. She began going outside at night just to lie on the ground, asking for rain. While she dearly wanted it to rain, Peggy instinctively knew she could not demand it. Instead, she focused on becoming receptive to the idea of rain, and lying there in close contact with the earth along the length and breadth of her body, she became more united with the land. From that place of centeredness, Peggy asked for and made ready to receive rain. One night she picked up a rainstick and began walking around her home ground and soon started dancing, moving in spirals and circles. This time she somehow knew that movement, rather than stillness, was called for. It rained late that night, and Peggy remembers that when she awoke to the sound of the falling raindrops she stayed in bed, just listening and drinking in the smells, attempting to simply receive the rain into her being, as thirsty as a plant rooted in the earth.

During an earlier drought, Peggy remembers feeling agonized over the suffering she felt around her. She became desperate for relief, and out of her desperation, she demanded the appearance of rain, and when that didn't work, she begged for the rains to come. None of this changed anything. Through her enormous angst, Peggy had been concentrating on the lack of rain, thus inadvertently energizing that state of being in the world. So when the next drought occurred she reacted differently, and saw different results. This time Peggy concentrated on achieving a state of receptivity—and made ready to receive the rain. Peggy believes that a key ingredient to her weather-working "recipe" is her attitude of "just doing my part" for the land in a way that allows for rain: no desperation, no demands. She says, "The spirits are here—all we have to do is acknowledge them." Relatedness, compassion, empathy, receptivity, desire . . . perhaps this is all it takes to work with the weather in a healing way.

Weather working can be as simple as a heartfelt request or prayer. From my journal during a summer of drought at home:

We have received no rain since the shower on April 28 or so. We continue to have lots of sun and very warm weather. Things are getting extremely dry. Woods are crackling dry and hot. The weather report yesterday spoke of a big storm, a low, stuck offshore and drenching Boston, but with no forecast at all for any of it to come farther north to us. Last evening I went outside calling to the storm spirits, the rain and cloud spirits, as well as all other weather spirits, asking on behalf of the land, to please come and give a little rain—if there was any to give, and if it served the highest good. Then I offered the spirits some tobacco. David also asked. Went to bed hopeful, but resigned to whatever.

The following morning I awoke to a patter of rain. I gave thanks, and then asked if the clouds had any more to give, though the sky looked like it would clear. So I gave it up. A little while later I glanced out our kitchen window and saw the sky looking promising again. So I went out and sprinkled tobacco once more, and right then the clouds also sprinkled! Soon after I went back inside, more rain began to fall. I hurried out to stand in the blessing of it as it came in fits and starts and then became a regular and gentle rainfall.

During this episode I learned that when you court rain, if it comes, don't rush indoors! Let it wet you, touch you—and love it.

How much of successful weather working is simply being in the right place at the right time? This sort of ambiguity can be our friend, helping us stay out of our own way so that we can focus on what's really important: a harmonious balance for our realms. I learned during another drought-filled summer that our presence, focus, and genuine appreciation—along with appropriate timing—can sometimes tip the scales.

David and I were working in a place we have visited and cared for over a span of several years. It was as drought-stricken as any I had seen. The normally lush grounds were bone dry and brown at a time when the predominant colors should have been shades of green. Shrubs were dropping their leaves, and only a few flowers bloomed here and there. The towering oaks and sycamores were doing a little better, with their enormous spread of roots and longer life spans, yet their leaves had a pinched look as well. It was another regional drought for the Northeast—and a time for humans to learn more about the preciousness of water.

Our group wanted to do something to end the drought, yet the journey teachings clearly indicated that the drought was a necessary experience for reasons that we didn't have to understand. We could, however, ask for some short-term relief. A couple of days later, during lunch hour, I felt I had to go outside, and immediately I noticed the beginnings of a promising cloud on the horizon. The day was hot and sunny, and the sky mostly clear except for this now very puffy cloud that continued to rise as it expanded. As I watched for ten to fifteen minutes, the cloud took on shades of gray and then blue-gray so that now it had depth, texture—and the possibility of even rain? I took a quick look around to make sure I was still alone, and then I started to sing a song of appreciation and acknowledgment of rain to come. I sang it over and over, spontaneously adding a little dance with my hands to the song—just like a child would, and like a child, I was having fun. There was something alive and joyful in this act of singing and dancing to a growing cloud, to the birthing of what turned out to be a brief but intense thundershower!

So what happened here? Conditions were promising. I showed up with my attention. I had a spontaneous feeling of a window of opportunity for something to happen. Through the portal of my genuine appreciation for the beauty of the cloud, I experienced an uncommon sense of connection with something greater than me. I felt playful yet sincere in my desire for some much-needed rain on behalf of that place I cared for. I offered the gift of a little song and dance. Was this a weather working or an expression of weather dancing with fortuitous timing? Who knows? The rain fell and we were blessed.

There are also those instances in which the weather spirits seemingly respond to the very presence of certain dedicated, evolved individuals—especially when they are leading large, spiritually oriented gatherings or ceremonies. David and I think of it as a way of weather working that is akin to grace. It appears to be a kind of sympathetic response from the spirits of weather to our human activities, and, as with any deliberate weather workings, the principle of ambiguity walks hand-in-hand with the miracle. This dynamic can be observed in relation to visits by the compassionate monk Thich Nhat Hanh. According to author and writing coach Kevin, formerly an Omega Institute staff member:

> On at least a couple of occasions, we had been in a long dry spell at Omega, and the day Thich Nhat Hanh arrived for one of his silent meditation retreats, it would rain. It would then continue raining for much of the retreat. Among staff members, the scheduling of his retreats became a form of weather forecasting—we knew we could count on rain during that period. The rains also lent a calming, hushed spirit to the retreats. The photo Omega most often uses to promote Thich Nhat Hanh's retreat shows him leading a walking meditation holding an umbrella!

Another example is the Indian Holy Mother Mata Amritanandamayi Devi, otherwise known as Ammachi. Those who accompany her on world tours speak of predictable occurrences of rain during Ammachi's retreats and purifying ceremonies, as well as accounts of Ammachi working intentionally for rain. In 1996 the northern New Mexico region suffered another summer of severe drought. According to Bente, volunteer helper for Ammachi in the United States, upon arrival for her tour retreat in Santa Fe, Ammachi was asked to bring relief to the parched land. Rain fell almost immediately, so much so that the tour workers asked her to temporarily stop it for practical reasons. Ammachi refused, explaining that she had made a sankalpa, a divine resolve, and would not take it back or postpone it for matters of convenience. In years past, on nights of the Devi Bhava ceremonies, when Ammachi would shower blessings upon all present—from hundreds to thousands of people—these celebrations were often visited by thunderstorms. Eventually, as the crowds outgrew the indoor shelters, the storms became less frequent.

There are numerous examples of what David and I think of as

sympathetic weather responses. Many practitioners of core shamanism who have participated in intensive healing circles have observed that when significant shamanic healing work occurs, especially in a group or circle of people, it rains. The promise of rain may be present throughout the weekend of a workshop, but the rain will often fall just when the healing work begins or is in progress. This is an affirmation of the inherent harmony of the work, and as another expression of the principle of reciprocity.

In ancient times the philosopher-historian Plutarch noted the phenomenon of heavy rainfall after major battles. More recently, the infamous 9/11 attacks on the New York City World Trade Center and the Pentagon in Washington D.C., were carried out on a brilliantly sunny day. A day or so later, a hard and blustery rain fell in both places. A fellow shamanic practitioner and resident of Manhattan e-mailed us regarding her concerns about the seeming violence of the weather. When we thought about it, however, to us it seemed like a blessing, and another instance of weather's sympathetic response. While the rain did impede rescue efforts, it also helped cleanse the immediate atmosphere of a heavy load of nasty airborne particulates from the still-burning fires.

Dr. Hank Wesselman—author, teacher, paleoanthropologist, and shaman—wrote for us his story of an instance where he attempted to influence the weather:

LONO THE RAINMAKER

In August of 2001, my wife, Jill Kuykendall, and I were leading a five-day shamanism workshop for a group of forty people on the island of Hawai'i. At the core lay an in-depth exploration of health, illness, and healing in the indigenous perspective, and since the event was taking place in the center of the Pacific, the small altar in the center of our circle included a bowl of light as well as a cluster of images symbolizing the great Polynesian spirits: Kane the creator,

Kanaloa the lord of the deep ocean, Ku the powerful, and Lono the fruitful. A small wooden bowl of sacred 'awa rested before them, offering our reverence and our gratitude.

Lono was especially important for our week's work. Lono is associated with healing and the practice of medicine, much like Apollo of the classical Greeks, and is connected to highly organized mental domains such as science and navigation. He is responsible for the processes of growth and increase, making him the patron of agriculture. Lono's also the weatherman, the wind keeper, and the bringer of rain.

This last arena of his expertise came very much to the forefront halfway through the week, when Jill and I emerged from sleep one morning to see the rain coming down in buckets outside. It was one of those drenching tropical storms that had moved in off the ocean during the night, and the living air was simply saturated with water. "Lono," I thought. "This is Lono's doing."

Now on the one hand, this storm was a blessing because the island had been experiencing drought. On the other, this was the day on which Jill and I had planned to take the entire group on an afternoon field excursion around the island to pay a visit to the volcano spirit Pele at her traditional home in the caldera of Kilauea. It's a spectacular place to visit on sunny days, located as it is on the island's southeast shoulder at 4,000 feet of altitude in Volcano National Park. But when the rain moves in up there, the elements are in charge and visibility can be reduced to zero.

I wrapped a sarong around my waist and walked out through the sliding glass doors onto the narrow lanai beyond our bedroom. The rain was really coming down, and I wondered briefly whether to cancel the trip. Then a thought appeared. As a practitioner of shamanism who had lived for many years in the islands, I seemed to have developed some rapport with Lono. As I stared at the rain and wondered if I could get him to turn it off, I happened to look through the bedroom window just as Jill sat up in bed and stretched. An idea emerged. I turned my hands up to the soggy sky and made my prayer.

"Hey Lono . . . Lononui'akea . . . have I got a deal for you."

I used his full name, out of respect, then made my case. I began by pointing out the undeniable presence of this monster storm sitting on the island. I explained that I valued its presence and life-sustaining function, then mentioned in passing our intention to bring a group of visitors to Pele that afternoon on the mountain. I observed that this was a very good thing, reflecting a new level of involvement with the natural world for dissociated Westerners. I finished by requesting a three-hour window of time in which the sky would be clear, with the sun sparkling over Kilauea while we paid our respects. Then I brought in the clincher—something to ensure that there would be no rain, not a drop, during those three hours.

"Lono," I concluded, "if you assist us with this, I will allow you to merge with me later and then I will make love with Jill." Remembering all those stories about Apollo's love affairs in the Greek myths, I figured it was worth a try. As Jill joined me on the lanai, wrapped in her own sarong, I knew with absolute certainty that no god could resist her. Now I had to clear it with her.

Jill watched me with amusement as I recounted the nature of the deal I had just made with the god Lono for three hours of clear skies at the volcano. She raised her eyes to the sky, and after a long, thoughtful pause, she simply said, "We'll see . . ." The downpour continued unabated during the morning session of the workshop. Those in charge of logistics approached me, uncertain, citing the long drive and the storm's undeniable presence on the mountain. I responded hopefully: "Don't worry, I feel that the weather will be clear on the mountain this afternoon." They were not reassured.

We left the retreat center at noon anyway, eating our lunches in the vehicles to save time, and as the drivers had predicted, it rained all the way to Hilo. The storm thickened ominously as we headed up the mountain, building in intensity as we gained in altitude. Then, on the final approach to the park, the windy, rainswept darkness appeared to brighten, miraculously. We drove through this brightness and were almost blinded by the brilliant sunlight on the other side. It was as though we had passed through a curtain in the mist. We could even see the summit of Mauna Loa rising more than 13,000 feet into the blue immensity of the sky above the vibrant green of the dripping fern trees.

We spent the afternoon touring the extraordinary geological site under clear skies. We made our offerings to the volcano spirit at the traditional place, accompanied by a Hawaiian elder who graced us with his presence and his wisdom. At one point, he turned to me and commented on the amazing shift in the weather in the early afternoon. The storm had apparently enveloped the entire island, with the exception of where we were right now. I glanced around, and seeing that we were alone, I revealed the nature of my agreement with Lono to him. He watched me evenly, then grinned. "You must have an inside track," he said with a laugh. Then he glanced at Jill, who was talking animatedly with some of the women, and shook his head with the wonder of it.

Sure enough, when we bid farewell to the elder and got back in our cars at the afternoon's end, that curtain of rain was waiting for us just beyond the park boundary. We drove through it into the windy darkness of the storm once more and headed down the mountain with the windshield wipers working double time. When we turned north from Hilo, something interesting occurred.

While driving along the coast road, one of the women suddenly pointed out to sea, and there, hovering above the ocean several hundred yards from the shore, was a rainbow unlike any I had ever seen before. It was as if a straight, vertical shaft of prismatic light was standing on its end upon the water, backed up by gray storm clouds. We all exclaimed in wonder, and as the conversation turned toward the unusual extremes of weather we had experienced that day, Jill then shared the story of my deal with Lono. All the participants laughed with the delight of it. I smiled and shrugged as I watched the rainbow keeping pace with us. There was no doubt in my mind that the rainmaker was out there, following our car back to the retreat center.

Dinner was awaiting us upon return, and very shortly, the story of my agreement with Lono was known to the entire group. Accordingly, when Jill and I headed for bed at evening's end, we were accompanied by many supportive and mirth-filled comments. Yet when the big moment came, we admitted to each other that we were very tired from the long day and needed to sleep. "Tomorrow, Lono," I thought as I began to drift. "Wait for tomorrow . . ." We dropped into sleep almost immediately, holding hands.

In the darkness just before the dawn, Jill turned and snuggled into my embrace with a breathy caress. I awoke, and the magic that touch creates was manifested in the love we felt for each other at its most magnificent levels of intensity. But there was also something else—something immediate, yet elusive. In retrospect, I wondered, had I felt a presence move into my field at the beginning of our dance, or did I imagine it? There was no way of knowing, as I was distracted. But when our dance was done and Jill and I held each other closely, savoring our union in passion's aftermath, I felt something or someone depart. It was subtle, yet quite clear. It was also at that moment that I happened to turn and glance out through the window. My breath caught in surprise.

There, just beyond the lanai, stood two vertical rainbows. They were side by side, and the red range of their visible spectra seemed particularly intense. I got out of bed and went out onto the deck. It is difficult to describe what I was feeling in those moments. With a whisper of sound, Jill moved into the circle of my arm and embraced me as I raised my free hand and offered my gratitude with magnitude.

"Lono the Rainmaker" is a personal anecdote that offers us valuable teachings for a fundamental understanding of weather working and its underpinnings. In this account Hank clearly demonstrates that truly harmonious weather working relies on an established relationship with a compassionate spirit: one who is somehow related to weather, and one to whom he can turn to for a favor. Furthermore, Hank did not ask from a place of personal whim or gain. His request was made on behalf of a group of people engaged in spiritual work who wished to honor a sacred site. Lastly, he offered a gift to this spirit—something that meant a lot to him! Above all, Hank weather-worked from a worldview of relatedness and respect—the essence of weather dancing.

PART FOUR

THE PRACTICE
OF WEATHER
DANCING

15

WEATHER DANCING

METAPHOR FOR A SPIRITUAL PRACTICE

*There is a way for working with spirits that is particularly
good for working with weather spirits. You invite them
to dance and you let them lead. Soon they dance you.
You present yourself as bait and when they swallow you,
you in part swallow them. You become their hand and
sometimes you are allowed an arm.*

STEVE SNAIR, DESCRIBING A
SHAMANIC JOURNEY, JULY 4, 2003

Within my spiritual teacher's model of concentric circles
representing the basic levels of our relationships with
weather—including influencing the weather—we see that weather
dancing occupies the innermost circle as the heart, the core of it all.
Furthermore, the kind of relatedness that weather dancing stands for is
capable of permeating all other levels of relationship, depending upon
how openhearted we can be. David and I could see the potential of
power and beauty in this, and as we deepened in our understanding,
we realized that weather dancing embodies far more than we had imag-

ined. We discovered that it is no less than a guiding metaphor for a transformative spiritual practice.

As such, weather dancing requires of us an ability to trust, a willingness to risk, and the dedication of our life and spiritual work toward a greater overall presence and experience of harmony in the world. On this path we seek wisdom and learn how to hear and speak the truth of our hearts. We align ourselves with the helping spirits and with the spiritual forces of weather and, in so doing, work with compassion and humility. Along the way we learn to honor what we are given in the process, be it that which we ask for, that which we yearn for—or something else.

Among our most important tools is the ability to focus our attentions and effectively stalk that which we seek, concurrent with a nearly relentless commitment to practice. Very early on we will encounter the need for an understanding of and right relationship with power. Throughout it all, we'll know we have gone astray somewhere if we lose touch with an expanding sense of gratitude—and joy.

To successfully negotiate our path of spiritual practice and open ourselves to its gifts of aliveness, beauty, and even moments of pure ecstasy, we must dedicate ourselves to a relationship of partnering, an intentional and mutual collaboration with the helping spirits of all the worlds:

I ask my weather teacher to please show me more about the nature of power in working with weather, and he replies, "Power is in the relationship." He reaches toward me and leads me into a graceful, intricate dance. I understand that he is reminding me to "follow the lead of the helping spirits" in this. We dance with intensity and passion. I respond to the compelling focus of presence in the moment as our emotions and movements intertwine. It is powerful! I revel in the excitement of my own energy as I raise and direct it in this mutual act of relating. Whirling with my feelings, I hear him say, "The power is the dance of relationship, and the ecstatic moments are there in the dance, in the alignment of our beings with the beings and energies of the weather."

The practice of weather dancing requires the kind of internal centeredness that begets balance that begets harmony. As a spiritual path it asks of us our willingness to undergo personal growth, the kind that never stops and is never completed. This willingness is a prerequisite that does not fade away as we proceed along our path. As we persevere we'll find that our growth is fostered in ways unique to each of us. (It either teases or wrings it out of us depending upon our nature.)

The practice of weather dancing also insists that we cultivate a genuine attitude of humility, or we could find the forces of weather ignoring or humiliating us—or worse—for excessive self-aggrandizement. At the same time it requires a healthy ego. We need an ego that is sufficiently strong so that we have the necessary self-confidence to willingly risk, and especially to risk our familiar sense of the rational. Our comfort levels—physical, mental, emotional, and spiritual—can and will be challenged. When we open ourselves to new opportunities for learning and personal growth, our egos will want to rebel from the possibility of failure as we encounter challenges and face the need to risk, again and again. The "demons" of self-doubt and lack of trust in the universe, in the compassionate spirits and sacred relatedness of all that is, lie in ambush at every twist and turn of our dance with weather.

Sandra Ingerman speaks forthrightly to her students about the "razor's edge" of the shamanic path they are attempting to walk. She cautions them to continually ask themselves where they are on their path. Have they fallen off the edge into realms of inflated egos? Or the opposite side, with too much self-effacement? Either is capable of leading us astray, to the point where we are lost in a maze of delusion and we can cause harm to ourselves and others.

An ego in balance allows us a clear sense of our own unique essence and personal boundaries. This helps us live with a real measure of ambiguity as we come to realize our general state of ignorance. It helps us persist, even as we learn to accept that we might never achieve what we may intensely desire—a satisfyingly rational understanding of the underlying, great mystery.

Our own successes and failures in trying to find and maintain "right attitude" have shown David and me just how tricky this is. Having a spirit element of weather choose to work with us can be an unexpectedly intoxicating experience. As when we ask a big favor of a friend, it is a genuine relief to feel noticed and worthy of an agreeable response, a sure indication that the relationship is in alignment with a mutual purpose. However, the jolt of elation and wonderment that accompanies a genuine interaction can instantly create within us an intense desire for more and more. Without a strong sense of clarity coupled with a balanced ego, before we know it we'll find that we have subverted a relationship intended to bring healing into something that can weaken us or damage others, as would a serious addiction. We'll also have strained our friendship, perhaps to the point of offensiveness.

To know that we don't know much is an excellent place to begin. This kind of attitude will help us stay clear of places of ego imbalance, especially if and when the spirits and forces of weather start responding to our efforts. From this perspective we are better able to perceive the need for weather working—to know when and where it is necessary to work, and if the need is genuine. There is no room for arrogance in our relationships with any of the compassionate spirits; it does not sit well with them and clouds the clarity of our vision.

Myron Eshowsky, well loved by his community as a shaman and teacher, shares the story of how he once lost his power to work with the weather spirits for many years. After relocating to Madison, Wisconsin, Myron repeatedly tried, without success, to revisit Indianapolis, where he grew up. In one memorable effort, he left Madison in late April, with temperatures in the mid-sixties. By the time he got to the countryside of northern Indiana, Myron relates what he encountered:

the most awful snowstorm you could imagine. It was coming down so hard you couldn't see anything. And the traffic stopped before me and behind me on both lanes. The snow was piling up and was up to my car window. I was running the car for heat as I had not taken much cool-weather clothing, and I had the thought that I would be buried in my car without gas.

Myron relates how he went to work calling on the spirit of the sun to break through the clouds and help melt the snow and sang a weather song he remembered from childhood. After a while he opened his eyes and saw the welcome sight of sunshine, and the traffic slowly beginning to move. He was directed by state troopers to either turn around and go home or prepare to spend the night in an emergency shelter, as the interstate highway would not be cleared until the next day. He chose to go home.

Back in Madison, Myron got in touch with a few friends to relate his experience of yet another bizarre failure to reach Indianapolis, and he heard himself say,

"You wouldn't believe what happened—the snow was awful and I was going to be buried alive in the snow, and I prayed and 'I made the storm stop.'" Well, the minute I said that I knew I had gotten carried away with myself, and the weather spirits laughed and said, "Oh yeah?" I had to do ritual for many years to humble myself in this domain.

Myron must have done his work of making amends well, because after this incident we both attended a Foundation for Shamanic Studies conference in California and decided to go to San Francisco for a showing of the highly regarded Sami movie *The Pathfinder*. It was early evening when we emerged from the theater and began to walk across a large, open area to reach the car. No longer was it the warm, sunny, late afternoon weather we had experienced earlier. In fact, the resident offshore fog was rapidly moving in, propelled by a stiff wind. Dressed only for a hot summer day, we were suddenly shivering from the penetrating chill of wind and damp. The "trek" to the car had a stressful edge to it, and we linked arms for a united front as we lengthened our stride. Yet, halfway there, I noticed something—the wind had lost its bite. In fact, I couldn't even feel the wind. I scanned around me and observed bits of trash, as well as a flag, the skirt of a woman nearby, and the small branches of a tree, all clearly indicating by their skipping and flapping that there was indeed a wind. So why couldn't I feel it? Why was I able now to relax on this little walk to the car? I looked at Myron and noted that he wouldn't meet my gaze, and that all he seemed to do was focus on the destination of the parked car.

It wasn't until we got to the car and separated, as Myron unlocked the doors, that once again I felt the wind whipping through my hair and clothing. That's when I realized for certain what he had been up to. We never talked about that working, and though at the time I wasn't conscious of my future path, I knew there was an important teaching for me here, one that I would not forget.

To learn more about the issue of ego and power in relationship to the weather I journeyed to my weather teacher to ask how weather working power is gained and lost. My teacher replied,

> It's not that we possess a power as in "power-over" with the spirits of weather. They, the weather spirits, see us, as humans, as powerless in their realm. We cannot blow as hard as the wind, nor sound as loud as thunder, nor bury the landscape as only a blizzard can—but we can align ourselves with them. Those who weather-work must align themselves with the spirits' powers.

Since we don't have power over the weather spirits, then there is no power to lose. However, what I can lose is good standing in my relationship with them. My teacher told me that I must learn to get their attention and call out to them in a language they can hear. How would I know this language?

"Ask them," he laughs.

In order to more fully realize the promise of connection and relationship that the practice of weather dancing holds, we need to cultivate a certain quality of attention. When we seek greater understanding of the unseen world all around us, we each pick up unique perceptions along the way. No one of us gets the whole picture. As we tune in, what sense can we make of our perceptions, of all that we are able to see, feel, hear, smell, taste, and intuit? What particular story is life and the world showing us? It takes intention, focus, and practice—lots of practice—to broaden our abilities to "see" and understand.

Our state of centeredness and well-being has much to do with the nature of our individual lens of perception. Do we have a personal radar that generally picks up signals of world troubles, conflict, sickness, discord, depression, or disaster? Or does our radar screen resolutely dwell only on signals of joy, beauty, lightheartedness, health, and happiness, thus effectively filtering out all else? This presents a duality of extremes, an apparent lack of balance. Yet what if we could learn to stand in the power of our center, unflinchingly, and take in both sides of the nature and doings of our world? From this stance of courageous compassion we are far more able to bless the hurricane and effectively offer help where it is truly needed. When we can intentionally include all elements as parts of the whole, we may find the real world, something akin to Zorba the Greek's passionate praise for his rich life, "the full catastrophe."

A worthwhile endeavor would be to explore how we can broaden our radar and magnify our abilities to tune in to the greater, overall reality. At any given time of day, the sea, for example, can present a different face of colors, shapes of waves, aromas, and sounds. We cannot gaze upon her visage once or twice and accurately describe the totality of her mood everywhere, or even for the day. Likewise for the "ocean" of our atmosphere, with its unending variety of expressions of weather.

A conviction of seeing or answering to only one particular side or aspect of a thing is to deny a balance of awareness of self and world. In other words, a practice of mindful attention to how we perceive, and knowing that we usually do so selectively, will bring us to a greater place of clarity so that we can then broaden our scope of vision, leaving room for more parts of the whole to successfully find us. The shaman's perceptive abilities need be as inclusive as possible, with a kind of awareness that comes from a desire and intention to regard, holistically, as much of the nature and mystery of reality found in all the world as possible. It's an open-ended stance of compassionate strength and balance that requires a courageous willingness to dwell in ambiguity, even as clarity is passionately sought.

From Heracleitus, one of the earliest Greek philosophers, we are left with this surviving fragment of wisdom: "From the strain of binding opposites comes harmony." The venerable Taoist yin/yang symbol illustrates this teaching. It is usually portrayed as a circle; within the container of the circle exist the sacred opposites of dark and light, female and male, internal and external, opposing one another, each holding an essence of the other, and eternally revolving in a dance of duality within the One. It is thought that the Celts saw the whole of reality as a magnificent knot of interwoven strands. Though theirs is not exactly a teaching of duality, the Celts understood the world as something more like "neither this nor that, neither here nor there"—yet all part of an integrated whole.

From a place of refined attention and deepened awareness, we are more prepared to bring the essence of weather dancing home as something livelier than an invention or convolution of the intellect. For this we turn to the gifts of metaphor. To work with metaphor is to open one's mind and psyche to nuances not readily available in more simple, concrete language and thought. To work with metaphor is to invite an opening into the consciousness of the sacred. In our culture few know the power of metaphor as it relates to the shamanic state of consciousness better than Michael Harner. For decades he has introduced the concept of sacred metaphor to his students. Metaphor can serve as a more accessible route to essence, that internal "magic." My spiritual teachers once told me that metaphor presents the "shadow of a thing," an expression of its true shape, devoid of details or any rendering that could mislead us. To understand the hidden nature of something through metaphor requires from us an active engagement of our essence to its essence.

Metaphors of the sacred challenge us to pursue clarity, though we may feel daunted at the outset. We might arouse an initial state of confusion or frustration when we probe beneath the surface of a thing. Our only encouragement is that through our efforts we'll stretch our abilities to grasp that which is not obvious. A willingness to remain alert, to cast our attentions about us in seemingly endless circles, allows us to tone and tune our abilities to follow the elusive mystery—and dance the dance of weather.

Attention to metaphor brings self-awareness, a key requisite for the success of any sort of relationship—with other people, with the animals living in our homes, with any element of nature, and especially with the weather. Metaphor gives us elbow room, offers us a spaciousness of understanding and invites us to fill in the spaces with our own deep knowing. It can be said that metaphors are intertwined with the structure of our unconscious self. If we were to listen carefully to our language, we would discover the hidden metaphors we all live by that define our take on the experience of life, metaphors that reveal our desires, our fears, our values, our hopes, and our choices.

For example, an outsider listening to the language of our culture would learn about the prominence of sports and computers through our metaphors. We frequently speak of "being on the team"; "the name of the game"; "dropping the ball"; "having the ball in your court"; "right off the bat"; "covering all the bases"; "being out in left field"; and so on. Additionally, we describe ourselves or situations we're involved in as "online"; we receive "input"; we "program" and "reprogram." Our use of the word *web* is an interesting one, used in our language to describe both the Internet and the great "web of the world" that hearkens back to our ancestral description of the underpinnings of reality.

Listening to the metaphors of our own speech can accurately reveal our general attitude toward Nature, exposing beliefs that we may hold yet be unaware of. Many of our culture's common expressions carry implications of conquest or threat regarding the natural world. "The hurricane's fury"; "the assault of the ants"; "a rogue wave"; "it's a jungle out there"— these are examples of some of our verbal descriptions of how we relate to Nature. Television commercials exhort us to "rub out those dandelion *invaders*." (Ironically, we use poisons—herbicides—to eliminate the very plants capable of cleansing our own bodies of environmental toxins!) Repeatedly, since earliest childhood, we have heard a preponderance of words expressing the metaphor of humans at war with Nature.

Fortunately, there are other metaphors out there for us: "The weather smiled on us"; "the playful breeze"; "sunlight dancing on the water"; "the man [or woman] in the moon"; "catching lightning in a bottle." From our ancestral heritage we are given the metaphor of Earth as our mother, as creatrix and source of life-sustaining nurturance. If enough of us in our culture were to take that one deeply into our hearts, so that it could inform our whole beings, our lives might dramatically shift. Our relationship to the world, environmentally challenged as it now is, would metamorphose into what we could only call the miraculous.

If we can regard weather in this middle world as a metaphorical expression, as an ever-changing representation of the life force of the outer world as well as our inner world, then what is the weather communicating to us? My spiritual teacher put it this way:

Weather is the metaphor, the doorway to the harmony you so desperately need in your world. Weather forces are "in your face" and cannot be completely ignored. Indeed, most people are fascinated by them. A relationship between humans and weather is born of a sense of relatedness to all and brings you to those places of harmony and love.

Weather is your ally. Use each change of weather as a teaching metaphor for your life.

A simple practice, such as observing the weather and seeking its metaphorical correlations to our lives, anchors us in the power of the present moment. Coupled with our love, this is a sure way into a conscious relationship with the spirits of weather.

David and I learned that to invite an enlivened, harmonious relationship with the spirits of weather into our lives, we needed to find personal metaphors to help us understand and clarify what we were about in this endeavor. Metaphors of the sacred help keep us and our aim true and help us discern and avoid the path of "power-over" in relationship. Through metaphor we can see—know—that in relating with the spirits of weather we recognize the profound truth of "all my relations," an honoring phrase attributed to the Lakota people.

To offer a working metaphor to others is of limited usefulness; it's better to find one through our own heart and efforts. We can meditate or journey to ask for a metaphor to enhance our understanding of what a relationship with the spirits of weather means, personally and globally. We can ask for a description of our own nature and life in terms of a weather metaphor. The changing shapes of clouds offer us opportunities to divine—to find helpful metaphors for our lives and questions, ones that provide the insights or advice we may need.

A metaphor from the helping spirits can reliably and creatively guide us in our questions concerning the possibilities and the ethics of an active, working relationship with the spirits of weather.

I fly up a vertical sunbeam, through a layer of beautifully colored clouds, and up, up through several more layers to reach the domain of my weather teacher. I ask him to offer me a metaphor that will inform and inspire my spiritual path with the forces and spirits of weather. I need a "guiding light."

Without hesitation he replies, "Dance. Dance is an act of engagement, an honoring, reciprocal movement, a coming together, merging, then pulling apart. It is alluring and enticing, and it can be solitary or performed in the spirit of alignment with another . . . aligning with the movements and energies of the partner, then redirecting . . . following and leading . . . a blending and a separating . . . a defining of self and other in the dance. It is an experience of sacred duality within oneness. Dance is an inspired play of change and movement. It is so rich. Watch the plants. See them dance in wind and rain. In drought when they wilt, they are dancing drought!"

He continues, "To dance requires presence and an offering of energy. To dance your soul is to be in beauty."

Knowing that I was struggling to find the right word or words to name our work, something that would not conjure up popular misconceptions of power and control in the minds of people who hear about it, my weather teacher gives me these parting words: "Dancing with spirits of weather implies much more than weather working. It is spacious and allowing. One must be in tune—in harmony—to dance well."

I returned from that journey with *weather dancing* singing in my ear, and I knew that I had not only my guiding metaphor but also the empowered word I was looking for to name and speak of our work.

16

CEREMONY

DANCE OF ALIGNMENT

"When we were young, the villagers did a Primicia *in the Catholic church after each planting," he said. "We stayed up all night, chanting and calling out to the Spirits for rain." Before dawn, torrents of rain would pour, announced by loud cracking thunder. The thunder would awaken the tender seedlings in the fields. "We did nine* Primicias *a year for planting, for harvests, for rain, for sick people, and sometimes just to show our love for the Spirits."*

DON ELIJIO PANTI, MAYAN H'MEN,
QUOTED IN *SASTUN*, BY ROSITA ARVIGO

Lodged in a round stone building, we were perched on the high-est, most exposed part of the Esalen Institute's narrow strip of the rugged Big Sur coastline. The circle had just formed for the closing ceremony to complete the week's work together. It had been a day of rest-less weather. Wild rain and windstorms occasionally spin up the coast from the south this time of year, carried along by the Pineapple Express (a jet stream bringing warm, moist air from Hawaii to the West Coast), and on this January day one was on its way. The outside world was blustery, and as people entered the foyer the wind tried to come in too. I knelt by the altar in the center of the room and felt tendrils of wet ocean-cooled air crossing the threshold.

Preparing to light the candle, I closed my eyes and let the words well up—simple words—a spontaneous honoring of the wind and a spoken invitation for the elements of weather to take notice of us, to join our circle in a supportive way. We all sang our soul songs as we drummed, rattled, and danced. The room seemed to expand, and the fire in the fireplace sang and danced with us. At some point I realized I was dancing as wind—whirling, dipping, letting my body express the love I feel for this element. Eventually, David beat the customary four drum rolls, our signal to stop.

Just as we settled back into a circle of repose, the wind gave us its dance. With startling strength a gust roared at us, blasting the outer wall, kicking the glass doors and windows into their own dance. We watched, wide-eyed, as the doors shook so heavily that a buckling seemed imminent. People along the outer wall scuttled over to the security of the stone hearth. Laughing nervously, we all waited to see what else might happen. The lights flickered off and on, then finally off, and in the firelight we listened to a relentless background roar punctuated by groaning and thumping sounds while the wind explored what it could. I felt the presence of a predator, as if the wind were looking for something or someone. We all jumped when it forced its way through the louvered windows with an eerie, piercing scream. Moments later the windows and doors stopped shaking, the lights flickered one more time, and the wind settled itself into a gentler mood. Now it rained— hard at first and mixed with hail, unusual for that area. Then that, too, eased up. A few minutes later, David and I stood at the altar drumming for the first journey of the evening.

David and I often think of weather working and other methods of relating to the weather as an alchemical process, as a relationship between the changer and the changing, where sometimes we are the one, and sometimes the other. What, then, is the crucible for this alchemy? Is there an overall cross-cultural method for creating alignment with the weather spirits, something that can enfold the seemingly disparate teachings, principles, and practices of weather working from the past and the present?

It was time, once again, to seek the advice of my spirit weather teacher. His reply was succinct:

> Weather is always relating to something. In weather dancing you are the ones who must learn to consciously relate to the weather. The use of ritual and the tools of ritual, such as dancing, singing, praying—engaging in that which aligns heart, body, mind, and spirit with your intention—creates a magnetic attraction for the weather spirits. This forms the space, and a way for us to dance together.

David journeyed to his teacher in the lower world to learn more about alignment. He learned that when we open our circles with drumming, singing, and dancing, we create alignment within the group and with the helping spirits we wish to welcome. This is an intentional, active act of alignment in ceremony.

There are both *passive* and *active* alignments, his teacher advised. All things must eventually align; this is the passive alignment of entropy. We wear clothing to prevent it, else we become the same temperature as the air. We paint wood to preserve its integrity, to forestall its eventual alignment with the surrounding elements. We have boundaries and need to protect them. Battle preserves boundaries, while alignment dissolves boundaries. Therefore we must learn about selective alignment. David's teacher added, "Align with that which attracts what you want. If you want to attract bees, align with the flowers. Practice becoming rain, snow, heat, wind . . . Aligning with the elements of weather is weather dancing."

Rolling Thunder, the well-known and respected Cherokee medicine man, understood the nature of alignment. His teachings encourage us to surrender our attachments to self-image and, instead, to focus on identifying ourselves as part of it all, as part of all manifestations of the life force. Doug Boyd expounds upon this perspective: "There are no dangerous plants or animals. For [Rolling Thunder], there is no fear. The wind and the rain, the mosquitoes and the snakes are all within him. His consciousness extends to include them within its very being."[1]

This is what is behind those breakthrough, peak experiences of ecstasy: our sense of expanded being-ness in the world. When it happens for us it is a rare and genuine state of grace, and it inspires a feeling of true belonging in Nature, with a consciousness of no separation—of unity. It is the essence of alignment.

In another journey, my spiritual teacher continued his earlier teaching:

When I arrive in his domain I find him standing on a hilltop, facing away from me. He appears to be waving and flailing his arms around—up, down, and over, expansive sweeps interspersed with shorter jabs and flutters. My teacher is conducting! And the sky is his orchestra. I watch voluminous white and gray clouds form and reform just above him. A breeze plays gently in my hair. I think I hear a distant rumbling of thunder once or twice that soon grows distinctly louder and nearer. Lightning that at first flickered in the distance now flashes in eruptions of brilliance as it comes ever closer. The breeze is now a wind that pushes me around. I start to tingle and hold my breath in anticipation of a dramatic crescendo. And then suddenly it all shifts—the sky calms, and as it clears my tension melts away with the storm clouds. Now I can see that the fingers of both of my teacher's hands are holding something and moving at the same time. When Grandfather finally turns to greet me, I see that he has been playing a flute.

He says, "Effort . . . there has to be an exchange of effort—an offering of your effort first—in the working, in the asking. Weather expends energy,

and to ask a cloud or a storm to bring rain requires a reciprocal act in which
you expend some of your energy."

Grandfather went on to explain that ritual is a way for us to retrieve and raise our own power as we direct our intention to align with the power of weather. Ritual and the acts of ritual are like a steep-sided, narrow canyon that the wide and slow river must flow through. As the river enters the narrowed space of the canyon walls and experiences the drop in elevation and boulders in its path, its entire form and way of being intensifies as it cascades in its dance over and around rocks, through chutes and down falls, heading inexorably to the sea. It is a changed river; it is an empowered river. Likewise, the container for the alchemy of the relationship of weather working is the sacred space of ritual and ceremony.

Additionally, Grandfather urged me to do more than "just ask," instead refining and individualizing my acts of relating to the weather spirits. He considers this a more respectful way to work. Therefore, offerings or exchanges of energy will depend upon what I am asking for and whom I am addressing. So whether the offering is praying, singing, dancing, honoring, or some other form, it requires an expenditure of energy on our part as we seek to align with the weather spirits. It is through ceremony and its elements that we can contribute our exchange of effort.

Tom Crockett, author and shamanic counselor, understands the importance of alignment with the power of the weather spirits in ceremony. He lives in a hurricane-sensitive area along the coast of southeastern Virginia, and he shared with us his experience with Hurricane Floyd and its serious threat to his home and neighborhood:

As he moved toward us, I settled in to do ceremony and journey out to meet him. I spent between two and three hours on Wednesday evening in ceremony. The rain was driving; the Thunder Beings were speaking. I have four stones I use for working with the elements and I used each one to pray with. I was very careful not to direct the storm anywhere else but to merge my energy field with the storm and ask the wind to blow gently around us, the earth to hold firmly to the roots of her trees, the water to flow past us without harming person or property, and energy of fire to keep us in power or to restore power to us quickly. I then went outside in the dark and the wild rain and planted the stones at each corner of our property. I "camayed" [spraying alcohol through the mouth as a blessing] with Florida water and prayed at each point.

The next morning as the hurricane bore down on us in the midst of dire predictions from the local weather people, I opened myself up and journeyed into the storm. I understood from the guidance of the storm that I should return to my body and meditate, expanding my energy body to include the house and the entire street. This was very intense and required all my focus. I surrendered to the storm and asked that it move quickly through. I also asked the wind spirits to keep us safe from tornado winds.

Three hours before high tide the water started washing up our street in waves. At two hours before high tide the water had made an island of our house. I was out wading in the water making sure our older neighbors were okay. Power and phones went out all over our area. It looked grim. I stood in the middle of the street with water up to my thighs and intoned the five directions against the howling wind. Within minutes, and an hour before high tide, the water began to reverse and the wind died out.

As I began to explore I found that our street had been spared any significant damage. Our power came back within an hour. Beyond our street major trees had been uprooted and power continued to be out. One street away there were houses a foot and a half underwater.

Now, my Western "left-brain" thinking tells me that the storm moved faster than anyone expected, shifting winds to the west and working against the tidal flooding. We were lucky. But I also felt linked to the energy of the storm in a way that was palpable. I felt like I had a connection that allowed me to influence in some subtle way the intensity and duration of the storm. I did ceremony afterward to honor and thank the energies I appealed to and tried not to allow ego to enter into this, but it did feel like I was able to channel some energy that affected the storm. The most significant thing for me was the experience of joining with the storm. I think I know now what it means to align with natural power.

As an alchemical container, ceremony, whether human-created or one of weather's, requires an organization of potential. A climatologist in Florida once described a hurricane's birth as a "circle dance" of thunderstorms,[2] metaphorically demonstrating that if and when a particular level of organization is met, something can be created that is far greater than the sum of its parts, something capable of effecting significant change for our world.

Furthermore, ceremonies or rituals are never limited to rote steps performed for an indifferent audience. Malidoma Patrice Somé, a wise man of the Dagara people, writes:

> There are two parts to ritual. One part is planned: people prepare the space for the ritual and think through the general choreography of the process. The other part of ritual cannot be planned because it is the part that Spirit is in charge of. . . . It is like a journey. Before you get started, you own the journey. After you start, the journey owns you.[3]

Both rituals and ceremonies can be minutely orchestrated, or they can have more spontaneity to their flow. They can be repeated over time or occur just once. They can be for one person or for an entire community. Their organization may be highly detailed and grandiose or spare and humble. I think of ritual as a more personally oriented rite than ceremony, and ceremony as larger in its format and scope, but the distinctions between the two are hazy. What is important is the spirit of the experience.

Greg, a longtime shamanic practitioner, intentionally calls upon the enormous power of approaching thunderstorms to enlist their healing help to restore harmony to the earth. In a personal ritual, he stands on his backyard porch and sings "The Thunder-Being Song" (a song we learned from Sandra Ingerman)—loudly, and for as long as he dares. The words of this song speak for themselves:

> *I call to the power of the Thunder Beings,*
> *I call to the power of the earth,*
> *I call to the power of the East and West,*
> *I call to the power of the North and South.*
>
> *Behold, the time has come,*
> *The time has come to unite as one,*
> *Behold, the time has come,*
> *To encircle the earth with our love.*

Greg has continued this practice for years, and on one memorable occasion a thunderstorm answered back. He described to us his ritual and what occurred:

I stand on the edge of the porch, getting a bit wet, and feeling the breezes and the electricity. As I sing over and over (at least four to six times) in full voice, I get emotionally connected to the Thunder Beings through the words. There's the recognition of the power of those thunder and lightning spirits, the immense power of Mother Earth, my relations in the Four Directions . . . some pushing through fear . . . and the love we share as we "encircle the earth" together.

I have a very tall poplar tree in my backyard that I've always used as my portal to nonordinary reality . . . I always give it a hug in my journeys. One night this past winter we heard a very loud boom during

a storm and a strong feel of electricity in the air. The next morning
I discovered pieces of the tree speared into the ground and scattered
about . . . typically pieces about 4 feet long and 5 inches wide. . . .
High up in the tree you can see the scar down the side of the trunk.
At the foot of the tree, next to the crack, was a small hole, less than a
foot wide and curling into the ground, at least a foot deep.

Though the lightning strike was nearby, Greg's home suffered neither damage nor electrical failure. He gifted us with one of the pieces
of wood from his tree, and so far as we know, he continues to offer his
"Thunder Being" songs on behalf of our world.

This hearkens back to the ancestral understanding that ritual and
ceremony are primary ways in which humans can do their part to hold
the world together—to maintain the cosmic order that engenders the
balance and vitality all beings depend upon for life. The recognition of
humans as vital to the well-being of the world is cross-cultural in its
scope. Taken seriously, it is an invitation to shoulder a great responsibility, for the harmony of both our world and the spirit world, for behind
it all we are all connected. Historian Calvin Luther Martin writes of
the Navajo people "who regard the world as utterly beautiful. Yet beauty
. . . unravels, succumbs to entropy. We were created, they say, to restore
the beautiful. . . . Humans breathe into the world the proper, sustaining
songs and stories; man and woman keep the world in motion in dance,
in ceremony and ritual."[4]

Many of the wisdom-teaching stories speak of some kind of reciprocal agreement made in the long-ago times between humans and the
spirits. Often a shaman is involved. One tale relates how a Yupik shaman was responsible for initiating such an agreement between his people and the sky spirits. He journeyed to the sky and found that the
spirits there appreciated human attention, and upon his return to earth
he created a ceremony that his people would perform in the proper season on behalf of the sky spirits. The sky spirits, in turn, would do their
part to provide the earth with food for the people.[5]

At midsummer the Tohono O'odham people, or Papago, of the Southwest harvest the fruits of the majestic saguaro cactus. Collecting the ripe fruit is otherwise known as "pulling down the clouds," and it marks the beginning of the Saguaro Wine Festival, a time-honored ceremony of thanksgiving and rainmaking. The people make jams, candies, and syrups with this fruit, as well as a sacred wine. For the wine, the juice of the saguaro fruit ferments for three days in the "rain house." According to Mike Chiago, a Tohono O'odham artist, "Rain songs are sung while the liquid ferments, and men and women dance at night. At noon on the third day, the headmen gather to recite long poems over the basket of wine. The planting of crops takes place after the wine festival, to make use of the rains that are bound to follow."[6]

In a slightly different version, once the ceremonial leader declares the wine ready, the people all gather around in a circle to sing, dance, and pray from that day until sunrise the next morning. Within the roundhouse special rites are performed for the wine. At some point the principal elders emerge outside with eight baskets of wine. Singing songs for rain, the circle of people drink the blessed wine. The rains follow and summer monsoon season begins.[7]

To this day indigenous peoples conduct ceremonies and rites of passage to connect—align—their children with the earth, the community, and the spiritual powers of the earth, sky, and ancestors. Katie, a clan mother of the southern Ohio Shawnee tribe, described to us her ritual of presenting her family's newest member to the world—and their vow to teach him what it means to be human:

On November 9, 2002, my husband and I introduced our grandson, Kicks First, to the Four Directions, ancestors, and spirits of our land. Damon (Kicks First) was three weeks old. The three of us turned to each direction and welcomed the spirits from each direction. Both of us were rattling. We then stated our promise:

"To the spirits of the East
This is Kicks First.

We promise to teach him to

Walk in the proper manner for a human.

We ask for your protection for him as he grows up."

The wind came up and started swirling around us as we turned south. So when we introduced him to the South, I said,

"To the spirits of the South and the air

and Thunder Beings,

This is Kicks First.

We promise to teach him to

Walk in the proper manner for a human.

We ask for your protection for him as he grows up."

When I was saying "We ask for your protection . . ." there was a single clap of thunder. The wind continued to swirl as we did the other directions and then died out as we finished. The sky was clear blue and it was fairly warm. We held the ceremony at about 2:00 in the afternoon. We did have a thunderstorm that evening around 8:00 p.m.

Ceremonies or rituals may be performed to dispel the forces of disharmony in our lives and world. Dr. James Swan writes, "My friend, Bill Fields, retired director of Indian Affairs for the U.S. National Park Service, says that the Hopi Indians say that they don't make it rain with their ceremonies. Rather, the ceremonies drive away the disharmony that prevents the rain from falling. The Hopis call the disharmony exorcised by their ceremonies 'akina.'"[8]

An example of a simple ceremony that is able to effectively restore harmony among both people and weather occurred during a photography expedition to the high country of the Himalayas and the east face of Mount Everest. Snowbound for three days by a large storm, the party of hikers, guides, yak herders, and yaks were restless and confused as to their options. The storm showed little sign of letting up, the yaks hadn't eaten in three days, and the herders were fearful for their welfare. To make matters more precarious, winter was coming on and they had significant climbing ahead. Wade Davis writes:

> I noticed Tandu, the quiet leader among the Tibetans, placing a large flat stone on the snow. Kindling a fire with dried juniper, he burned incense and green boughs, then added offerings of tsampa, yak butter, and tea, all the while singing a deep melodious chant that drew everyone out of the tents into a wide circle around the flames. The ritual puja, a ceremonial prayer, in this case for good weather, had two immediate and gratifying effects. First, it brought our group together, dispelling in a moment any thoughts of retreating over the pass. Second, the sky cleared.[9]

Ceremony also provides a place and time where we can invite the spirits to join us for a particular working. Anthropologist, author, university professor, and longtime resident of New Orleans Martha Ward shares her experience of the workings of a voodoo conjure-dance ceremony on behalf of the city and its environs during hurricane season. As Martha describes it, the ceremony to turn the hurricanes begins with a focused intention or prayer and an altar of offerings to the spirit Erzulie. The main body of the ceremony revolves around a particular form of dance, the conjure dance, in which the dancers invite the spirit to join them, to dance through them for the purpose of manifesting the stated intention.

> Since the late 1990s the national meteorological services have been predicting that more and more severe hurricane seasons will hit the U.S. Other scientists have been pointing out the unique vulnerability of south Louisiana and the island of sinking land at its heart, the city of New Orleans. On July 18, 1998, La Source Ancienne, the strongest Voodoo congregation in the city, performed a dance with one strong and stated intention: "to turn hurricanes." The ceremony honored Erzulie Dantor, a loa or spirit in the Haitian Vodou pantheon, with the things she likes: flowers, candles, fruit, candy, sweet liquors, perfume, jewelry, and French pastries. She smokes Virginia

Slims and loves fried pork skins. Erzulie is a powerful spirit, easily provoked. One side of her personality is full of anger and vengeance although when properly treated, she will roll up her sleeves and go to work for serious petitioners. . . .

Each hurricane season since 1998 I have participated in and observed the Voodoo dance. I pray that the Voodoo's intention will hold though I decide to cut them some slack if it fails. After all, a hurricane is the most powerful natural force on the planet.

On September 11, 1998, Tropical Storm Frances with her 70- to 72-mile-per-hour winds dumped 22 inches of rain on my neighborhood in a few hours. Parts of historic old St. Charles Avenue were under four feet of water. Frances was a very severe storm who did extensive damage—but she was not a hurricane, defined as winds that exceed 74 miles per hour. Okay, I said, the offerings and dancing we did on July 18 that year said nothing about tropical storms. Despite the damage, Frances was not a hurricane.

Then Hurricane Georges left the coast of Africa and moved in a resolutely straight line across the Atlantic, never deviating a degree off a course that would take it straight up the mouth of the Mississippi River. No one could remember a hurricane that so clearly had our name on it. He ripped through the island of Hispaniola as a Category 4. Hundreds died; their bodies showed up for months. He hit Cuba, crossed [its] mountains, and weakened to a Category 2, bypassing southern Florida on a heading straight for New Orleans. Gulf Coast residents began our preparations.

If the Voodoo can't turn it—I bargained on their behalf and reasoned with capricious Fate—perhaps their efforts can mitigate the effects of the storm. A disorganized Category 1 would not be so bad. On Friday, September 25, I bought another lamp, more oil and wicks, batteries, food, film for the camera, masking tape, plastic covers, and an axe. I filled the car with gas and went to the bank for cash—the things I took for granted [would] be down for weeks. I made lists, checked the radios again to make sure they work.

My paramedic daughter was on duty at the mayor's office where the health department had collected 500 body bags; some graduate students had stationed themselves at the levee board offices, pumping stations, and the special-needs evacuation center. The mayor announced a complex list of mandatory and voluntary evacuations; the archbishop excused all Catholics from attending Mass on Sunday. On Friday night and Saturday morning, I returned calls and checked on people I knew [were] vulnerable. By Saturday afternoon Hurricane Georges had strengthened to a Category 3, moving up in velocity and intensity, still heading directly at us.

On Sunday morning, Georges, still on course, was 100 miles from the mouth of the river. The Weather Channel showed the storm heading directly for New Orleans on the worst possible trajectory. The forecasters said that the hurricane would push Lake Pontchartrain over the flood walls and levees and into all of the communities around the lake, dump 20 to 25 inches of water on the first day, more in succeeding days, and bring a 20-foot tidal surge flooding all coastal areas and pushing saltwater up the Mississippi as far as New Orleans.

Then Georges hesitated. He turned one-half degree to his right—east. His first turn, a wobble that left south Louisiana on the dry west side. Hurricane Georges landed along the coast with no loss of life and less property damage than Tropical Storm Frances. Each season since 1998 has followed the same hair-raising pattern: through the summer and fall, New Orleans is under a series of watches and warnings. Then a tropical storm brings damage, flooding, disruption, even some deaths. All the hurricanes, however, turn away or dissipate without explanation.[10]

The ceremony to turn the hurricanes was duly performed during the month of July 2005, and later that summer, on August 29, the city of New Orleans, as well as much of the Gulf Coast, was struck by Hurricane Katrina. Just as Hurricane Georges' shifted his path,

Katrina did veer to the east just before landfall and so did not deliver a direct hit to New Orleans. The giant storm also stood down from a class 5 to a class 3 just as she came ashore. Her immense size, however, ensured that New Orleans was subjected to hurricane-force winds and rains. Most of the tragedy that befell New Orleans came from the levee breaks and resultant flooding that occurred after Katrina's pass. Though city and government officials had ample foreknowledge of the size and power of this storm, as well as New Orleans's vulnerability to catastrophic flooding, the situation proved too much and promptly overwhelmed the overall immediate human response and ability to deal with the tremendous suffering of thousands of people and animals. The city's plight inspired both the worst and the best in people: acts of crazy violence and greed two-stepped with those of brilliant and heroic compassion. The unfolding drama held the nation spellbound for weeks. As of this writing we don't know how long it will take for New Orleans to become a tenable city once again. May it and the other Gulf Coast towns be redesigned and rebuilt in greater accordance—alignment—with the forces of Nature, so that the ceremonies of thanksgiving and protection can prevail.

Don Matsuwa was a respected, revered shaman of the Huichol people from the mountains of Mexico who had practiced shamanism for at least sixty years. In the 1970s, when he was in his eighties, he visited New York and California. A man filled with vitality and good humor, Don Matsuwa is said to have wept as he worked in ceremony, seeing the frightful lack of balance in our world, and he offered timely advice that our culture cannot afford to ignore:

> This place that you live in and many other places in your country suffer from drought, too much rain, shortages, many problems. There is a reason for this misfortune, for you have not been doing ceremonies, gathering together, thanking the earth, the gods, the Sun, the sea for your lives. This is missing here. Without celebration,

the gods are unhappy and bring misery to us. The ceremonies, gathering together, celebrating together—this is the love or energy that the gods live on. . . .

Don Matsuwa described how he had performed another ceremony during an earlier visit to our land, how he had chanted with his heart, and several hours after the ceremony's conclusion, clouds had gathered and "a powerful rain" come. He gently chastised, "You should have told me sooner that you had such problems. I would have come earlier to do a ceremony in order to change the situation." He went on to say that when a state of imbalance has existed for a long time, such as what we suffer now, the consequent disharmony is not easy to correct. It can take a long time and much work of gathering together in ceremonies to realign ourselves with the elements of Nature. Don Matsuwa added that in his country, the people work in anticipation of disasters and offer ceremonies to avoid them.[11]

All ceremonies are composed of various elements that are utilized worldwide. The use and workings of prayer, meditation, symbols, offerings, chanting, singing, and dancing all provide ways to stimulate us, to help us concentrate, to focus our intention, and to show up in our power as we engage and align with the spirits in ceremony. Each ceremony will have its own intention and combinations of elements, put together with an invitation to the helping spirits, and through these we are able to cocreate, to conjure, to manifest in this world. The appropriate tools and methods of ceremony can come through to us no matter who we are or where we are or what our educational backgrounds or lineages are. All we have to do is ask—and give the spirits an opportunity to be heard. Shamans recognize the sacred responsibility of humans to dream the world anew, and it is through ceremony that the dreams are empowered.

17

ETHICS OF
WEATHER WORKING

*We fear the cold and
the things we do not understand.
But most of all we fear the doings of
the heedless ones among ourselves.*

Eskimo shaman, quoted in
The Star Thrower, by Loren Eiseley

Attempts to influence the weather can genuinely serve our world as a form of shamanic healing, for the health of both the environment and the community, but the razor's edge lies in the *appropriateness* of any workings we may contemplate. Weather working as shamanic healing depends upon the essential elements of our friendships with the weather spirits coupled with the guidance and assistance of our reliably compassionate helping spirits.

There is a real distinction between relating to and actively engaging with the spirits of weather. It is one thing to honor and appreciate weather's elements and their spiritual natures; yet it is this and something more to align with the weather to achieve certain results. We can enjoy a good and honorable relationship with a friend without telling our friend what to do all the time, beyond asking for the occasional favor.

As we grew into our relationships with the forces and spirits of weather, David and I were surprised to experience a diminishing desire to try to change anything! To us, this is a good sign that our aim is true, although it is always a thrill when the weather spirits do agree to a request, which reassures us that we are aligned, if only for one instance.

David and I learned something about appropriate weather working one evening with our drumming circle. It was midsummer 1998, and we were in the thick of a withering drought in the Northeast. The moss- and lichen-carpeted woods crackled with each step, the perpetual spring at the meadow's edge had vanished, the beaver dam had nothing to hold back, neighbors' wells were running dry, and cisterns hadn't seen rainwater since late winter. Regional reservoirs were at record low levels. We worried that the local coyotes, deer, moose, and other animals wouldn't be able to find any watering holes.

Our drumming circle had journeyed and practiced together since we first began to explore weather shamanism, so on this night we all felt unusually primed to go to work. My anticipation was so great that I could practically smell that rain coming. We had the good sense to remember, however, that we might not know everything about the situation, and that we should call on our helping spirits for a more reliable perspective. We took an exploratory journey for the advice we needed. Some of us went to the upper world, some to the lower world, and some to the middle or other world—wherever we could find the compassionate tutelary spirit of our choice. In the end, the teachings that we each came back with surprised all and disappointed some, though we trusted the wisdom of it:

"Leave it alone. Do nothing. Deal with it as best you can—conserve water and dream of balance restored in its time."

"This drought is necessary. It is needed to heal—to heal the land in ways you do not understand—and it is needed to heal the ignorance of people. Through this ignorance, people live in disrespect for the natural world."

"Because of their lack of respect too many people abuse the waters that give them life."

"The animals know how to live here and will manage well enough."

"People have forgotten the sacredness of water and how to live with water. Therefore, the rains are withheld for a time—long enough to attract the attention needed for more people to yearn for harmonious relationships with water, with weather, and with Nature."

"This drought is a healing. Do not interfere."

In the face of this teaching we had to back off. There would be no community drought-busting this night, nor until we heard otherwise. But we continued to yearn for rain, and we stayed with the pain of withering plants, tinder-dry forests, and scared, upset people. Whenever I asked for some relief, it was always when I could feel that the clouds of the moment might have a little rain to give. And that's what we got. We celebrated each shower. A hurricane remnant in early autumn plus the onset of winter snows gradually improved things until eventually the drought ended.

Rolling Thunder lived according to the life principle of a right time and place for everything, including his own being. One of his students, Doug Boyd, explains that this principle cannot be grasped through the intellect, that you must intentionally live it, every day and night, to understand what it means to be a part of everything. Eventually, as you become one with it—align with it in surrender to the dictates of right timing and place—the principle of life responds to your will. This is how, for Rolling Thunder, there were no "unwanted rains."[1]

Yet there are those times when it is crucial to attempt to intervene in a particular weather's course—when the time and place are right. Mary Elizabeth Thunder once participated in an emergency weather working by Rolling Thunder. He awoke her and another guest just after dawn as he hurried out the door toward a large open space on a nearby golf green. As she ran after him all she heard him say was that a tornado or hurricane was coming and they had to stop it. The sky was darkening ominously as green-black clouds rolled in.

> He gave each of us an Eagle feather. Then he took out his sacred Eagle wing and started yelling and chanting. I was very nervous with my small Eagle feather, doing—I hoped—as instructed, holding position and praying for the clouds to break up. As [Rolling Thunder] walked around the golf green and continued to yell and chant, the clouds began to break up. I'll never forget him standing there with his arms out to the Universe, and the Universe responding.[2]

Buddhist monk Thich Nhat Hanh also speaks of an internal reality of connectedness with Nature and lives his life accordingly. He encourages us to go deeply into the reality of knowing ourselves as truly a part of it all, so that from this place of belonging and understanding we'll be able to take right action. Thich Nhat Hanh calls for the aware human to work for the maintenance of balance and overall harmony in the world—as the old-time shamans did for their communities.

> The individual and all of humanity are both a part of Nature and should be able to live in harmony with Nature. Nature can be cruel and disruptive and therefore, at times, needs to be controlled. To control is not to dominate or oppress but to harmonize and equilibrate. We must be deep friends with Nature in order to control certain aspects of it. . . . We should be able to prevent to a large degree the destruction that natural disasters cause, but we must do it in a way that preserves life and encourages harmony.[3]

Whenever we weather-work, there are choices to be made. We have to straightforwardly ask ourselves, why do we want to do this? Will it promote harmony and restore balance? Are we working to heal, or are we working on behalf of our own personal desires, to serve our egos for any reason? My spiritual weather teacher gave me a guideline to follow:

> You must come from the heart. Both the desire and the need must come from the wisdom of the heart. There may be a desire to work for rain, but no need for it. Any working like this will serve only ego. This can create trouble. To have desire without the need is empty of heart.

Once a decision to work is made, then the first concern regarding any act of weather modification or weather working must be about the possible immediate and longer-term effects, not only in the specific area, but also downwind for the greater region. For example, when a hurricane threatens, do we weather-work to just send it on in any other direction save ours, or do we ask that it dissipate, though we may not completely fathom the role it is playing in the world? David and I know a gifted individual who trusts his ability to cocreate in the world and impulsively did a simple "working" to move an oncoming hurricane over, just a bit, so that his hometown would be spared a direct hit. He happily watched the nearly immediate results on a weather website on his computer until he saw the storm spiral into the heart of another town, exactly in the direction he had indicated. He had to wonder if his attempted "spiritual nudge" influenced the storm's course. The reality is that in these days of high population density, those of us who wish to ask a storm to move over are hard pressed to find a clear path.

It is the shaman's responsibility to consult with the spirits not only to master specific techniques but also to learn how to work with the forces of Nature to bring about what is best for the most people, animals, plants, land, and ideally, the entire world. Middle-world weather spirits are not necessarily obliged to work for compassionate ends. Cross-culturally, shamans think of power in the middle world as an amoral, neutral force, neither "good" nor "bad." The qualitative aspect of this power derives from *how* the power is directed and *what* its objectives are. The calling, for those practicing weather dancing, is to align with these forces and spirits from their own place of heart and wisdom, in collaboration with the reliably compassionate helping spirits of the upper and lower worlds. This partnering can include trustworthy and compassionate spirit allies of the middle world as well. In this way, no harm comes from weather working.

Weather workers who are not aligned with harmonious forces can create substantial harm. Even though these people intend no harm, when they work from a place of carelessness or hubris—basically ignorance—their workings can go awry, causing great difficulty for others and lifelong regret. Then there are those who intentionally work to cause suffering for revenge, to satisfy a grudge, or to cause a loss of power or prestige to a competitor or enemy.

The Warao of the Orinoco Delta of the Amazon require a high degree of maturity in their prospective weather shamans, for Warao weather shamanism is a complex tradition embodying numerous levels of purpose and meaning that often overlap one another. There is no simple definition of a "good" or "dark" shaman; with few exceptions, both can work for healing or harm. A Warao weather shaman can call on wind, rain, or thunder and lightning to smite or harass an individual rival or another hostile community. However, the same shaman can then choose to heal a sickness or injury caused by those same elements of weather. When personal motive predominates over a compassionate consideration for the good of all, it is not possible to know how some shamans will use their powers of influence.[4]

The Warao rain shaman possesses the apotropaic power to attract or repel rain. Depending upon the timing of any weather working of this sort, the shaman can either help or hurt a community. In addition to causing potentially grave problems of food shortages and spoilage—hence the specter of famine—too much or too little rain can also have a decidedly harmful effect on people's health, tormenting them with a variety of "weather afflictions" such as colds, muscle aches, chronic coughing, gastrointestinal malaises, frequent episodes of conjunctivitis, fevers, and the serious respiratory illnesses of bronchitis and asthma.

A Warao rain shaman looks something like an elderly mendicant in the village, soliciting, and expecting to receive, foods, items, and favors as needed. This illustrates an ethically gray area in which the shaman is willing to invoke trouble and hardship in the interests of ensuring proper behavior among the villagers:

> Everybody caters to the wishes of the old man to keep him from turning his power against them. . . . The rain shaman makes his people aware of the interrelationship among climatology, botany, and human behavior, pointing out that regional and local famines are the result of his anger and the rain lords' wrath provoked by human stinginess and egotism. Constantly calling on his people to be considerate of others by sharing food and helping the disadvantaged, he conjures up the frightful images of hunger and starvation to enforce selfless normative behavior.[5]

It is said that most Warao shamans, including fully initiated curing or healing shamans, can blow against a storm to avert it, but only a certain class of weather shamans receive the training and power of *nahanatakitani,* allowing them to invoke the lords of rain and conjure up damaging storm rains, winds, and lightning.[6]

On another continent, there is the venerable tradition of wind and storm conjuring attributed to the Finns and Lapps (Sami), predominantly of northern Sweden, Norway, Finland, Denmark, and Iceland. These shamans (usually called witches, sorcerers, or wizards) were said to be able to tie winds in knots and unleash them at will. Such power was perhaps first mentioned in writing by Homer in his epic poem *The Odyssey,* in which Aeolus, the deity of winds, gifted Ulysses with a leather bag of winds tied up with a silver cord. Written records from as far back as the 1500s commonly reported the sale of wind knots to sailors to ensure an expedient and safe voyage. A passage from the 1680 *English Atlas,* by Moses Pitt, describes something of the Finns and Lapps (Sami) with their wind and storm workings:

The strings they make use of to raise or quell the winds, which they sell to Mariners for that purpose. They consist commonly of three knots, the first of which being untied, affords a favourable wind; the second a brisk gale; and the third a violent storm; as has been approved to the great danger and loss of several Mariners, that have given account of it in publick.[7]

In 1674 an English version of a work by the French surgeon Pierre Martin de la Martiniere, titled *A New Voyage into the Northern Countries,* described an episode he witnessed while on an expedition to the far northern realms. The expedition was becalmed as it neared the Arctic Circle. A few seamen went ashore at the nearest village in search of a sorcerer for help. They asked for a wind to take them to a destination apparently too far for the sorcerer's powers to fully reach, but they took him up on the assistance he could offer them. The sailors brought the sorcerer and three of his coworkers to their sloop, where they bargained and settled on a pound of tobacco and ten silver crowns in return for a "Linnen Cloth about a foot long, and four fingers broad, in which having tyed three knots, they told us that would do." The cloth was fastened to the edge of their "fore-most Sail," and each time a knot was untied the results were immediate. All went well with the first and second knots, and each wind was favorable. Then the ship entered into confusing territory where the compass varied in its readings, so that the men surmised there must be lodestone in the surrounding mountains. Finally, after two difficult days and nights, they cleared the mountainous terrain and their compass could finally register true. Only now they were becalmed again. This time, when the captain untied the third knot, a violent northwest wind rose up and the men were forced to endure a storm of three days' duration, of such power that their ship was dashed upon the rocks. Apparently all the men prayed hard for salvation, and fortunately they managed to escape the fate of drowning predicted for those who untie the third wind knot.[8]

There are also stories of storm raising by those practicing the "black arts." In colonial Massachusetts, both Increase Mather and his son Cotton Mather, pillars of the Puritan community, wrote about the northern European practice of selling the winds, and the wickedness of such activities. In 1693 Cotton Mather wrote in his *Wonders of the Invisible World,* "Undoubtedly the *Devil* understands as *well* the way to make a *Tempest* as to turn the *Winds* at the *Solicitation of a Laplander.*"[9]

In 1726 Daniel Defoe published *A System of Magick* and discussed the "black arts." He described those "black-art men" who could be bribed to raise frightful storms, yet who were also approached for their abilities to bring rain for planting, or to end drought, or to protect cattle from lightning. Again we have human motives for altruistic concerns intertwined with those of profit, anger, and revenge. However, within the same work, Defoe goes on to write of other weather workers who, if a seaman were to offer them money to raise a storm instead of a fair wind, would become very angry and refuse any payment, declaring that "their Power comes from a good Spirit, that never does any Hurt in the World, but always does things kind and good, and for the Benefit of Mankind."[10]

In our modern era, Ted Owens gives us another example of "gray" ethics in weather working. An unusually gifted man, he repeatedly demonstrated profound abilities as a weather worker. Craving public acclaim and respect, Owens made sure that many of his workings were preadvertised and documented. During the course of his weather-working career he repeatedly contacted federal, state, and municipal authorities to offer his services, but he was generally ignored or, worse, ridiculed. Fortunately, he attracted the attention of several capable researchers, including Dr. Jeffrey Mishlove, who, years after Owens's death in 1987, wrote a book on Owens's exploits and ideas titled *The PK Man: A True Story of Mind over Matter.*

Endowed with innate psychic and psychokinetic powers, Owens could influence the material world with his mind—and with the collaboration of certain middle-world forces. At first he described a working relationship with the forces of Nature, but later Owens attributed the extra assistance as coming not from Nature but from alien "Space Intelligences." Whomever or whatever he was working with advised and helped him in his weather-working ventures, no matter if the results caused relief or suffering.

Numerous documented and notarized testimonials attest to Owens's uncanny ability to affect the weather. Mishlove later interviewed many of the people involved, who confirmed their experiences with Owens. In one instance, Kenneth Batch and Charles Jay of Merton, Pennsylvania, asked Owens to show them his purported influence over lightning, and Owens readily agreed. Their affidavit states that on a suitably stormy day, they stood on an apartment balcony with Owens and asked him to direct a lightning strike to the top of City Hall. No less than three brilliant strikes appeared over the building. Then the men asked for lightning in the opposite direction, and after Owens pointed his hand, lightning struck just where he had indicated. According to these witnesses, no other lightning bolts occurred that day except when and where Owens pointed.[11]

In another instance, on October 25, 1972, the day after government officials warned that due to the fuel shortage situation the U.S. public could face real hardship if there was a severely cold winter, Ted Owens wrote letters to several people announcing that he would create for his hometown of Norfolk, Virginia, a mild, summerlike winter so no one would have to suffer for lack of heating oil. News clippings from that winter depict the east coast of Virginia north to Philadelphia and New York City as experiencing record warmth and lack of snow. In Norfolk on December 5, 1972, the temperature reached 73 degrees Fahrenheit, breaking a forty-seven-year record. New York City, on January 18, got up to 66 degrees, another record high. Conversely, the deep South experienced a colder winter with unusual snowfall occurrences.[12]

Ted Owens seemed relatively unconcerned with the results of some of his weather workings such as storm raisings and influencing the course of hurricanes. His desire for acknowledgment too often superceded moral inhibitions. It could be argued that our culture would have benefited from a willingness to study his abilities and better understand what might be available to humans who choose to look beyond the norm, but the consequences that were forced upon people and communities as a result of some of his "demonstrations" crossed ethical boundaries into unacceptable territory. There's nothing like a storm to grab attention, and Ted Owens made use of this sacred element of weather.

From directing lightning strikes while standing on the roof of a skyscraper in downtown Philadelphia with a witness in 1967 to changing the course of hurricanes both toward and away from Florida, storm raising in Cape Charles, Virginia, drought busting in London, Australia, Florida, and California, and wreaking vengeance upon cities such as Chicago in October 1975 and Cleveland (where he had been treated contemptuously by an interviewer in a radio talk show) in 1972, Ted Owens lived in a world unable to accept his abilities, no matter how well demonstrated and documented. It can be said that Owens was his own worst enemy in his ambitious search for respect. Over the years he remained misunderstood and grew increasingly bitter.

Perhaps if things had gone differently, our modern world might have found a greater stance of balance with Nature. Mishlove, who knew Owens and meticulously documented his weather-working activities, wrote,

> It is not clear to me what Owens' motives were in these early years. In fact, I doubt he knew himself. Obviously, he was attempting to attract attention to himself. Often he seemed to do so with reckless disregard for the suffering produced in the wake of his demonstrations. It is indeed possible that Owens' *enfant terrible* behavior represents the puerile manifestation of an emerging evolutionary talent latent in all humanity.[13]

In contrast, Sandra Ingerman writes in her seminal book, *Medicine for the Earth,* about some of her weather workings and the ethical safeguards she employs. For her there is no issue of personal gain in any of her attempts to influence the weather. Her guiding principle is to ask for the highest good for all life. She endeavors to keep a close watch for any ego inflation and generally tries to choose for her ceremonial workings times at which it would be difficult for her to determine the amount of influence her efforts exerted upon the weather. For example, she looks for those cloudy days where rain could be possible to attempt to call down rain. Ingerman advises, "It's also important not to take credit if you are successful in working with weather. When we move into a place of self-importance, saying, 'Look at what I did,' we forget that we are just one small piece of the puzzle."[14]

18

HEALING WITH WEATHER

Techniques must be mastered, but the best healers have a special calling to work with natural elements in a unique way, their "medicine," Indians call it. Their methods are an expression of their nature kinship; nature healers work with allies more than with antibodies.

JAMES SWAN, *NATURE AS TEACHER AND HEALER*

Weather heals. We see this when long-withheld rains fall upon parched earth so that the cracks in the ground mend and the withered grasses green up again. Weather heals us. When we are in physiological balance with seasonal weather changes, life goes well for us. Otherwise, the change of seasons is a time of vulnerability for our well-being.

It was clear to David and me that honoring the weather brings balance and well-being both to the one doing the honoring as well as to the weather itself. Sometimes that honoring can become an intentional alignment with the weather spirits on behalf of healing and restoration for specific areas of the earth and their local plant, animal, and human communities. Now we wanted to know whether we could work with the weather for more specific, individualized kinds of restoration. In other words, is it possible for shamans to enlist elements of weather as personal allies in their practices to heal the sufferings of others?

I journeyed to my original spiritual teachers to ask whether it is possible to heal others with the elements of weather. They answered "Yes, absolutely, you can heal with the forces of weather." Then they sent me off to my weather teacher, who was floating inside a sparkling whirlwind when I arrived. As I watched, his garments and other items were pulled away from his body, one by one, and released out into the sky. Seeing this happen, I understood that this element of weather has powerful "extraction" abilities.

I then realized that during all these years of my life, ever since childhood, whenever I have dreamed of a tornado, the whirlwind has been helping me—extracting some fear, some difficulty, from my being and life. The dreams I called "nightmares" were actually healings. It all fell into place as I stood there before my teacher and the sparkling whirlwind: the entire sequence of dreams—all of those dark and threatening tornadoes, my panic and efforts to escape, the people I tried to help—and then the changing tenor of the dreams as I grew and walked my shamanic path, up to the last three big dreams of recent years, with their powerful teachings. I continued to watch as, upon the whirlwind's departure, all of Grandfather's clothing and personal items returned to him with a shine of newness. Clearly this weather element carried an ability to transmute, to renew.

Soon after this journey I received a long-distance telephone call from a mother whose teenage son was undergoing a life crisis, in what she described as a several-years-long emotional and spiritual challenge to his sense of identity, self-worth, and place in the world. His entire family suffered along with him as they tried, again and again, to help their son and brother. All involved were presently dealing with the aftershocks of the wrenching decision to place him, against his will, in a program thousands of miles from home. As I listened to this mother's voice I felt moved to work on their behalf. Once she assured me that her son knew she was asking for spiritual healing and that he felt desperate enough to agree to any sort of help—a breakthrough in itself—I knew I could proceed.

When the timing felt right, I journeyed to my spiritual teachers of the upper world, the ones who most often assist me in healing work. Those compassionate spirits instantly agreed to work on the youth's behalf, but unexpectedly, they sent me off to see my weather teacher. This time Grandfather had no words for me. Instead, he motioned with his arm and I saw the same sparkling whirlwind appear, only this time I was the one to enter into its revolving vortex. As I did so, I spontaneously merged with its essence, and together with my power animal, we headed back to the middle world to where the healing was to occur. As I saw the son's spirit, I called out to him that we were here only to help, and that he should relax and receive the healing. At this point I was literally on my feet in my healing room at home, working in two realities at the same time.

As the sparkling whirlwind and I approached the teenager, we gently but powerfully descended and enveloped him with a relentless, sucking swirling that stirred up and withdrew the negativity of confusion and self-loathing that held him hostage, keeping him apart from those who cared and from any joy in life. I was also aware that the despair of drug abuse was a part of this—a dank and oppressive energy. What wasn't ejected out into the universe was transmuted into beauty, and I felt grateful for this, as I was deeply immersed in it all. As in the journey, my physical body twirled around and around the healing room, and I collapsed just as the work was done.

I didn't know what to expect in ordinary reality from this work, though I knew a healing had been provided at the spiritual level, and I didn't share the details with the mother. I had planned to journey again for a more "conventional" form of healing, such as a soul retrieval, but before I could do so, his mother called. Just by the tone of her voice I felt an enormous sense of relief and gratitude for all the helping spirits and their compassion. Something noticeably good had happened for the young man, and he was able to make a shift in his attitude, which was the beginning of his journey home.

Cross-culturally there are many in the world who understand the intimate relationship between humans and elements of weather. In traditional Chinese, Hindu, Diné (Navajo), and Mayan medicine ways, conditions of health and disease are described and treated in terms of weather. The ancient Greek god of the medical arts, Aesculapius, who still serves today as spiritual muse to physicians and other health practitioners, was the son of the sun god Apollo. Aesculapius is associated with a healing atmosphere. The classical Greek word *asklepios* denoted a gentle radiance of the sky such as we experience in the air after a storm.[1]

For thousands of years practitioners of traditional Chinese medicine espoused that a life lived in harmony with the cycles of Nature is essential for good health and longevity. When practitioners of this form of medicine assess a patient's state of health, they typically note the kind and quantity of wind within the patient's being. These healers work with the yin and yang, male and female forces of earth and sky. When those forces lose their balance in the sky, we experience tornadoes, hurricanes, or other natural disasters on the earth. Likewise, when the balance of these forces is lost within the human body, sickness or death may result.[2]

Similarly, for the Diné of the Southwest, wind is as much a part of a person's physical and emotional health as it is a force that creates and sculpts our environment. In their tradition, winds become a part of us from our beginnings in the womb. They keep us alive and guide us throughout our lives. Maleficent winds can move in and ruin us if we lose touch with the beneficent winds. Wind impresses its mark on each of us. The spiraling whorls on our fingertips are everlasting reminders that wind fosters us, and to lose good relationship with wind is to lose the ability to live well, if at all.[3]

As David and I looked more closely at this new (to us) modality of healing, we discovered that other peoples in the world have established traditions and ways of working with the elements of weather for purposes of diagnosis and for the restoration of health and well-being. The Tzutujil Mayans see humans as composed of internal weather patterns that mirror and respond to the emotions and health of the external "Big Weather" patterns of Earth. Symptoms of loss of health are described in terms of "weather bloods." The shaman knows the names of the spirits of these various "weather bloods" and how to attend to the desires and demands of these spirits when attempting to heal a patient. Tzutujil-trained shaman Martín Prechtel cautions that this can be a dangerous business, for if the spirit's name is called and the caller is ignorant of how to deal with—or feed—that spirit, then the caller is also at personal risk.[4]

There are shamans who specialize in diagnosing illness with the aid of lightning. Mayan diviners work with a combination of the Mayan calendar and "the speaking of the blood"—the movement of "sheet lightning" within the body. Barbara Tedlock, anthropologist and shaman, underwent a shamanic apprenticeship training with K'iche' Mayan shamans in Guatemala. Like Prechtel, she learned that the body is a microcosm of the world, embodying its own terrain of features such as mountains, plains, lakes, and winds. The "sheet lightning" moving in her body that she divines and diagnoses with is the same as that which we see moving in the atmosphere of the outside world:

> I discovered the flowing and shimmering of my own bodily vital energy, called koyopa or "sheet lightning." Initially these ecstatic feelings seemed strange, and I was frightened that I was becoming possessed by something outside myself. But during my months of shamanic training I eventually learned how to accept and even welcome the movements of sheet lightning since it produced a remarkable bodily-based intuitive form of knowledge called "the speaking of the blood." This gift of accessing bodily intuition has been central to my spiritual understanding and shamanic practice ever since.[5]

In addition to diagnosis, lightning is a potent tool for healing from Africa to North and South America. The Zulu and other tribal people of South Africa speak of a lightning bird, who deposits an "egg" when lightning strikes. These eggs are prized for their powers, and if they are found, medicine men can use them in their healings and charms. Zambian rain doctors work with lightning bird eggs to repair various injuries caused by lightning.[6]

Tudy Roberts was a respected medicine man and Sun Dance and Ghost Dance leader of the Wind River Shoshone people. He successfully doctored many people, and it is said that he received his healing instructions and powers through his dreams. One account of his works describes how he was asleep on the ground after a Sun Dance ceremony and dreamed that three men appeared to him. They were Indians dressed in contemporary, clean clothing and each wore a hat with a feather in it. They communicated to him through song and advised him to call in the help of "black clouds and lightning" to cure a lightning-struck person. The spirit men then told Tudy how to make a certain doctoring tool for this purpose, and that tool could also be used to help himself if he wasn't feeling well.[7]

Walking Thunder, a contemporary Diné medicine woman, speaks of the presence of wind, lightning, and thunder in her healing work:

> We believe that tiny lightning can enter your body and cause you to move. If you get sick, you have to push more lightning back in there to recharge yourself. When medicine people feel the lightning, they'll get a chill or a body twitch. This is how lightning works in our healing. When lightning moves in your body, that's the Thunderway with the Wind. This is behind the twitching of a holy person.[8]

Walking Thunder names certain healing ceremonies that she uses, such as the Thunderways of the Wind, the Cloudways of the Wind, and the Courage Sunburst of the Wind. She uses the Thunderways to put a "new wind" in a patient, who may physically feel the wind as it enters his or her body. Weather elements such as clouds, wind, lightning, and rainbows can figure in the sacred sandpaintings that Walking Thunder creates for her patients.

David and I continued to explore what it could mean for us in our culture and times to heal with the assistance of the spirits of weather. In another of our workshops, Diana journeyed and returned with an important teaching on weather's capacity for healing us as individuals, which is dependent upon our ability to receive:

I went up to my teacher. He brought me outside his hogan and back down to the membrane surrounding the earth, and there was a huge mountain of a man. He had a flowing white beard and he was laughing and jolly, and when I introduced myself and asked my question, he laughed so hard that the wind from his laughter blew me head over heels around the world.

He told me it is about balance and harmony, and it's weather's job to cleanse out the negativity and balance it with positive energy. . . .

He explained that when we hate the weather we are refusing the healing it brings and blocking the cleansing for ourselves as well as that part of the planet. [We must] accept the weather, welcome it, and know it is part of the bigger picture.

More than anything else on our path of learning to relate and work with the weather spirits, David and I have been asked to accept and honor the weather. This has always been the prime directive for the success of our relationships with the spirits of weather. As Diana's spiritual teacher pointed out, we get in the way of the healing that weather brings when we hate it, rather than reaching beyond our personal likes and dislikes to a place of respectful acceptance.

We learned more about what can happen when we are not in good relationship with the weather when Sheila attended our weather-dancing workshop in Nova Scotia. She came to the circle with a long-term difficulty, an illness resulting from a dysfunctional relationship with the weather, in Sheila's case the wind. The power and presence of wind made Sheila feel ill. She could not tolerate the feel of wind and was afraid to venture outside on windy days. Despite all this, she gamely showed up at our workshop prepared to fully participate in all the group explorations, even those with wind. During the introductions Sheila announced that she hoped to overcome her inability to function outdoors.

To open to the possibility of remediation for her broken relationship with wind was an important first step in her process, for Sheila, a healer, was more accustomed to working for others than asking for help for herself. David and I kept track of Sheila during the course of the workshop and admired her willingness to work with her fears and intense dislike of wind. As we hoped, the weather spirits matched Sheila's bid for healing and compassionately pushed her limits. A few weeks later, we were relieved when Sheila wrote to us:

> I continue to explore with the weather spirits and even went for a walk with my husband along the ocean shore on a very windy day. It was great fun! I am so grateful that I no longer have difficulty with the wind. I now find comfort in the greatness and mystery of the many expressions of the weather spirits.

The following is another account of how weather supports and heals us. This is a story of a woman who disliked most everything in her life except the weather, and how weather gifted both her and her shamanic practitioner daughter, Dory, at her passing. In Dory's words:

> First, it's important to know that my mother was a very rude, bossy, and completely dis-spirited individual who had no love for anyone or anything . . . except the weather. She literally never bonded with any of her children and had no interest or like for animals, flowers, or other physically living things. She had no

hobbies and no interests except weather, and she was a religious but not spiritual person. I could count on one hand the number of times I felt or experienced joy coming from her. She was miserable, discontented no matter where she was, and did not enjoy life for one minute she was here, as far as I experienced.

Her only "hobby" was keeping a weather diary. I think it really all started because she and my father argued about the weather all the time. One would say we had the biggest snowstorm last year on such a date, and the other would contradict and say it was a different date. So my mother, in her quest to be *right,* began keeping a daily diary of the weather wherever she was on any given day. Unfortunately, I believe the diaries were lost in one of her many moves, because we found only one year's worth when we moved her to the nursing home.

On July 3, when I arrived at my mother's bedside, I knew she would die that day. Despite our lack of connection and her not having a clue about who I am or what I do, I automatically stepped into my shamanic role with her. I knelt beside her and told her about what she would likely experience as she was dying. She pooh-poohed it and said she would believe it when she saw it for herself. I was with her all day and watched her transition from being embodied to becoming less and less embodied as the evening came in.

As the sun set she moved into an altered state and began communicating (out loud) with some of her deceased relatives. She had the most incredible glow about her; I was in absolute awe at what I was observing. She looked at me with eyes that actually *connected* with my spirit and said, "You were right . . . so beautiful . . . this is so beautiful . . . so many people . . . they are all beautiful."

There was a bit of time between that communication and the next. Her next statement, with, once again, an all-encompassing spiritual glow, was: "Weather is beautiful." I was particularly aware of the fact that she did not say *"The* weather is beautiful" but simply *"Weather is beautiful."*

I truly believe she was communicating with the spirits of weather and that they were taking her to the next level of her spiritual journey with them. It was absolutely a million degrees in her room and I was quite physically uncomfortable. As she slipped into a coma with a huge smile on her face, a thunderstorm moved in, complete with powerful lightning bolts and lots of rain.

Wow, Mom . . . you went out with the storm.

My mother died at 1:00 a.m. on the morning of July 4, never having spoken another word. I was gifted with seeing her spirit leave her body through her mouth, like a light gold wisp of a cloud.

In another circle participants journeyed with the question, "Can weather spirits help with healing?" They returned with an overall affirmative response and the following teaching: "Weather spirits do no actual healing themselves, but through their work they create opportunities for us to engage in healing. Healing is our responsibility and our obligation. *They set the stage, they bring focus, they bring chaos or continuity, each at the right time.*"

This particular teaching made a lot of sense to us, especially in light of the workings of storms. We have seen how the element of storm can be a profound force of cleansing and rejuvenation for our world. Additionally, participants in our workshops have returned from their journeys with descriptions of storms as agents of healing for us, too: "Storms are the healers of the world." "Storms balance the energy of humans, who do not remember their original instructions." In shamanic parlance, storms function like extraction healings by removing disharmony and sources of disharmony, and as soul retrieval or power retrieval healings by restoring that which was lost. As one workshop participant put it, this is accomplished "as they swirl and pick up all of the hurt and negativity and transform it."

I met anthropologist and artist Jeanne-Rachel Salomon at one of Sandra Ingerman's five-day soul-retrieval training programs. During that week, we spent an after-hours evening together in an intimate discussion of our lives and passions. When she heard me speak of my personal dedication to the weather, Jeanne-Rachel shared her story of a significant healing she had asked for and worked hard to receive, and the thunderstorm that made it possible. Her husband had died half a year before and her grief led her to contemplate suicide. Then, as if things couldn't get worse, she was diagnosed with a cancer of her uterus:

> Then my survival instinct kicked in. Having had just learned about shamanic journeying and shamanic healing, I began to wonder if I could not heal myself. With no experience in regard to the process of shamanic healing and with nobody to turn to for help, I decided to give it a try. I asked the spirits of the place where I lived to assist me, and, along with the steady drumbeat from a shamanic drumming tape, I made a journey into my body and went right into the uterus. I found a black mass that was as hard and impenetrable as stone. Since I had not previously thought about what to do once inside my body, I had only my hands to work with, and as much as I tried, I could not even scratch this black material. With the feeling of having utterly failed, I gave up.
>
> The date for surgery was scheduled, and I was instructed to arrive at the hospital at 8 p.m. the night before. A friend volunteered to drive me there, and when she arrived at my house, an enormous thunderstorm started. The rain was so heavy that the driveway was soon flooded, and it became impossible to even get from the front door to the car. We decided to wait till the rain was over.
>
> But this was not an ordinary thunderstorm. Something prompted me to utilize the time until we could leave for the hospital to give one more try to shamanic healing. Again I asked the spirit forces for their assistance. Again along the drumbeat from the tape I ventured into my body. Again there was the black stone, which reminded me of onyx. Mentally I took out my sculptor's tools, a chisel and a mallet, and started to chip at the black mass. To my delight some

small chips came off! Although the black material was very hard and difficult to penetrate, I managed to chop off bigger pieces of the glasslike material. Some hurt me with their sharp edges, and I had to squint my eyes for protection. Yet I was very determined in my work, and while in ordinary reality the house shook repeatedly under heavy thunder, in nonordinary reality I chipped away piece after piece of this black stuff.

The work proved somewhat difficult in another aspect: the space in my uterus was so small that there was hardly room for me to move. But I would not give up till I had taken out everything that did not belong there! After long and laborious work, suddenly, as if a window had been opened, this formerly pitch-black space was flooded with sunlight! I rested my tools and looked up: the shiny mother-of-pearl-like walls were bathed in the soft light of rosy and pale yellow colors; there was such a beautiful glow to the space that I knew I had succeeded, that I had accomplished my goal! I removed the last pieces of the black material and threw them out, and, with my back against the wall, I even used my feet to push out the debris that was left.

When I returned to ordinary reality, the thunderstorm had spent its power, and my friend drove me to the hospital. The next morning the surgeon could not find any trace of cancer that had been detected during biopsy.[9]

Cross-culturally and around the world, humans have acknowledged their relationship with the four basic elements of creation: earth, air, fire, and water. Within the primary four categories of elements, we can find all the beings and forces of the natural world. Indeed, we find ourselves as well. Eliot Cowan, teacher of plant spirit medicine, writes, "The connection with Nature is exhilarating and beautiful, but it is not a luxury. Connection with Nature is health; health is life. . . . This is so because we are Nature; we are made of dirt, rain, sunshine, minerals and gases."[10]

And so we, too, are able to experience health and healing through the elements of nature. Jeanne-Rachel was most fortunate to seemingly "stumble" upon the source of help she needed to effect her healing. For her, as well as for the shamans and others who work to relieve suffering and who intentionally seek help from the natural world for their practices, a compassionate collaboration or partnership with the elements of weather—be they whirling winds, lightning, thunderstorms, or potentially any of weather's manifestations—can gift us with miracles of healing.

19

CARRYING ON

We dance the shining mind change,
boundless connections that we are . . .

LINDA CRANE, FROM
"THE CRANE DANCE" IN *HOW WILD?*

I am running through high desert country, and the smells of sage and bitterbrush welcome me as I revel in the chance to stretch my legs and run like the wind. The breeze shifts around from one direction to the next, encircling me with its enlivening presence, much as the surrounding mountain ranges enfold the valley of my home. I am heading for the wind-sculpted, old cottonwood tree as it stands alone in all that spaciousness of land and sky. In greeting, I briefly caress its trunk and then climb toward the top branches, not at all minding the feel of rough bark on my skin. As I reach the top, a large winged one swoops in and we're off, ascending with incredible speed to the vast and numinous realm of the upper world.

I find my spirit ancestor-teacher surrounded by a vast openness of sweeping vistas. Up close are lichen-covered rocks nestled among a variety of plants growing low to the ground, and everywhere the winds restlessly weave all around and through us.

He tells me that for our ancestors, weather was kin. They were aware of it each day, all day and night, in one way or another, as they lived intimately with all kinds of weather. I see visions of our ancestors interacting with the weather, greeting the first weather of the day and commenting to one another about "who" is here. I see people offering acknowledgment to the beings of weather directly through their words, songs, gestures, and offerings of food or other substances. I see a group of people singing and dancing in a circle, and I ask my ancestor-teacher if this is a ceremony about weather. He nods, and I understand that throughout their lives our ancestors were deeply conscious of the life-sustaining workings of weather. The old ones knew their lives depended upon their ability to live with and relate to these powerful forces.

My teacher sadly adds that I would be surprised at how asleep many, many people are today in their most basic awareness of weather. The drumbeat changes, and my ancestor-teacher invites me to return to learn more about the old ways, even as I work to discover new ones. I respectfully thank him and return to ordinary reality.

Native traditionalists of today have not forgotten any of this wisdom and still work, much as they have for thousands of years, to ensure that life continues not only for their own communities, but for us all. They, too, understand and demonstrate the importance of personal attitude for the greater well-being—how necessary are our individual expressions of love, honoring, and gratitude for our lives and all others, seen and unseen, with whom we share this middle world. These traditionalists know how vitally important it is for us to take part in the work of maintaining balance and harmony in our world. Perhaps there is also a spiritual legacy of honoring and weather working for each of us from somewhere in our ancient past.

David and I feel that weather dancers of today have a crucial role to play and an important tradition to uphold—even as any tradition must continue to evolve. The longevity and genius of shamanism is that, in part, it is not hidebound to methodology. As such, shamanism is always metamorphosing as it evolves in response to the current, always-changing circumstances of the world (like the weather!). When we don't have to push against a codified set of established traditional ways, we can more readily receive the gifts of core cross-cultural knowledge and practices in our search for what is needed and effective, here and now.

There are weather workers whose vocation is handed down to them through their lineage. It is said that to this day, there is a "rain queen" of the Lovedu tribe. The story goes back to 1600, when the daughter of Mambo, the ruler of the region we now know as Zimbabwe, stole a rain charm and escaped with her son to the mountains to form the Lovedu tribe. This charm was passed down in the family, and generations later it came to Mujaji, another daughter of a king. Mujaji learned how to successfully work with the charm, and upon her death, she passed the rain charm and its secrets on to the next queen, and so on. All subsequent rain queens were named after their original ancestress, Mujaji, and charged with the responsibility for the ongoing seasonal cycles and working for rain in times of drought. They could also use their abilities to deny rain to their enemies. It is said that the most important ingredient in their workings is the permission of their ancestors, and upon their death, as each becomes an ancestor, the charm with its secrets is passed on to the next.[1]

Wovoka, the Paiute prophet, healer, and weather shaman of the 1800s, is said to have received certain weather-working abilities through his father, as well as through his revelation experience. Yeshe Dorje Rinpoche, the contemporary Tibetan Buddhist monk and rainmaker, related, "My family has stopped hail for centuries. This gift has been passed on from father to son."[2] Yeshe Dorje also acknowledged his spiritual father, Yogi Tashi, as a great practitioner and teacher for him.

Whether born or initiated into spiritual traditions, Yeshe Dorje, Wovoka, the daughters of Queen Mujaji's line, and the Hopi people with their famous rainmaking ceremonies are all upheld by a clear and strong sense of support from their lineage or religion as they live and grow in their spiritual path. Those not born with this helpful clarity and guidance often feel a sense of loss. Among our circles of novice and experienced shamanic practitioners, David and I repeatedly hear people lament that, having rejected their religions of origin, they are now "spiritual orphans."

Those of us who wish to practice weather shamanism today but have no known ancestral lineage of weather workers can take heart from the fact that we may, nonetheless, be at something of an advantage. To be sure, there are significant challenges to our growth as shamanic practitioners (our worldview for one), yet unshackled and cut loose from cultural moorings as we may be, rather than considering ourselves adrift, we can benefit from one of the primary strengths of shamanism: its inherent spontaneity. Shamans tend to be eclectic in their practical willingness to utilize what works, and a lack of unquestioned allegiance to a particular tradition or religion can be an asset for our spiritual growth.

And we can never forget that as with the Hopi people, Yeshe Dorje and Wovoka led intensely spiritual lives. They understood the necessity of dedicated focus and effort—hard work—to wholeheartedly remain on their path. In this also, we have to remain wary of our culture's predilection for dilettantism regarding spiritual ways. It is all too easy to play at things and risk deluding ourselves into thinking we are living our practice.

Johnny Moses, master storyteller and traditional healer of the Northwest coastal tribal peoples of British Columbia, teaches that the spirits and ancestors are "always there in the forests and the mountains, waiting for us to visit them, but we are the ones who have to visit." Furthermore, we have to show that we are truly willing to show up for the teachings and are worthy—strong enough to receive and carry the work, the medicine, the power. Ancestral teachings and traditional peoples today say that this requires suffering. Moses describes his people's meaning for the word *suffering* as not "a negative thing; it refers to forces that are pressing or pushing on us that we can feel very strongly. Suffering helps us become strong so we can withstand the winds and storms of life."[3]

If we do feel called to work with the weather for purposes of greater harmony and balance in our world, then it is imperative to keep our sights focused on the spiritual nature of this path. The world doesn't need more acts of weather modification and relationships of power-over. Though the ancestral, indigenous ways of weather working vary from people to people, underneath it all is the understanding that "rainmaking is regarded as a sacred occupation. There is a mental and spiritual preparation."[4]

George Wachetaker, a Comanche shaman, stated that it takes him at least ten days of spiritual preparation before an actual ceremony of weather working can begin. During a drought in Florida in 1971, a radio station in Pompano Beach hired Wachetaker for his rainmaking services. It is reported that approximately 1,500 people gathered in a circle in a parking lot where the ceremony took place. What the onlookers saw was Wachetaker lighting a fire, chanting, dancing, and sipping from a bowl of water. What they experienced, four minutes after the ceremony, was a torrential downpour, and a moment where, according to the radio program director Casey Jones, "we just didn't believe it." At first people bolted to the storefronts for shelter, and then they broke out into "wild applause."[5]

If the helping spirits beckon any of us toward a path of weather shamanism, then we'll need to learn how to create our own unique, working relationship with the spirits and forces of weather. As weather dancers, the truly important calling is to love the weather and to relate to weather from a place of personal authenticity. No one else can prescribe exactly how to do this for any one of us. Essentially we're on our own, unless we come from and live within an indigenous, ancestral tradition of established ways of relating. What we can find, however, is a "bare bones" map, something that in the spirit of core shamanism reveals the underlying common ground, the bedrock shared by a variety of similar and dissimilar traditions that shows up over and over, no matter what direction we look toward.

From the ancestral traditions of Africa, Malidoma Patrice Somé's description of human relationships with the sacred reflects that bedrock of shared understanding found wherever the shamanic worldview exists: "The connection to Spirit and the Other World is a dialogue that goes two ways. We call on the spirits because we need their help, but they need something from us as well. . . . They look at us as an extension of themselves."[6]

As shamanic practitioners, we have to understand that the need and the desire for harmony between the worlds is mutual—yet it's not all up to the spirits. And so we, too, have an important role to play in our willingness to work with the helping spirits. Somé's tradition is not alone in its recognition of the necessity for intentional collaboration between humans and those of the spirit world. As he says, "If Spirit is looking up to us, and we are looking up to Spirit, then we are looking up to each other, and human beings should take from this a certain sense of dignity."[7]

As we grow strong and sure enough on our path, we'll be better able to appreciate the freedom to learn directly from the helping spirits—who, of course, can be the most demanding taskmasters of all, so we aren't getting off easy. Someone from an established tradition may also learn directly from the helping spirits, but he or she has to reach beyond cultural prescriptions or bonds to bring in something new. To go against established tradition can be a formidable task, and even dangerous, a challenge the old shamans may have had to face from time to time. Either way, we are all supported and tempered by our circumstances. What counts most in shamanism, other than ethics, is the willingness to bring forth what is needed in the world now. And that may be something that is entirely new or something ancient that is renewed for today.

Those of us practicing shamanism within our culture have a doorway through which we can intentionally create favorable change for our world. Through appropriate acts of spontaneity, we can continue to follow the lead of the helping spirits so that the work and knowledge can evolve and stay fresh. Throughout, the presence and power of love makes it all worthwhile—and possible—as it weaves everything together.

There are many among us who do have an innate spiritual connection with the weather, and if this ability is consciously nurtured and intentionally developed in service to greater balance and harmony, then these people can offer healings that are real and useful—and essential to our times. And if we aren't aware of any inherent gift or ancestral lineage, yet we have a love for the weather, for the earth, and for our lives, then it is enough. This is all we need to begin on our way of successful weather dancing, in every sense of the metaphor.

Hear me well . . .

*You have all that you need within you to add a greater
    light to the web.*
Go
Dream me a new dream,
Weave me a new web,
Spin me a new song,
Make me a new world.

Let the Peace of the Light and the Storm be within you.
Blessed be us all.

"Spider Woman Speaks," Ramona Lapidas,
received during a shamanic journey

NOTES

CHAPTER 1
THE DOOR BLOWS OPEN

1. Nan Moss and David Corbin, "Shamanism and the Spirits of Weather: More Pieces of the Puzzle," *Shamanism: Journal of the Foundation for Shamanic Studies* 12, no. 2 (1999), 11–16.

2. Stephen Rosen, *Weathering* (New York: M. Evans & Co, 1979), 274.

3. Brian Fagan, *The Little Ice Age* (New York: Basic Books, 2000), 92.

4. Thom Hartman, *The Last Hours of Ancient Sunlight* (New York: Harmony Books, 1999), 151.

5. James Swan, *Nature as Teacher and Healer* (New York: Villiard Books, 1992), 148.

CHAPTER 2
A DIFFERENT VIEW—A NEW STORY

1. Johannes Wilbert, *Mindful of Famine: Religious Climatology of the Warao Indians* (Cambridge, Mass.: Harvard University Press, 1996), 191.

2. Tamra Andrews, *Legends of the Earth, Sea, and Sky* (Santa Barbara, Calif.: ABC-CLIO, 1998), xii.

3. Michael Harner, *The Way of the Shaman* (New York: Harper & Row, 1990), xiii.

CHAPTER 3
CHANGING THE WEATHER

1. Daniel Pendick, "Cloud Dancers," *Scientific American Presents* 11, no. 1 (Spring 2000): 64–66.

2. Ibid.

3. William J. Burroughs, *The Climate Revealed* (Cambridge, U.K.: Cambridge University Press, 1999), 180–81.

4. Josh Rosen, *Owning the Weather* (Spine Films, 2005). Documentary produced for the Science Channel.

5. William J. Burroughs, *The Climate Revealed,* 181.

6. Daniel Pendick, "Cloud Dancers," 69.

7. John and Marcia Donnan, *Raindance to Research* (New York: David McKay Company, Inc., 1977), 133.

8. Nick Begich and Jeane Manning, *Angels Don't Play This HAARP: Advances in Tesla Technology* (Anchorage, Alaska: Earthpulse Press, 2002), 6.

9. Daniel Pendick, "Cloud Dancers," 69.

10. James Swan, *Nature as Teacher and Healer,* 250.

11. Richard Nelson, *Make Prayers to the Raven* (Chicago, Ill.: University of Chicago Press, 1983), 40.

12. Gary Lockhart, *The Weather Companion* (New York: John Wiley & Sons, 1988), 195.

13. Michael Hittman, *Wovoka and the Ghost Dance* (Lincoln: University of Nebraska Press, 1990), 63.

14. Ibid., 69.

15. Vincent A. Gaddis, *Native American Myths and Mysteries* (Garberville, Calif.: Borderland Sciences Research Foundation, 1991), 121.

16. Marsha Woolf and Karen Blanc, *The Rainmaker* (Boston: Sigo Press, 1994), 49–61.

17. J. R. Moehringer, "Romancing the Clouds . . . ," *Los Angeles Times,* February 23, 2003.

CHAPTER 4
STEPPING THROUGH

1. Martín Prechtel, *Secrets of the Talking Jaguar* (New York: Tarcher, 1998), 106–7.

2. Ibid., 129.

CHAPTER 5
THE MIDDLE WORLD

1. Michael Harner, lecture at Pymander Bookstore, Westport, Conn. (February, 1996).
2. Brian Greene, *The Elegant Universe* (New York: Vintage Books, 2000), 41.
3. Ibid., 270.

CHAPTER 6
FORM

1. David Abram, *The Spell of the Sensuous* (New York: Vintage Books, 1997), 9.
2. Ruth Holmes Whitehead, *Six Micmac Stories* (Halifax, Nova Scotia: Nimbus Publishing and the Nova Scotia Museum, 1992), 6.

CHAPTER 7
WHAT IS WEATHER?

1. Martín Prechtel, *Secrets of the Talking Jaguar,* 231–32.

CHAPTER 8
CHAOS, ORDER, AND POWER AT WORK

1. David Schoen, *Divine Tempest* (Toronto: Inner City Books, 1998), 21.
2. Tamra Andrews, *Legends of the Earth, Sea, and Sky,* 242–43.
3. Tom Cowan, "The Evil Formorians," *Gnosis Magazine* (Winter 1999), 49.
4. Richard Nelson, *Make Prayers to the Raven,* 30.
5. Tamra Andrews, *Legends of the Earth, Sea, and Sky,* 245.
6. Ibid., 244.
7. Joan Halifax, *Shaman* (London: Thames and Hudson, 1982), 11.
8. Tamra Andrews, *Legends of the Earth, Sea, and Sky,* 15.
9. *Journeys through Dreamtime* (Amsterdam: Time-Life Books, 1999), 25.
10. E. C. Krupp, *Skywatchers* (New York: Wiley and Sons, 1997), 50.
11. Tom Cowan, *Fire in the Head* (New York: Harper, 1993), 105.

CHAPTER 9
THE FACES OF WEATHER

1. Ruth Holmes Whitehead, *Six Micmac Stories,* 6.
2. Tamra Andrews, *Legends of the Earth, Sea, and Sky,* 92.

3. Barbara and Dennis Tedlock, *Teachings from the American Earth* (New York: Liveright, 1975), 154–58.

CHAPTER 10
THE SACRED NATURE OF STORM

1. Stephen Rosen, *Weathering*, 2.

2. Jerry Dennis, "Lake Squall, 1967," in *Soul of the Sky*, edited by Dave Thurlow and C. Ralph Adler (New Hampshire: Mt. Washington Observatory, 1999), 3.

3. E. C. Krupp, *Skywatchers*, 80.

4. Tamra Andrews, *Legends of the Earth, Sea, and Sky*, 115–16.

5. Ibid., 241.

6. Ibid., 61.

7. Joseph Bruchac, "Otstungo, a Mohawk Village in 1491," *National Geographic Magazine* 180, no. 4 (October 1991), 81.

8. Tamra Andrews, *Legends of the Earth, Sea, and Sky*, 106.

9. William Lyon, *Encyclopedia of Native American Healing* (New York: W. W. Norton, 1996), 307.

CHAPTER 11
ENLIVENED RELATIONSHIP WITH NATURE

1. Tom Cowan, *Fire in the Head*, 111.

2. Nan Moss and David Corbin, *CloudDancing: Wisdom from the Sky* (Port Clyde, Me.: Middle World Press, 2004), 9.

3. Tom Cowan, *Fire in the Head*, 130.

4. Tom Cowan, *Yearning for the Wind* (Novoto, Calif.: New World Library, 2003), 132.

5. Martín Prechtel, *Secrets of the Talking Jaguar*, 152.

6. Ibid., 151.

7. Bruce Bower, "When Stones Come to Life," *Science News* 155 (June 5, 1999), 360–62.

CHAPTER 12
DANCE OF POWER

1. Calvin Luther Martin, *The Way of the Human Being* (New Haven, Conn.: Yale University Press, 1999), 23–24.

2. Daniel Bianchetta, lecture at the Esalen Institute, February 28, 2006.

3. Joan Halifax, *Shamanic Voices* (New York: Dutton, 1979), 66 [Italics ours].

CHAPTER 13
TO HONOR HURRICANE

1. David Schoen, *Divine Tempest,* 21.
2. To learn about transfiguration, see Sandra Ingerman, *Medicine for the Earth* (New York: Three Rivers Press, 2000).

CHAPTER 14
WEATHER WORKING

1. Johannes Wilbert, *Mindful of Famine,* 184–85.
2. Ibid., 194.
3. Tamra Andrews, *Legends of the Earth, Sea, and Sky,* 38.
4. Silvio Albino, "Skies Open Up at Rainmaker's Behest," *Shore Line Times* 124, no. 3 (September 20, 1995).

CHAPTER 16
CEREMONY

1. Doug Boyd, *Rolling Thunder* (New York: Dell, 1974), 71–72.
2. Florida State University climatologist James O'Brien, quoted in Madeline J. Nash, "Wait Till Next Time," *Time* (September 27, 1999).
3. Malidoma Patrice Somé, *Healing Wisdom of Africa* (New York: Tarcher, 1998), 142–43.
4. Calvin Luther Martin, *The Way of the Human Being,* 24–25.
5. E. C. Krupp, *Skywatchers,* 56.
6. Ann Marshall, "Rain," *Native Peoples* (Summer, 1993): 70.
7. Jamake Highwater, *Ritual of the Wind* (Toronto: Methuen Publications, 1984), 137–39.
8. James Swan, *Nature as Teacher and Healer* (New York: Villard Books, 1992), 35.
9. Wade Davis, *Shadows in the Sun: Travels to Landscapes of Spirit and Desire* (Washington D.C.: Island Press/Shearwater Books, 1998), 87.
10. Martha Ward, *What in the World Is Conjure?* (unpublished draft, 2005).
11. Joan Halifax, *Shamanic Voices,* 251.

CHAPTER 17
ETHICS OF WEATHER WORKING

1. Doug Boyd, *Rolling Thunder*, 71–72.

2. Mary Elizabeth Thunder, *Thunder's Grace* (New York: Station Hill Press, 1995), 168.

3. Thich Nhat Hanh, "Love in Action." In *The Soul of Nature*, edited by Michael Tobias and Georgianne Cowan (New York: Plume, 1996), 129.

4. Johannes Wilbert, *Mindful of Famine*, 96–104.

5. Ibid., 93.

6. Ibid., 104.

7. Ernest J. Moyne, *Raising the Wind* (Newark: University of Delaware Press, 1981), 44.

8. Ibid., 32–33.

9. Ibid., 45.

10. Ibid., 80–82.

11. Jeffery Mishlove, *The PK Man: A True Story of Mind over Matter* (Charlottesville, Va.: Hampton Roads, 2000), 92–93.

12. Ibid., 98–99.

13. Ibid., 59.

14. Sandra Ingerman, *Medicine for the Earth*, 238.

CHAPTER 18
HEALING WITH WEATHER

1. Stephen Rosen, *Weathering*, 193.

2. Jwing-Ming Yang, *The Essence of Taiji Qi Gong* (Boston: YMAA Publication Center, 1994), 39–40.

3. James Kale McNeley, *Holy Wind in Navajo Philosophy* (Tucson: University of Arizona Press, 1981), 17–49

4. Martín Prechtel, *Secrets of the Talking Jaguar*, 231–32.

5. Barbara Tedlock, *The Woman in the Shaman's Body* (New York: Bantam, 2005), 79.

6. Tamra Andrews, *Legends of Earth, Sea, and Sky*, 130.

7. Ake Hultkrantz, *Native Religions of North America* (Prospect Heights, Ill.: Waveland Press, 1987), 79–81.

8. Bradford Keeney, ed., *Walking Thunder: Diné Medicine Woman* (Philadelphia: Ringing Rocks Press, 2001), 124.

9. Jeanne-Rachel Salomon, *Towards an Ethnography of Transpersonal Consciousness: Quantum-Anthropological Enquiry into the Noetic Self of Man* (unpublished thesis, May 2002), 23–25.

10. Eliot Cowan, *Plant Spirit Medicine* (Newburg, Ore.: Swan-Raven & Co., 1995), 3.

CHAPTER 19
CARRYING ON

1. Tamra Andrews, *Legends of the Earth, Sea, and Sky,* 154–55.

2. Marsha Woolf and Karen Blanc, *The Rainmaker,* 8.

3. Timothy White, "Northwest Coast Medicine Teachings: An Interview with Johnny Moses," *Shaman's Drum: A Journal of Experiential Shamanism* no. 50 (Winter 1998), 44.

4. Vincent A. Gaddis, *Native American Myths and Mysteries,* 122.

5. Ibid., 121.

6. Malidoma Patrice Somé, *Healing Wisdom of Africa,* 61–62

7. Ibid., 62.

BIBLIOGRAPHY

Abram, David. *The Spell of the Sensuous.* New York: Vintage Books, 1997.

Andrews, Tamra. *Legends of the Earth, Sea, and Sky.* Santa Barbara, Calif.: ABC-CLIO, 1998.

Arvigo, Rosita. *Sastun.* San Francisco: Harper, 1995.

Begich, Nick, and Jeane Manning. *Angels Don't Play This HAARP: Advances in Tesla Technology.* Anchorage, Alaska: Earthpulse Press, 2002.

Best, E. *Maori Religion and Mythology.* New York: AMS Press, 1977.

Bower, Bruce. "When Stones Come to Life." *Science News* 155 (June 5, 1999): 360–62.

Boyd, Doug. *Rolling Thunder.* New York: Dell, 1974.

Bruchac, Joseph. "Otstungo: A Mohawk Village in 1491." *National Geographic Magazine* 180, no. 4 (October 1991): 68–83.

Burroughs, William J. *The Climate Revealed.* Cambridge, U.K.: Cambridge University Press, 1999.

Cowan, Eliot. *Plant Spirit Medicine.* Newburg, Ore.: Swan-Raven & Co., 1995.

Cowan, Tom. "The Evil Formorians." *Gnosis Magazine* (Winter 1999): 46–51.

———. *Fire in the Head.* New York: Harper, 1993.

———. *Yearning for the Wind.* Novato, Calif.: New World Library, 2003.

Crane, Linda. *How Wild?* Barrytown, N.Y.: Barrytown/Station Hill Press, 2005

Davis, Wade. *Shadows in the Sun: Travels to Landscapes of Spirit and Desire.* Washington D.C.: Island Press/Shearwater Books, 1998.

Dennis, Jerry. "Lake Squall, 1967." In *Soul of the Sky,* edited by Dave Thurlow and C. Ralph Adler. New Hampshire: Mt. Washington Observatory, 1999.

Donnan, John and Marcia. *Raindance to Research.* New York: David McKay Company, Inc. 1977.

Eiseley, Loren. *The Star Thrower.* New York: Harcourt Brace, 1978.

Fagan, Brian. *The Little Ice Age.* New York: Basic Books, 2000.

Ferris, Timothy. *The Whole Shebang.* New York: Simon & Schuster, 1997.

Gaddis, Vincent A. *Native American Myths and Mysteries.* Garberville, Calif.: Borderland Sciences Research Foundation, 1991.

Greene, Brian. *The Elegant Universe.* New York: Vintage Books, 2000.

Halifax, Joan. *Shaman.* London: Thames and Hudson, 1982.

———. *Shamanic Voices.* New York: Dutton, 1979.

Harner, Michael. *The Way of the Shaman.* New York: Harper & Row, 1990.

Hartman, Thom. *The Last Hours of Ancient Sunlight.* New York: Harmony Books, 1999.

Highwater, Jamake. *Ritual of the Wind.* Toronto: Methuen Publications, 1984.

Hittman, Michael. *Wovoka and the Ghost Dance.* Lincoln: University of Nebraska Press, 1990.

Houston, James. *Songs of the Dream People: Chants and Images from the Indians and Eskimos of North America.* New York: Atheneum, 1972.

Hultkrantz, Ake. *Native Religions of North America.* Prospect Heights, Ill: Waveland Press, 1987.

Ingerman, Sandra. *Medicine for the Earth.* New York: Three Rivers Press, 2000.

———. *Soul Retrieval: Mending the Fragmented Self.* New York: Harper, 1991.

Journeys through Dreamtime. Amsterdam: Time-Life Books, 1999.

Keeney, Bradford, ed. *Walking Thunder: Diné Medicine Woman.* Philadelphia: Ringing Rocks Press, 2001.

Krupp, E. C. *Skywatchers.* New York: Wiley and Sons, 1997.

Leonard, Schierse Linda. *Creation's Heartbeat.* New York: Bantam, 1995.

Lockhart, Gary. *The Weather Companion.* New York: John Wiley & Sons, 1988.

Lyon, William. *Encyclopedia of Native American Healing.* New York: W. W. Norton, 1996.

Marshall, Ann. "Rain." *Native Peoples Magazine,* Summer, 1993, 70.

Martin, Calvin Luther. *The Way of the Human Being.* New Haven, Conn.: Yale University Press, 1999.

McNeley, James Kale. *Holy Wind in Navajo Philosophy.* Tucson: University of Arizona Press, 1981.

Mishlove, Jeffery. *The PK Man.* Charlottesville, Va: Hampton Roads, 2000.

Moehringer, J. R. "Romancing the Clouds." *Los Angeles Times,* February 23, 2003.

Moss, Nan, and David Corbin. *CloudDancing: Wisdom from the Sky Guidebook.* Port Clyde, Me.: Middle World Press, 2004.

———. "Shamanism and the Spirits of Weather: More Pieces of the Puzzle." *Shamanism: Journal of the Foundation for Shamanic Studies* 12, no. 2 (1999): 11–16.

Moyne, Ernest J. *Raising the Wind.* Newark: University of Delaware Press, 1981.

Nash, J. Madeline. "Wait Till Next Time." *Time,* September 27, 1999.

Neihardt, John. *Black Elk Speaks,* twenty-first-century ed. Lincoln: University of Nebraska Press, 2000.

Nelson, Richard. *Make Prayers to the Raven.* Chicago: University of Chicago Press, 1983.

Pendick, Daniel. "Cloud Dancers." *Scientific American Presents* 11, no. 1 (Spring 2000): 64–69.

Prechtel, Martín. *Secrets of the Talking Jaguar.* New York: Tarcher, 1998.

Rosen, Stephen. *Weathering.* New York: M. Evans & Co., 1979.

Schoen, David. *Divine Tempest.* Toronto: Inner City Books, 1998.

Somé, Malidoma Patrice. *Healing Wisdom of Africa.* New York: Tarcher, 1998.

Swan, James. *Nature as Teacher and Healer.* New York: Villiard Books, 1992.

Talman, Charles F. "The Weather." *The Mentor,* July 1, 1916.

Tedlock, Barbara. *The Woman in the Shaman's Body.* New York: Bantam, 2005.

Tedlock, Barbara and Dennis. *Teachings from the American Earth.* New York: Liveright, 1975.

Thunder, Mary Elizabeth. *Thunder's Grace.* New York: Station Hill Press, 1995.

Thich Nhat Hanh. *Love in Action.* Parallax Press, 2005.

Waters, Frank. *The Man Who Killed the Deer.* Athens, Ohio: Swallow Press/ Ohio University Press, 1970.

White, Timothy. "Northwest Coast Medicine Teachings: An Interview with Johnny Moses." *Shaman's Drum: A Journal of Experiential Shamanism,* 50 (Winter 1998): 44.

Whitehead, Ruth Holmes. *Six Micmac Stories.* Halifax, Nova Scotia: Nimbus Publishing and the Nova Scotia Museum, 1992.

Wilbert, Johannes. *Mindful of Famine.* Cambridge, Mass.: Harvard University Press, 1996.

Woolf, Marsha, and Karen Blanc. *The Rainmaker.* Boston: Sigo Press, 1994.

Yang, Jwing-Ming. *The Essence of Taiji Qi Gong.* Boston: YMAA Publication Center, 1994.

ABOUT THE AUTHORS

Nan Moss, C.S.C., and David Corbin, M.S., C.S.C., are faculty members of the Foundation for Shamanic Studies (a worldwide organization founded by Michael Harner, Ph.D.) and are certified by the foundation as shamanic counselors. They teach beginning and advanced courses for the foundation at locations throughout the Northeast, including Boston and New York City. They also teach the foundation's most advanced courses, the two-week and three-year programs in advanced shamanism and shamanic healing on the East Coast. Additionally, they lead five-day shamanic workshops and month-long intensives at Esalen Institute in California.

Their interest in the spiritual aspects of weather is a longstanding one, and they have been teaching and researching this topic since

1997. In 1999 they began presenting their introductory workshop, WeatherDancing: Shamanism and the Spirits of Weather, in the United States and Canada. They are the authors of *CloudDancing: Wisdom from the Sky,* a set of shamanic divination cards and guidebook using cloud images, and have written articles on the spirits of weather, which have appeared in *Shamanism,* the journal of the Foundation for Shamanic Studies.

In addition to their training in core shamanism with Michael Harner and the Foundation for Shamanic Studies, Nan and David have also studied with indigenous healers from various cultures, including Siberian, Tuvan, Saami, Chinese, and Native American. They are founding members of the Society for Shamanic Practitioners.

Nan and David have a private shamanic healing and counseling practice in Port Clyde, Maine.

INDEX

BOOKS OF RELATED INTEREST

Original Instructions
Indigenous Teachings for a Sustainable Future
Edited by Melissa K. Nelson

Shamanic Experience
A Practical Guide to Psychic Powers
by Kenneth Meadows

Shamanic Spirit
A Practical Guide to Personal Fulfillment
by Kenneth Meadows

As in the Heart, So in the Earth
Reversing the Desertification of the Soul and the Soil
by Pierre Rabhi

Earthwalks for Body and Spirit
Exercises to Restore Our Sacred Bond with the Earth
by James Endredy

Green Psychology
Transforming Our Relationship to the Earth
by Ralph Metzner, Ph.D.

The Universe Is a Green Dragon
A Cosmic Creation Story
by Brian Swimme, Ph.D.

The Deva Handbook
How to Work with Nature's Subtle Energies
by Nathaniel Altman

INNER TRADITIONS • BEAR & COMPANY
P.O. Box 388
Rochester, VT 05767
1-800-246-8648
www.InnerTraditions.com

Or contact your local bookseller